Dancing in the Light of the Moon

Dancing in the Light of the Moon

Published by Freedom Publishers

ISBN: 9798838474575

1

Sita Sharma sat in the back of the new model Ambassador beside her mother, Sanaya. The car idled alongside an oval stretch of lawn. On the far side of the lawn was the Mumbai High Court, a place she had often heard of but never seen. For the past two months her father had spent his days there, returning home with a nightly report of how the trial progressed. After briefly tucking her and her siblings into bed, he and her mother would closet themselves in their shared office lined with law books and discuss strategy for the coming day. Colleagues dropped by at all hours, and there was only one topic of conversation. If they could convict Raju Khan, her father said, it would change everything.

Sita examined the building, which was surrounded by reporters, camera men and interested bystanders. The court looked like a castle or a cathedral and was obviously built during the time of the British Raj, a period of history her tutor had drilled her on repeatedly. The Indian flag hung above a parapet between two towers, limp in the breezeless, hot June morning.

"This is the day, Sita," her mother said. "Your father has pushed to make this case happen, he has been bullied and threatened, but he has not backed down. Your father is a man of integrity," she said, glaring at Sita as if she had ever doubted this. "If he can put an underworld boss away, despite all the bribes Khan has surely paid out, then there is hope for this country. And today the Judge will declare his verdict." Her mother took a deep, shaky breath. She sat bolt upright, elegant and austere in her black silk salweer kameez, the classic pants and tunic pairing that Sita greatly preferred to the western-style business ensembles worn by other female barristers. Her mother scanned the crowd, eyes wide, jaw tight. Sita wondered for the first time if perhaps her mother had not brought her along for the educational experience. Perhaps she had simply needed someone to stand beside her.

"We should go in. One of your father's aides is saving us a seat."

Entering the courtroom, the crowd of people was so packed that she almost took her mother's hand. But she was too old for such things and Sanaya did not appreciate it when her children acted like babies. Today, for the first time, she had styled Sita's hair in a mature chignon much like her own. Sita patted her beautiful pouf of thick hair nervously, staying close as her mother led them up the rows of long wooden benches.

A familiar face waved to them from the second row from the front. The young man looked relieved to see them.

"Mrs Sharma, Miss Sita, I will let Prakash know you are here."

Sanaya nodded her thanks to the Law Clerk, but Sita's father had already seen them. A handsome man in his mid-forties, Prakash Sharma flashed them his infectious smile, though today there was a nervous edge to it. The day prior, the other two defendants had been acquitted. Sita had heard him joke that, if Khan was acquitted, they might as well just move to Goa because their life here would be over. She would be sorry for her father if he lost, but she did love the beach. They had vacationed in Goa the year before, and her memories of swimming in the ocean at sunset were still vivid, the sunlight like an orange path, unrolling before her on the water.

Swimming sounded wonderful right now. Even with the high, airy ceilings, the room was sweltering. On little foldout tables set around the room, metal rotating fans endeavoured to move the heavy air. Her father gave her mother a last, meaningful glance, then turned back to his team and whispered something to Mr Khanna, one of the senior barristers at her father's firm.

"Is it always so hot in here?" Sita whispered.

"No, a power surge knocked out the air conditioning yesterday. This is why I could not bring Chandra," she said, referring to Sita's younger sister. "You know how she complains. Not like you," her mother added, allowing a small smile of approval.

Sita stood up straighter. Though her mother might have intended to head off more complaints with this rare compliment, it was true. She was the eldest; it was her responsibility to set the example. As such, she tried to never complain.

The Judge entered, and the packed room quieted. When he sat, those with seats did so as well. The Judge, a small elderly man, reminded her of Mahatma Gandhi with his round spectacles, bald head and white moustache. He banged his gavel once, and the crowded courtroom went silent. Brooding anticipation hung in the air like invisible smoke. Even though the room was filled beyond capacity, only the fans could be heard.

On the Defendant's side, Raju Khan sat beside his team of four barristers. He was easily recognisable from the news coverage of the case. More than once, Sita had come down to breakfast to see his face in black and white, the newspaper stained with tea from a cup that had been slammed down in frustration.

"He's a mob boss. He traffics drugs, people and prostitutes. He could wallpaper his house in money. Of course he bought some journalists and editors!"

From the garden, she had heard her mother say this to her father.

"And will he buy the Law Clerk, the Jail Warden, the Judge?" her father had hollered. "The corruption in this country must stop somewhere! The law must apply equally to all! We must win this case!"

Another morning, she came down to find her father smiling as he buttered his toast. The headline that morning read: "King of Mumbai Underworld Unable to Bribe His Way Out?"

Now she stared at the man himself as her father took the floor to offer his closing statement.

"Ladies and gentlemen, your Honour," Prakash bowed his head to the Judge. "Over these past months, you have heard from forty-six witnesses. You have had to view over one hundred and eighty-two incriminating photographs as well as four video tapes depicting serious crimes in play. Some of these we will not soon forget, much as we might like to." He paused to allow the gravity of the crimes to resonate through the crowd.

Raju Khan watched her father impassively. His glossy moustache outlined a sneer, and his hooded eyes drooped with indifference, perhaps even boredom. Now and then, he reached into his pocket to grab a handful of peanuts which he tossed effortlessly into his mouth, dropping the shells onto the floor by his feet.

"Unlike his co-conspirators who were acquitted yesterday, the evidence against Raju Khan is overwhelming. He has been arrested many times before this, but this is the first time he has seen the inside of a courtroom, the first time that justice is within reach. Through all levels of Mumbai's society, this man has worked like a poison. Though the defence team would have you believe he is a family man and entrepreneur, my team has proven beyond a shadow of a doubt that Mr Khan is a murderer, a thief, a money launderer, and a human and drug trafficker. Today, we have the chance to cleanse our city of his toxic influence."

One of the Defence Barristers took the floor next. As her father had predicted, he began by speaking of Mr Khan's family, his charitable organisations, and the many people who were reliant on him as their employer. Winding himself up, the Barrister began to decry the prosecutor's smear campaign, the persecution of an innocent man and the loss of liberty and good name which Mr Khan had placed at her father's hands. Mr Khan continued to crack peanuts, nodding approvingly.

Beside her, Sita's mother exhaled sharply in quiet outrage.

Sweat beaded on Sita's brow as the man went on and on. At last, he concluded, having repeated his basic arguments five times over. All present now turned to the Judge who hammered his gavel down once.

"Mr Khan," he began. "You have been tried for murder, money laundering, theft, human trafficking and drug trafficking. This Court finds you—" Here, the Judge picked up his glass of water and took a sip, a slim smile plying his lips as he enjoyed the suspense. "This court finds you guilty on all counts."

Sita looked from the Judge to her father, then her mother, then Raju Khan. Shock registered on all their faces. Sita's mother took her hand and squeezed it as the prosecutor's team let out a cheer. The courtroom exploded in chatter, most of the people standing near them sounding relieved, even elated. But Mr Khan's cold gaze had turned furious, and his four barristers were already pointing fingers at one another, trying to assign blame before it fell at their feet.

"Your father did it," Sanaya said, speaking quietly in Sita's ear. "This is not just about Mr Khan. The people of India can have faith in their government, in the courts. They will write about Prakash in history books."

Sita watched as Mr Khanna, the senior barrister, patted her father on the back, looking as shocked as everyone else. Feeling that she'd just witnessed an event of great importance, she followed her mother back out to the car.

They had to hurry home to plan the celebration.

Nilopha, the children's nanny, sat on the daybed in the light-filled living room, listening as seven-year-old Ravi read his lessons to her. On the floor, eighteen-month-old Ganesh crawled across the handsome red carpets. Chandra, her glasses smeared and face still pinched with annoyance at being left at home, sat on one of several cushioned ottomans, idly tracing the intricately carved wooden table beside her. All looked up as Sita and Sanaya entered the room. Nilopha stood as quickly as her bad hips would allow and hurried forward.

"Well? Tell me the good news!"

Sanaya's smile said it all. She embraced the older woman. Sita thought, not for the first time, that her mother was beautiful.

"We won. That crook is going to jail!"

Nilopha patted Ravi's shoulders as he came forward and threw his arms around his mother's leg. Sita doubted he understood what was happening, he just liked to see his mother smile.

"Toys and books away, children!" Nilopha said, clapping her hands. "We must prepare for guests!"

Sita found herself shooed up the grand curved staircase with the others.

In her and Chandra's room, decorated in gold and pink, she looked in the mirror. She had her mother's almond eyes, high cheekbones and delicate lips. But there was something of her father in her face too, that same infectious smile that made people want to open up to him, to trust him.

Taking down the chignon, her hair fell in soft waves over her shoulders. She'd turned fourteen several months ago. Her face had lost its baby fat, and curves had started to appear on her slender frame. She was becoming an adult. In the past months, despite all the activity and upset in the house, she had not fully realised what important work her father was doing. For the first time, it occurred to her that one day she too might do important work.

After Nilopha had tucked them in and took to her own bed with a headache, Sita and Chandra got back up to watch the party from the top of the stairs. Ravi was already there, lured forth by the languorous buzz of the sitar on their mother's favourite classical album. Sanaya had decorated the beige great room with dozens of candles and tiny lights. The room glittered, candlelight reflecting off gold-stitched saris and the bright silver cuff-links of Western-style suits. The room was filled with her father's colleagues and well-wishers, all fashionably dressed and sipping champagne. Sanaya had hired kitchen staff as well, and a young man carried a tray of sweating, fluted glasses through the crowd.

Her father stood at the bottom of the stairs. Looking up, he caught sight of Sita and her siblings and winked at them, then began to make his way through the gathering. Sita recognised Mr Khanna, standing beside a police officer by the teak banquet on which the buffet-style food had been set out. Her father stopped to greet them, and they both clapped him on the back.

Between the railings, Sita gazed down at all the excitement with wonder and pride, fascinated by the beautiful dresses, jewellery and elegant hairstyles. In stark contrast, she wore her long, white cotton nightgown along with a pair of leather sandals.

"These people are all here because Papa won?" asked Ravi.

She was only surprised that he didn't follow this question with five more. Their father called it having an inquisitive mind.

"It was a very big case against a very bad man," replied Sita. "They say Papa is a hero."

"Do you think Papa's picture will be in the newspaper tomorrow morning?" asked Chandra. She took a handkerchief and wiped her flat, stubby little nose; she was constantly suffering from one ailment or another. She looked at Sita, her eyes a muddy brown beneath a fringe of frizzy hair and glasses. Not a beauty, but, like Ravi, she had always been at the top of her class.

"Yes, I'm sure of it." Sita made a mental note to wake very early and get to the newspaper first. "Look, Papa is going to say something. Be quiet, I want to hear this."

"I know it is getting late and many of you have to make the long drive back to Mumbai this evening," said

Prakash. "So, please just give me a few moments of your time."

Someone tapped a knife against a glass, and he smiled in appreciation.

"First, let me thank you all for coming to my home here in Pune. It is an Honour and a privilege to have so many of my friends and co-workers here tonight, for this is a very special celebration."

The crowd of thirty men and women clapped politely.

"I'd like to thank you all for your support. While we were able to secure one major conviction today, please remember that two others were acquitted," Prakash continued. "So, we must be humble. But despite this minor setback, I consider this trial to be an important victory for our legal system."

Another brisk round of applause followed. Sanaya, standing at the front of the gathering in a gorgeous blue satin outfit, beamed at her husband.

"As you know, nearly all our critics said that our legal system could never secure the conviction of a notorious kingpin within the Mumbai Mafia. They accused our laws and our procedures of being corrupt and incapable of doing any good. But this ruling today shows that this is just not so. Our courts can work, our courts can convict and our courts can clean up our country and put it back into the hands of honest, respectable Indians. Thank you again for coming and let us continue what we have started here today."

The audience gave a third round of applause, slapping Prakash's back as he passed by as if he were a big celebrity. Within minutes, the chitchat resumed as people found their places among their respective cliques.

After walking over and whispering something into Sita's mother's ear, Prakash walked back up the stairs.

"What are you three doing up so late?" He tried to sound stern, but he had never been very good at this role. Sita thought he looked relieved to escape the party. "You should have been in bed hours ago. Look at the time! It is well past eleven. And where is Nilopha?"

"Nanny went to bed already, Papa," replied Sita. "She had another one of her headaches. Can't we stay up and watch for just a little while longer? Chandra and Ravi don't have school tomorrow."

"What about you, Sita? Are you up-to-date on your studies? Last week your tutor informed me that she caught you sketching saris instead of studying again."

"It was a Kappulu like the woman down there is wearing," she said, nodding towards an older woman in an emerald and gold costume. "It drapes from left to right instead, with that thin pleat in the back—"

Prakash hushed her at his wife's approach. Sanaya had made it clear that Sita should not waste her time on fashion. Anticipating what she was going to say, Prakash backed off and squared his shoulders sternly.

"What are you three doing up so late?" she asked in a concerned voice. "And Sita, look at you. You can't be seen in those clothes, especially by strangers. You're a young lady now. How many times have I told you to begin acting like one?"

"Sorry, Mama," replied Sita, her head down. "Do you think we can stay up for a short time longer? We won't come down. No one will ..."

"Absolutely not! I want you three in bed right this moment."

Sita turned toward their father for support. But she could tell by his expression that he wasn't willing to take on this battle.

"Okay, children, I will tuck you in," said Prakash, placating. "Now hop into bed! All of you, at once."

Ravi went off to his room while Sita and Chandra returned to their own. After a short visit with Ravi, Prakash came to say goodnight to the girls.

"Papa?" said Sita, as her father tucked the mosquito net in around the mattress.

"Yes, Sita," he replied with a warm smile.

"Can we take the car and drive to the park tomorrow? It has been such a long time since we did anything as a family. With your work and..." Sita stopped herself from completing the statement. She tried not to complain to him about his excessive hours away. "Please?"

"I can't, Princess. I must prepare for another major case that is coming up next week. When this is all over, we will take a long vacation together. I promise."'

"Can we go to Goa again? Let's go to the same hotel with the pool and the restaurants, right on the beach... Can we go there again, Papa? Please?"

"Anywhere you'd like," he replied, though he looked away as he said it. "I'm sorry I've been so busy, but the work I'm doing is very important to me—to us all."

"Papa, why is Mama always so strict with me?"

"She is not..."

"Yes, she is!" Sita insisted. "I can't watch TV or see my friends very often. I hate not being able to go to school with the others. I have been out for nearly two years now. When can I go back again? I don't like studying at home—it's boring! I'm tired of the same tutor every day."

"Your mother worries about you. She wants you to get the best education you can. That school you were attending before wasn't good. After this year is over, we will enrol you again in another school, one that is much better. I promise."

"Really?"

"Yes, now get some sleep."

"Congratulations again, Papa."

"Thank you, Dear Heart. Good night."

Her head sunk into the feather pillow, her eyelids heavy. Tomorrow she would get to the newspaper first, to see if Papa's picture was in the paper. Nilopha had promised to make idlis for breakfast, and the texture of the steamed rice dough pancakes filled her with a sleepy anticipation. She could leave the newspaper by Papa's seat at the table before he awoke. Her mind began to drift then her eyes shot open -- the dress, the one

made of mango chiffon with the Gol saree draping—
she'd meant to draw it this evening! She debated for
a moment, then closed her eyes again. It was late. It
could wait for tomorrow. If it was good, she'd send it to
her friend Amara in her letter.

13

2

Sita awoke to the gentle pressure of her nanny's hand over her mouth. Opening her eyes, she met Nilopha's terrified gaze. The woman put a gnarled finger to her lips.

"Quiet, Dear One," Nilopha whispered, voice tight with terror. "Not a word! I want you to wake up your sister and follow me to your brother's room. Immediately! But whatever you do, don't say anything and don't make a sound."

"What is happening, Nilopha?" asked Sita, rising to a sitting position.

"Shhhhh! Just do as I say and be quiet!"

"Where are Mama and Papa?"

"They can't come now. They are downstairs. Now listen to me. There is danger in this house—grave danger. I need you to help me get the others out of here. After we collect the boys, we will leave through the window in my room. Do you understand me?"

"Yes," replied Sita with great apprehension. Nilopha had been her nanny since she was born but never had Sita seen such fear in her eyes.

Sita quickly approached Chandra's bed. Her sister woke and looked at them blearily, annoyed at the interruption.

Nilopha put her hands on the girls' shoulders.

"Chandra, I want you to immediately go to my room and wait. Close the door, and don't make a sound. When you pass the staircase, I want you to crouch down on all fours. Do not look down."

"Why must I do this?" asked Chandra, confused. Her hand fumbled to find her glasses on the nightstand.

"We are playing a game," replied Nilopha, forcing a smile. "It's like hide and go seek."

"But I'm tired," Chandra complained. "Can't we play in the morning?"

"Chandra, do as Nilopha says," Sita insisted, tamping down her own fear. "You can sleep late tomorrow. I promise."

"Okay, I'll go. It doesn't sound like much fun at all," she added, doubtful.

Nilopha peered down the hall, making sure Chandra did as she'd been told. "Sita, you come with me. You take Ganesh, and I'll take Ravi. It will be hard to keep them from crying at this late hour but try not to wake them. Do you hear me? I can't do this alone. I need your help."

"Please, tell me what is happening!" Sita begged, beginning to cry.

"Later, Dear One," replied Nilopha, as she wiped the tears away with trembling hands. "We have to go immediately. And whatever you do, stay away from the stairs."

"Will we really be leaving the house?"

"Yes."

"What about the clothes we all have on? They are our sleeping clothes."

"We don't have time to do anything about that."

"But..."

"Stop it, Sita, and do as you are told!" Nilopha hissed.

Nilopha and Sita entered the boys' room. Without waking them, they managed to pick them both up and carry them to Nilopha's room. The old woman led, struggling with her burden.

As she passed by the staircase, Sita stopped and looked down. Her breath caught in her chest, and bile rose in her throat. Her arms and legs went weak.

Her father's beaten, lifeless body was lying just in front of the couch. Beside him, her mother pleaded hysterically with a man who stood directly in front of her.

There were four men present. One was an associate of her father, a Mr Khanna. The other was a man whose picture had been in the paper a lot lately. His name was M.S. Khan, and he was one of the two gangsters acquitted of the crimes in the case her father had just finished trying. He was an exceptionally tall man, well over six feet, with a huge round belly. The remaining two were police officers, still dressed in their uniforms. Both had been to the house on numerous occasions. One had even attended the victory party her father had thrown several hours before.

Frozen, Sita watched as one of the officers struck her mother hard across the face with his nightstick. Along with a steady stream of blood, several of her teeth fell to the Afghan carpet.

"Your husband never should have taken on this case," shouted Mr Khan, full of rage. "We warned him many times, but he didn't listen. Now he is dead. And soon, you and the rest of your family will experience the same fate. I don't see anyone celebrating his victory over my brother's conviction now. Do you?"

"Please don't hurt my children," she pleaded, reaching for his leg. He pulled back before pushing her aside. "They're innocent. Please, I will do anything. They had nothing to do with this. Don't harm them. I beg you. They're just babies."

"It is much too late for that, Madam. There is no changing what has already happened. After we kill you, your children will be next. And believe me, we will do it slowly and painfully. We warned your husband, but he didn't listen to us. He never should have taken on that case. He should have listened."

He lifted his foot and kicked her in the head. She fell to the floor, crying hysterically.

It took a firm push from Nilopha for Sita to move. Without any further delay, they entered the old woman's bedroom and gently placed the sleeping boys onto the soft bed. Then Nilopha locked the door.

"I need you to listen to me." The old woman gently stroked Sita's face. "I must go over to the window for a few minutes. While I am there, I want you to sit beside your sister on the other side of my bed. Try not to wake your brothers." Nilopha waited to ensure that Sita understood the instructions. "And whatever you do, don't tell her what you just saw! Okay?"

"Don't leave us!" Sita pleaded. The impact of what she had just observed was beginning to register. Her entire body trembled from head to toe.

"Don't worry. I will only be on the other side of the room. I will not leave you."

Nilopha limped over to the window, her arthritic joints struggling with the latch. Sita stood to help her, and together, they threw it open wide.

"Sushanta, Sushanta!" Nilopha whispered, trying to get the guard's attention.

A moment later, he came staggering over to the side of the house. Dressed in a lungi and cotton t-shirt, his meaty face offered only its usual blank expression.

"What is it?" he asked in a loud voice.

"Shhhh," Nilopha scolded. "Hurry and climb up here to this window. Make it quick!"

The guard, clearly oblivious to what was happening inside, did as he was told, placing a garden ladder against the building and climbing up.

"What are you doing up at this time?" he slurred, as he clumsily fell through the window. His breath stunk of cheap alcohol. His bloodshot eyes betrayed his intoxicated state.

She pulled him aside, whispering so the other children could not hear. "Sahib has been killed, you fool. Madam and the children will soon be next. You must take them away from here."

"What are you talking about? The men who came tonight are friends of Sahib."

"Trust me, Sahib is dead. I saw him killed with my own eyes. And when they have finished with Madam, they will come looking for all of us, including you and me. Do you understand?" Nilopha asked, looking repeatedly over her shoulder at the closed door. "We are all in grave danger! Now, you have to take the children to the train station for me. No place in Pune will be safe for them after what just happened."

"Let me go and get the police," replied Sushanta, beginning to sober up a bit and turning back toward the window ledge.

"No! Two of those men downstairs are police officers," Nilopha hissed. "One of the others, a barrister, works for Sahib. Didn't you recognise him from the party?"

Shaking her head at him, she pulled a wad of rupees from her pocket and thrust it into his hand. "I hope this will be enough. It is all I have. Now, Sushanta, go with the children to the station, and buy five first-class tickets to New Delhi. This way they will give you a cabin to yourself. Once you have the tickets, take the children, get on the train, close the cabin door, and don't talk to a living soul. Buy some food and something to drink before the train leaves. Mineral water or juice is best. And get some milk for little Ganesh. Do you hear me? I will contact Sahib's sister, Auntie Nadia. She will be waiting for you at the station when you arrive. Take the 4:30 a.m. express. It will get you there the next day."

"I can't do this by myself," Sushanta confessed. "You have to go with them. I don't know anything about taking care of children. You know I don't have any of my own. Besides, what if they find me with them? They might..."

"You know I can't climb down that ladder with my bad hips," replied Nilopha, not letting him finish his statement. "Sushanta, you have been working for Sahib for nearly five years now. He has been good to you even with all of your drinking and gambling. How many times has he got you out of trouble? It is time for you to repay his kindness. All you have to do is stay inside the cabin with the children and when the train comes to a stop in New Delhi, their Auntie will be there to take the children. Don't be a coward, Sushanta. I know you can do this thing. I will call her now, but I want you to hold onto her name and address just in case something unforeseen happens."

"What will you do after we leave?"

"I will try to sneak out the back door once the call has been made. Don't worry about me—just go!"

Nilopha wrote the address on a small piece of paper. The guard stuffed it into his shirt pocket with the money.

"Sita, Chandra, come over here now," Nilopha instructed.

Sita took her sister's hand and pulled her forward.

"This isn't a game," Chandra whispered in weak protest.

"I need you both to listen to me very carefully, Dears," Nilopha said with tears streaming down her face. "Sita, I want you to quietly wake Ravi, but don't let him say anything. Chandra, you need to pick up Ganesh and hold him very tightly. Try not to wake him. You will then all leave through this window. Sushanta will help you to get down the ladder. Then Sushanta is going to take you to the train station. The five of you will take a long train ride to New Delhi. I want you to be good, mind Sushanta and stay inside the compartment. Don't talk to anyone, and don't leave the space unless you absolutely must. Sushanta will see that you have food and water. When you arrive in New Delhi, your Auntie will be waiting for you on the platform. She will care for you until this can all be sorted out. Do you understand what I'm saying? Can you be big girls for me?"

"Where are Mama and Papa?" Chandra demanded.

"They are both very busy now!" Nilopha snapped. She gave Sita her most stern expression, her message clear. For now, she must keep the horrible secret to herself. As Sita began to cry, Nilopha gently grabbed her arm and led her a few feet away to a corner. "Sushanta, please go now and help Chandra and Ganesh to the ground. Sita and Ravi will be there in a moment."

"I don't understand. Why doesn't someone go and get the police?" Sita gasped between sobs.

"Didn't you see those men, Sita? At least two of them work for the police. They are not to be trusted under any circumstances. Do you hear me? The police are in on everything that has happened here tonight. Promise me you will stay far away from them. Promise me!"

Sita nodded, sobbing harder. "Did they really kill my father?"

"I don't know. After you have all safely escaped, I will try to get help for your parents."

"One of the men said that they were going to hurt us."

"That is why you must leave immediately. Don't say anything to the other children. They are too young to understand any of this. When the time comes, your Auntie will know what to say and how to say it. You are going to have to be strong, Sita. For the next few days, you are going to need to take on the role of mother as well as sister."

"I can't do this—I'm frightened!"

"You must. Sushanta will take you on the train, but he does not know how to handle children. You will have to keep the family together. This is what your mother and father would have wanted. Now go."

Nilopha guided her towards the bed to wake Ravi.

At a nod from Nilopha, Sita offered him a watery smile. "We're going on an adventure," she told him, voice weak. With sleepy acceptance, he followed her to the ladder where Sushanta was waiting. He took Ravi, and she followed a moment later.

"Keep the family together, Sita." Nilopha whispered out the window. "That is all I ask of you. Stay together."

"I will," she said, her night gown snapping around her legs as the warm breeze tugged and caught at it.

A moment later, they all had disappeared into the darkness.

3

Sita and the other children followed Sushanta through a familiar hole in the boundary wall, into the park that bordered their home. Whenever the guard looked back, which was often, his eyes were wide and sober, though his slack jaw did little to inspire real confidence. Still, Sita stuck close to him, hurrying her sleepy siblings onward, past the playground area they often visited, over the large mandala that had been painted on the cracked concrete and down a set of stone stairs. Distantly, behind them, they could hear fire sirens.

"Why are we going this way to the train station?" Chandra asked. Sita shushed her and Chandra's thin lips compressed into a frown, but she did not repeat her question. Ravi, amazingly, had not quizzed them about the strange events of the night at all. Looking at his sweet, cherubic face only made it more difficult not to cry. They passed a fountain, the water lit with green lights. Ravi smiled, delighted and blissfully unaware of what had happened.

"Sita, what about our clothes?" asked Chandra, pulling on her sister's arm to get her attention. "Why can't you tell me what you know?"

"Never mind," Sita replied, trying her best to hold back her tears. "Keep walking and hold on to Ravi's hand."

"My feet are getting tired," Ravi said. "When are we going back home?"

"Listen, all of you," said Sita, gathering the others into a small huddle. Sushanta stood off to one side and waited impatiently. "You are going to need to do something for me. Soon we are going to catch a great big train that will take us to New Delhi. Do you remember we all went there two summers ago? Well, we are going there again. We will visit Auntie for a short while. Don't worry, it will be lots of fun. You'll see." She did her best to force a smile.

"But where are Mama and Papa?" asked Ravi, reaching down to shake a small pebble out of one of his sandals. "Why aren't they coming with us?"

"They will meet up with us soon enough," replied Sita, pulling her brother into her arms to give him a reassuring hug. "Just do as I say and everything will be fine. Okay? Since Papa is not here now, you need to be the man of the family. Can you do that for me? I need to take care of little Ganesh. Since he is still just a baby, this will require a lot of my attention. So, I'm going to need all the support I can get from you."

"Yes," he replied, accepting the responsibility. On many other occasions when their father had travelled on his frequent business trips, Ravi was asked to take on this role. He liked it when he was treated like a big boy.

"Good. Then let's get going, shall we?"

Near the main entrance to the park, a gang of young men who had finished cruising for the night watched as this motley crew passed them by.

"Are you kids lost?" asked one of the teenagers as the others broke out into laughter. "This is not a place to be out so late. Don't you know that bad things happen in parks, especially in the middle of the night?"

There was a second round of laughter.

"Don't listen to them," Sita whispered, grabbing her brother's hand. "Just keep walking."

Once outside the park, the family made their way through the old bazaar on Gandhi Road. No customers haggled, no vendors bargained. The silence weighed on them, oppressive. The usual smells of curry and hot oil were now faint and stale, and trampled marigolds marked the location of the flower stall. The only people present at this late hour were a handful of security guards who walked around in slow circles to stop themselves from falling asleep, a half dozen dogs that slept huddled together in a large pack and the occasional rat that scurried along the dark alleyways that branched off into darkness. To avoid slipping on the rotten produce that was scattered along the road, the group was forced to slow down and negotiate these hazardous obstacles.

The sight of Mumbai Central Station was a relief. The clock on the central tower read four am, but despite the early hour, the vaulted interior was bustling with people, some waiting to board trains, others waiting for passengers to arrive, while still others sold baked goods or squatted on their haunches to nap.

"Have everyone stand here beside this pillar," Sushanta said to Sita, his eyes scanning the station. "I need to make a few arrangements now." He left them leaning against the enormous marble pillar. On the gleaming floor, just a few feet away, an enormous compass rose pointed to all the many directions they might go.

While she desperately wanted to break down and cry, this was a luxury that would have to wait. There were too many things to worry about: keeping the family together, ensuring they got on the right train and finding Auntie at the New Delhi station. She pushed her grief and sorrow to the back of her mind. There was no other way.

Ganesh finally woke up in Sita's arms. For the first few minutes, he looked around the station as if trying to figure out what had happened to his world. Then he began to cry.

Ordinarily, Ganesh was no trouble at all. Considered by everyone to be a beautiful, easy-going baby with his round, pudgy cheeks, sparkling eyes and irresistible smile, he was easy to fall in love with. The only thing that marred his perfection was a large red birthmark on his left arm in the shape of India. Pointing to this prominent blemish, Prakash would brag that the birthmark was a sign that India was truly in his youngest son's blood.

Finally, Sushanta returned with a large bag of food and drinks and a collection of blue tickets, the colour that denoted first class accommodations.

"What took you so long?" asked Sita. "We've been waiting forever." She continued to rock Ganesh up and down in the hopes of getting him to fall back to sleep, but nothing seemed to console him.

"Forgive me. There was a long line to get the tickets," Sushanta apologised, hurt that his efforts were not more greatly appreciated. "Now, follow me. We do not have much time before the train departs."

They hurried along the extended cement ramp that led to the Delhi-bound train. After climbing up the steep stairs to the first-class car and helping Sita with her burden, Sushanta located the right compartment and escorted the children inside.

"Okay, now, your train leaves in just about twenty minutes."

"What do you mean by your train?" asked Sita. She took several steps aside away from the ears of the other children. "You are going with us!"

"I only had enough money for three first-class tickets." He bowed his head, avoiding Sita's eyes. "Ganesh, being an infant, doesn't need a ticket. If I had got one for myself, there would not have been enough money to buy any food. You all need something to eat for the long journey, and Ganesh needed milk."

"But Nilopha said you were to travel with us! You have to do what she says. She told you to come along!" This mutiny was unheard of.

"I am not going," Sushanta insisted. "When you get to Delhi, stand on the platform. Your Auntie will be there waiting for you. You will be safe there."

"But we are just children—we can't travel that far by ourselves!"

"You're fourteen years old. When I was your age, I used to take trains by myself all the time. Just do as Nilopha said. Don't talk to a living soul, stay inside the cabin and when you get there, look for your Auntie. Oh, and don't open your windows. When the train stops, people sometimes try to reach inside or climb through the window. Be careful of this."

"I demand that you do as I say! You work for my parents. That means you work for us too. You have to go with us."

Sushanta handed over the bag of food. It contained bananas, biscuits, two bottles of mineral water, a container of milk, and ten Fruiti mango drinks.

"Do as I say, and you'll be fine," said Sushanta, as he stepped outside the cabin and shut the door. Without another moment's hesitation, he turned and began to walk toward the exit.

"Sushanta, you get back here!" Sita shouted, desperate. "You get back here now!"

He continued on. Only when he was out of sight did she realise he had not given her the piece of paper with her aunt's address. She thought of running after him. He would be at one of the tea stalls, the only place to get alcohol at this hour. But what if the train started? Chandra would never be able to take care of the others by herself. Abuzz with anxiety, Sita stayed put. She would just have to trust that her Aunt Nadia would be waiting for them.

Within the first twenty minutes of the train ride, Chandra, Ravi and Ganesh all fell fast asleep. Sita, after making sure the window and door were locked, tried to close her eyes and get some rest, but each time she faced the darkness, she was haunted by the sight of her mother and father in the living room. The fact that they were both dead was inconceivable. Even though she replayed the scene over and over again in her mind, she just couldn't accept it. Parents were supposed to grow old and eventually die. That was what had happened to her grandparents. They were not supposed to be hurt at the hands of others in the prime of their lives.

She clung to the hope that what she had seen was somehow wrong. Perhaps, even now, her parents were searching for them.

Just over an hour into the trip, there was a light knock on the door. Not knowing what to do, Sita sat up in her seat and listened. A minute later, the knocking continued, this time with more force. With no answer, a key was inserted into the lock, and the door was opened.

"What is going on in here?" asked the conductor, his suspicious eyes taking in the sleeping children. "Why didn't you answer my knock?"

"I didn't hear you, sir," Sita confessed, trying her best to produce a smile. "Sorry, we had all fallen asleep."

"I need to see your tickets," stated the conductor, appearing to accept this explanation.

"Certainly."

Sita picked the tickets up off the small table and handed them over.

"Are you and these other children travelling by yourself?" he asked, looking for a sign of an adult.

"Yes, I am taking them all to New Delhi."

"How old are you?"

"I'm nearly eighteen," Sita lied. "I do this all the time. I have been travelling on trains like this for many years, since I was fourteen. My father dropped us off at the station in Pune, and when we arrive, my auntie will be waiting for us."

He gave them one more look. "Very well. Have a good trip. Keep the door locked."

"Thank you."

Sita drew a sigh of relief when the door was shut, and she was left alone again.

The remainder of the journey was long but uneventful. When the children were hungry, they ate. When they were tired, they slept. Despite the warning given by Nilopha and Sushanta, Sita opened the window several times to purchase small food items from passing vendors during one of the frequent station stops. In the bottom of the bag, Sushanta had left three ten-rupee notes. She used this money to buy what she needed.

Throughout much of the trip, Sita was unable to sleep. Her mind kept replaying what she had seen.

While the others slept, she cried. When they awoke, she occupied them with games. Only when they had reached their Auntie would she tell them what had happened. Auntie would know what to do, how to fix things. How to tell her siblings this impossible news.

And besides, maybe Auntie would investigate and find that she was worried for nothing. She pictured her parents opening their eyes and rising from the floor, her father grinning with his bright white Bollywood smile and taking a bow, like a magician. It was not impossible, that she'd been deceived somehow. She must have been. They only needed to reach her Auntie, and it would all be sorted.

4

The train finally crept into New Delhi Station a few minutes before 9:00 the following morning. The building, painted a vivid red, orange and green, was bustling with commuter traffic. Every minute, a thousand people crisscrossed one another on their way to destinations in the capital city.

Only after most of the other passengers had departed the train did Sita unlock the door of the private car. With Ganesh held tightly in her arms, she directed the worn out and bewildered group to a location near the centre of the building, a good vantage point to locate Auntie. Ravi's eyes were puffy with sleep, Chandra's face pale with worry.

"Now, I want you all to keep a close eye out for Auntie." At least a portion of her nightmare would soon be coming to an end. "After Auntie picks us up from here, she will take us home, and we will all be safe."

Standing together in a tight group, ten minutes passed and then another ten. Auntie was supposed to have been waiting for them at the station.

"Don't worry. She is coming for us. We just have to be patient," she repeated, willing herself to believe it. "Chandra, stop crying. And Ravi, I want you to keep your fingers out of your mouth. Be a big boy." She slapped his hand for the third time. "This place is so very dirty. We will be in Auntie's house soon. Once there, we can all take a nice warm bath and then go back to sleep. It'll be okay, I promise you."

After forty endless minutes, her brave face was crumbling. Auntie Nadia—what was her last name? How in the world would she go about tracking her down in a big city like Delhi? The thought of going to the police entered her mind several times. Each time, she dismissed it. Nilopha had said not to trust them.

A pair of policemen approached them. Sita waved, as if she had seen someone she knew and walked the group a little distance away. The policemen passed them by without another glance. She slumped, exhausted. Her little subterfuge had worked but for how long? As this question bore down on her, she stared off into the crowd. Only then did she notice a woman watching them from the other side of the tracks.

The woman smiled at her, and Sita froze, as if discovered, though the woman was no obvious threat. Dressed in a simple blue sari with a long white scarf that hung over her shoulders and draped down to her slim waist, her appearance was genteel, beautiful even, with her heart shaped face and bewitching gaze. She smiled wider, and Sita again moved her little group, uneasy about the attention. The police were walking past again. She motioned for her siblings to move to another post, out of their way. Glancing across the tracks from their new position, she found the woman had watched this manoeuvre with interest. Then Ganesh began to cry, and she bounced him on her hip. When she next looked across the tracks, the woman was gone.

"Sita, where is Auntie Nadia?" Chandra's voice was a thin whine. "You said she'd be here when we arrived. That was a long, long time ago. I feel so stupid standing here in these night clothes."

Sita turned to hush her, startled to find the woman in the blue sari now standing only a short distance away. The woman stood quite still, staring off into the distance. Sita couldn't shake the feeling that she was listening,

"I'm hungry," Ravi joined in, repeatedly tugging at Sita's sleeve. "Why isn't Mama or Papa here with us? I miss them. When are we going home?"

"Shut up, both of you and wait!" Sita snapped as Ganesh began to wail at the top of his lungs.

"Shh, shh, I know, you're hungry and tired," she said to him, bouncing him gently on her hip. He was drawing attention. Soon the police might feel the need to inquire about the child's health and well-being.

"Hello, Sita, is that you?" The woman in the blue sari stepped up to them, offering a sympathetic smile. Up close, Sita noticed that the woman's left eye twitched uncontrollably. But her manner of dress and speaking resembled that of Sanaya's friends, though she was younger than her mother was.

"Who are you?" asked Sita. Taking an involuntary step backward, she gathered all of the children into a tight circle around her.

"I'm here to pick you up. Your Auntie Nadia sent me. My name is Mrs Gupta. I'm her next-door neighbour. Unfortunately, she was unable to come, so she called and asked me to wait here at the station until you arrived. I'm sorry for being so late. The traffic in the city this morning was horrendous. My driver just now pulled into the parking lot. So here I am." The twitch in her left eye grew worse as she smiled again.

"But why wouldn't Auntie Nadia come herself?" asked Sita, full of doubt. "Nilopha said she was going to be here. She promised me so. After what happened back..." Sita stopped short of finishing the statement. The woman might not know about their situation. Perhaps it was best if she didn't.

"Well, you see, my dear, your Auntie wasn't feeling very well. With your uncle travelling and her in bed with a high fever, she asked me to bring you home to her right away." Mrs Gupta watched Sita's reaction closely. "Now before we leave, please remind me of each of your names. Your Auntie told me, but they slipped my mind. I'm afraid I've never been very good at keeping peoples' names straight. Please forgive me."

The woman must have been looking for them when Sita first spotted her. She must have been listening to make sure they were the children she had been sent to pick up. There was no other explanation.

"This is my sister, Chandra, and my brother, Ravi."

"What about the little one?" asked Mrs Gupta, reaching out to gently squeeze his right cheek. This gesture further exacerbated his crying which rose to an even higher pitch.

"His name is Ganesh," replied Sita. "He is very tired and hungry. I am sure he will settle down after we safely arrive at Auntie's place."

"Tell me, how old is the little guy?"

"He's nearly eighteen months."

"He is very cute and in such good health. What a nice little boy." The dark, bewitching eyes focused fully on Ganesh for several moments before she asked, "Aren't you four a bit young to be travelling alone on a train? This is no place for children. It can sometimes be very dangerous. There are bad people around who prey on others. You have to watch out for them."

"We are old enough!" Sita insisted.

She smiled again. "I guess you are. And where are your parents now?"

"They are back in Pune. Now, can we please go?" The woman had too many questions. And she wasn't willing to talk about her parents. It was too painful.

"Very well, let's be off. Do you have any bags I can help you with?"

"No, we have none."

"That's curious. Then I guess we should be off. Okay?"

"Children, follow me," Sita ordered. "And keep close together. I don't want any of us to get lost in this crowd."

After negotiating the flocks of morning commuters coming and going, Mrs Gupta led the group out to a massive parking lot that was located on the right side of the building. As they manoeuvred past the many cars, a late-model Ambassador pulled up beside them. Her parents had a similar car. Almost everyone in India with a car had one of these nationally-made vehicles, but this one had seen better days, the bumper and doors dented and the paint rusting off. The driver of the car, a middle-aged Sikh who sported a long black beard and wore a large yellow turban around his head, jumped out and began opening up all of the doors.

Sita hesitated before she opened the back door. Would her upper-middle class aunt really have a neighbour who drove such a rust-bucket? It seemed so unlike her, Auntie, to send a stranger to pick them up.

"Why don't you and the others climb inside," Mrs Gupta suggested, helping Ravi into the back seat. "I'll ride up front with Mr Singh, my driver."

Before she had a chance to voice a doubt, Ravi and Chandra were both inside the car. Sita climbed in after them, Ganesh in her arms.

Once everyone was settled inside, Mr Singh looked at the four children in the rearview mirror and then turned toward Mrs Gupta. "What is with the four of them?" he asked with a low voice.

"I'll explain later," she replied. In the rearview mirror, Sita saw her wink at him, her anxiety ratcheting up a notch.

"Where to?" he asked, as he attempted to start the engine which took nearly a minute and several coughs to engage. But Mrs Gupta answered so quietly Sita could not hear her answer.

Twenty minutes passed as the car made its way down a labyrinth of narrow streets and alleys that seemed to take them deeper and deeper into the bowels of the old city.

"This doesn't look like my auntie's neighbourhood." Sita made the comment calmly, to avoid creating fear in her siblings. Unease pressed on her chest, making it hard to breathe.

"You're right, it isn't," replied Mrs Gupta with a warm smile. "I have to pick up some medicine for your Auntie, and there is a pharmacy nearby that sells drugs that a person can trust. My family has been using this place since I was a little girl. Many of those other shops that sell medicine in this city can't be trusted; they are not at all reliable. We will stop here for a short time, and then we will be on our way again. You will see your Auntie soon enough. Trust me."

They pulled up in front of a small chemist's shop. Outside, a dozen customers vied to be next in line to get their drug or potion. The sun had already begun to cloud over, and the street looked grey and dismal. Next door to the chemist's was a shop selling souvenirs, though no one in sight looked like a tourist. The window displayed tie-dyed shirts and rows of carved elephants, painted magenta, gold, emerald and turquoise. In the colourless street, they only made her tired eyes hurt.

Mrs Gupta climbed out, walked over to the driver's window and instructed, "Take them across the street to the hotel. We will stop there for a cold drink and something warm to eat. Go ahead and order some Chinese noodles. They'll be very hungry after such an extended journey. I'll arrive there momentarily." She then turned toward Sita. "When you get to the hotel, my driver will escort you all into the waiting area located on the ground floor. I know the owner of the hotel very well, and she won't mind. It is already dreadfully hot outside. This chore I have to do for your Auntie may take me a bit of time. Instead of waiting in a hot car, you four can rest inside a nice air-conditioned room."

"Please don't leave us!" Sita insisted as tears began to flow down her face. She was surrounded by millions of strangers. At least she knew this woman's name.

"Why those tears, my dear?" asked Mrs Gupta, wiping them off with the end of her shawl. "Don't you worry, I will be back shortly." Without saying another word, the woman walked away. The car proceeded to the hotel.

After pulling in front of the four-story building, a boy no older than twelve years old came rushing up to open the door. He wore a T-shirt and a tattered green lungi. Across his thin face, a long scar ran from ear to nose.

"Bring them to the common room," ordered the driver. "I'll be right inside. If anyone asks, tell them that they belong to Mrs Gupta, and she will arrive soon."

The boy nodded, gesturing them inside with both arms as if he were herding cattle.

The waiting room, which was dark and shadowy, contained two brown couches and a half dozen wooden chairs. Off in the corner was a small black and white television set that was tuned to one of the Hindi movie channels. Before leaving the room, the young boy watched a few minutes of a fight scene that was unfolding on the set. Ravi too went straight to the television.

"I thought Auntie was coming to pick us up," Chandra stated, her voice barely audible above the roar of the ancient air conditioner.

"Mrs Gupta just had to make a quick stop," Sita assured her. But her own worries and doubts ran in a similar vein.

She sat down, her hand touching the arm of the couch. It was damp from drops of condensed water that had fallen down from the AC. The heavy scent of mildew filled the room, making her nauseous.

"I don't like that lady," Chandra confessed. "She doesn't seem like one of Auntie's friends. There is something about her that frightens me."

"Don't worry, I'll keep a close eye on her," replied Sita, sharing Chandra's suspicions. But what could she do? The woman did know her name and appeared to have come on Auntie's behalf.

"I'm back." Mrs Gupta unexpectedly entered the room, the hotel boy at her heels. In his hands he held a tray of food and drink that contained three bottles of Coke, a small carton of milk, a large tray of fried noodles and some warm naan bread.

"Eat as much as you like," Mrs Gupta said. "Once you've finished, we will all be on our way again. Is that okay? Good! Now eat!"

Sita's stomach rebelled against her mistrust of the woman. She was starving. They'd eaten little other than crackers and biscuits since leaving Mumbai. Now the enticing smells of the warm food were too much to resist. Ravi and Chandra were already shovelling in hearty mouthfuls. Ganesh squirmed in her arms, interested as well.

"Here, I can feed him so you can eat," Mrs Gupta offered.

Sita hesitated only a moment, then handed her youngest brother over to the strange woman.

She woke with a gasp, as though emerging from deep water. The space was black, and her heart pounded in her ears. The last thing she remembered was having a meal in the hotel lobby with her brothers and sister. When had she fallen asleep? Where was she?

As she attempted to stand and explore her surroundings, she stumbled and nearly fell to the floor. Dizzy and disoriented, she tried again, this time using the wall to prop herself up. Confused and uneasy, she felt along the wall for a light switch. When she finally located one, she hastily turned it on only to discover that she was no longer in the hotel waiting area. She was instead in a tiny room with two iron cots on either side. A large fan dangled from the ceiling. With each rotation of the blades, it wobbled as if it might fall to the floor. The sheets on the cots were grey, the cracked tile floor filthy. Chandra and Ravi were both passed out on one of the cots. There was no sign of Ganesh.

"Where is Ganesh?" she screamed. She pulled at the handle of the door. It was locked from the outside. How could she have fallen asleep without ensuring that her baby brother was safe? "Chandra, Ravi, wake up! Where's Ganesh?" But even a violent shaking could not rouse either of them from their coma-like state.

A key clinked against the lock. She backed up against the opposite wall.

"I see you are finally waking up," said Mrs Gupta, appearing in the doorway. "I'm afraid that your little

Ganesh is presently at a local hospital. After you all fell asleep yesterday morning, he became violently ill. Because you were all so tired from your long journey, I didn't bother to wake you up. You needed your rest. So instead, I myself rushed him off to see a doctor. His fever was very high. It was a dangerous situation. It is a good thing I was there to help." She smiled benevolently and crossed her arms across her considerable bosom.

"Where is this hospital?" asked Sita, nearly hysterical. "How do I get there?"

"I'm afraid it is very far from where we are presently staying," Mrs Gupta responded with another superficial smile. "But don't you worry. We took him to one of the best doctors in the city. We had to drive very far to do this. But it was worth it. He will get the best care that money can buy. I will see to it myself."

"What happened to my Auntie? Why didn't you take us to her yesterday? And how did we get inside this horrible place? Look at it. It's disgusting!"

"I'm afraid your Auntie said she can't take you in just yet. I spoke to her this morning. Because of her own illness, she asked me to watch over you for a few days."

"I don't believe you," said Sita, taking several steps forward. Under the present circumstances, her Auntie never would have sent someone else to pick up the family, even if she was ill herself. Why hadn't she come to this conclusion sooner?

"I want to know where Ganesh is right now. Tell me an address. We will all go there."

"I told you, he is fine," Mrs Gupta insisted, her voice taking on a sharp edge. Her smile faded as her left eye began to twitch spasmodically.

"I don't care what you say! We are going to see him right this moment!"

"And how do you propose to do that? Do you have any money for transport? How are you planning on paying the medical bills for Ganesh? They are already very high. He needed some special medicine that cost me a lot of money. How will you pay for that?"

"I want to talk to my Auntie then. Right now."

"I'm afraid she doesn't want to talk to you."

"I don't believe you. You're not telling the truth. I don't think you even know my Auntie. If you did, you'd know she never would have sent someone like you to pick us up. I shouldn't have listened to you. I was tired, and I made a mistake. Now we're all going. And I want to know where Ganesh is right now, or else!"

"Or else what?" asked Mrs Gupta with fire in her eyes. She walked up to Sita and gave her a hard slap across the face.

"We'll go to the police!" replied Sita, holding her hand across her cheek.

"I don't think so. I saw the way you looked at the police in that train station. You don't want the police in your life. I don't know why this is, but I know it to be the case. Even if you did bring in the police, I'd state that I never saw you before in my life. They'd take you away to a vagrant centre, and your family would be split apart. Is that what you really want?"

"Then we will find him ourselves," Sita cried out. "I am not spending another moment in this place with my family."

The second slap knocked her off her feet.

"I'm sorry, but you and your family can't leave just yet. You owe me money—lots of it."

"What are you talking about?" asked Sita between her sobs. "We don't owe you anything."

"You stayed in that hotel room for several hours. That cost me money. And you also ate food that I had to buy. And look, I bought clothes for you." Mrs Gupta pointed to three sets of second-hand clothes that were lying in a pile beside the bed. "You can't wear those clothes you have on anymore. They look ridiculous. Oh, and then there are the medical bills I have already paid for your brother. That all adds up. You are not going anywhere until this is paid off."

"I have read about people like you before," Sita snarled, pointing her finger at Mrs Gupta. "You are like a con artist—a crook. I don't care what you say, we are leaving here this very minute. We do not owe you anything."

Mrs Gupta smirked. "Go ahead, try to wake up your brother and sister. The drug they consumed yesterday is very potent. It will be several more hours before they awaken. I'm surprised you are conscious already. You see, this is going to be your new home for a while. You will soon learn that the place has few windows and only one door which is locked and always guarded. You and your family will work here until you've paid back what you owe me. Only then will you be free to leave. If you try to run off before your debt has been repaid, I promise you will never see your brother again. And if you are caught doing so, you will be severely punished. Do you understand me?"

Stunned, Sita walked over to the cot and sat down. She understood what the woman had said, yet it made no sense. It seemed as if Mrs Gupta had said they were prisoners, or even slaves.

A second wave of tears began to flow down her face which was still stinging from the slaps. All at once, the anger she felt moments ago was replaced with fear and a sense of helplessness. What could she do? How could she convince this witch to let them leave?

"Please, let us go," Sita pleaded, dropping to the floor as she reached for Mrs Gupta's feet. "You don't understand. We do not belong here. Please, I beg you. Let us go. Take me to my Auntie. She will pay our debt. She will even give you extra money. She has lots of money. She will pay you whatever you want. Please, I beg you."

"Get away from me," Mrs Gupta replied, using her shoe to push Sita aside. "Now, you think about what I have just said to you. And when your brother and sister wake up, I want them to change into those clothes and wait. I also want you to explain to them that they must do whatever they are told or they will suffer consequences.

And remember, there will always be someone watching over you. Always!"

Sita didn't say anything. She needed time to think. "I have to use the toilet," she finally confessed, realising that her pleas were pointless.

"Mr Singh, come in here!" The driver who had taken them to the hotel showed up at the door. "Follow her to the toilet. And don't let her out of your sight. If she so much as hesitates, you have my permission to slap her very hard."

With Mr Singh following a few feet behind her, Sita went down a long, dark hallway. The first room she passed was an office containing several folding chairs and a metal desk. Two metres further down the corridor they came to a large open room. Inside, at least two dozen boys and girls sat quietly on the floor, doing something with a dark blue liquid and hundreds of plastic containers. The children watched with a glazed curiosity as she and the driver passed in the direction of the toilet. The chemical smell that permeated that room and the corridor was almost more than she could bear.

"There it is," Mr Singh declared, pointing to a curtain at the end of the hall. "Now hurry."

As Sita entered the stall, a pair of large rats ran between her legs. With remnants of faeces and urine that hadn't been cleaned in many days, the place had an overwhelming stench. In her entire life, she had never experienced such filth. She gagged several times from the overpowering odour and tried not to breathe until her business was finished.

After returning to her room, gasping for fresh air, she curled up into a ball on the bed, trembling. It was she who had brought this on the family. She was the eldest. She was the one who was expected to be the parent. But over the course of a twelve-hour period, she had lost her youngest brother and led her other two siblings into a den of evil. She had failed. They were trapped.

When Chandra and Ravi finally awoke, Sita tried her best to stay calm and explain that they had to work for a few days to earn some money so that they could get Ganesh out of the hospital. Neither of them understood any of this.

Two days before, they had been living in a beautiful, clean house with parents that loved them and servants that took care of the family's every need. Now they were being held captive and forced to reside in a decrepit, rat-infested building where they were told they'd have to work from dawn until dusk. Over and over again, they begged to go home, to see their parents, their Auntie or anyone else who might be able to rescue them from the nightmare that had now taken over their lives.

But there was no escaping this new world that they were now living in. Mrs Gupta wielded unlimited power and control over them. Their lives were no longer their own.

5

For the next five weeks, the routine never varied. The morning started with a rude wakeup call just before 6:00 a.m. Breakfast consisted of a single japati bread, a small cup of vegetable curry and a glass of lukewarm tea.

Twelve hours a day, the child workers were expected to fill thousands of small plastic bottles with a blue dye that was mixed with a variety of toxic chemicals. Once packaged, the dye combination was purchased at a cut-rate price by publishing houses and small industries for a range of industrial purposes.

Within the first three hours, the lethal fumes given off by these chemicals caused Sita and the others to feel lightheaded and dizzy. By mid-afternoon, pounding headaches set in. Some days, her nose would start bleeding, and a few of the children who had been there longer wheezed as they breathed, as though they had some sort of respiratory infection. The dye also stained their skin. The first day, she washed her hands as vigourously as she could with soap and water, staying in the bath stall long enough that Mr Singh threatened to come in and hurry her along. But the stain of servitude would not even lighten.

The room they worked in had ceiling fans but no windows, and as the day passed, the room grew hotter and hotter. The endless repetition of the task, along with the heat, made it hard to stay awake, but if they slowed down or closed their eyes, they would be beaten. Their two guards were a pair of brothers, teenage boys who took turns at their job in order to limit their time in the noxious air.

The guards would let them use the bathroom, but this was their only break. The only other concession to physical needs was a large bucket of water with a cup which was passed around freely to keep the children from getting dehydrated. After all, it wouldn't be cost effective for them to die too quickly, Sita thought, rage simmering beneath her fear.

The brothers performed their routines robotically, without any emotion and with very few spoken words. The most dangerous time was when either one of them first arrived on his shift. This was when they went around looking for a reason to strike someone. If they couldn't find anything to correct, they would often strike someone anyway. As time passed and the heat and boredom set in, they'd take naps. These unsupervised times offered an opportunity for the inmates to escape, but since the only door to the building was always locked, there was really no place to go.

At least once or twice a day, Mrs Gupta would arrive to arrange for the finished products to be sent elsewhere; none of the workers knew where. She had a small warehouse out back that was large enough to accommodate several days' worth of packaging.

The first day, they had been told the rules. "If I catch you talking or if you stop working," the older brother had trailed off, slapping the stick he carried against his hand with a malicious grin. Sita, Chandra and Ravi had nodded, kneeling on the floor to join the others. Sita had jumped, nearly spilling dye on herself as the stick came down across her thighs.

"What was that for?" Chandra had cried.

The brother had hit her across the back, and she'd whimpered.

"I said, no talking," he had said, laughing to himself.

From then on, Sita watched the guards closely from the corner of her eye, on edge every time they came near. She couldn't say anything to comfort Chandra. She moved so that her leg touched her sister's, but this small physical contact was all she could offer.

By 7:00 p.m., the second and last meal was served. It usually consisted of leftovers warmed from the morning meal, often with water added to thin and stretch the quantity. Exhausted and nauseated by the toxic fumes and the dye leeching deep into their skin, most children were totally worn out and simply sought the refuge of sleep.

Sita kept her head down and did the work demanded of her, observing what she could. She could tell who had been there the longest by the vacancy of their stares. Over the course of only a few weeks, she watched a boy who had been there nearly six months grow more dazed, confused and irritable. The headaches and cough she had begun experiencing were so severe for him that he could hardly fill the bottles. Indeed, he hardly seemed to understand what was said to him. One day, he was no longer there. The next day, without any explanation, an older girl replaced him.

During the first few weeks, the entire family suffered from recurrent bouts of diarrhoea. Having always drunk boiled and filtered water at home, they were not accustomed to the wide variety of microbes that flourished in the local tap water. To cure these recurrent symptoms, they were given a range of powerful anti-diuretics. Mrs Gupta made a point of repeatedly explaining to Sita that this additional cost would be added to their original debt. It was also pointed out that they'd be responsible for paying for their room and whatever food they ate while working at the factory. With no way of knowing how much the three of them were earning on a daily basis, it was impossible to know when such a debt could be paid off, if ever.

Night was the only time that the family members could communicate with each other without being scolded. With all of the children sleeping in a common room, Sita, Ravi and Chandra huddled close together as they whispered to each other.

"When are we going to get out of here, Sita?" Chandra whispered, scratching at the flea bites on her legs. Every night since arriving, she had cried herself to sleep.

"I don't know," Sita confessed as she gently stroked her sister's matted hair. "Mrs Gupta said we will not be let go until we pay back what we owe her. Once that happens, we can all leave. If we try to leave before then, we may never see your little brother again."

"Haven't we worked long enough?" Chandra hissed. "It's been weeks! I can't do this anymore. That smell is so awful. My head hurts all the time. And look at my fingers. They are always blue now. I hate everything about this place. Please, Sita, help us get out of here!"

"Why doesn't Auntie take care of us?" Ravi chimed in. "And where are Mama and Papa? I miss them so."

She still hadn't told him. Chandra knew, though, and their eyes met over his head.

"Go to sleep," Sita said, pulling the tattered blanket over his body. "Go to sleep."

The next day, Sita waited until the guard was fast asleep, then made her way to the office. Bleary eyes watched her as she left the work area.

Six weeks had passed, and it was time to confront Mrs Gupta. They had done enough work to pay back their debt. It was time to leave.

But as she neared the door, she paused. Two voices drifted into the hall: Mrs Gupta and her driver, Mr Singh. "Tell me again, how much did they finally give you for that little boy? What was his name? Ganesh?" the driver asked. He sounded as though he'd had several drinks already.

"I got 65,000 rupees up front," replied Mrs Gupta, clearly pleased with the deal. "If they keep him for over three months, I will get another 20,000. The adoption broker said he was just what the family wanted. He had good strong features, fair skin, a nice smile and a soft character that was easy to manage. Deals like that don't fall from the sky very often. I must have done something to please the gods to receive this gift from their bounty."

"Didn't anyone ask where you got him from?" asked Mr Singh as he poured himself another drink. A clinking sound was made as the bottle struck the glass.

"I told them that he was orphaned when his parents were killed in a terrible car accident and that I was their only surviving relative. The broker didn't seem to care much about the source. It didn't make any difference to him. He just needed a warm body to fill another order for a toddler, not an infant. After the couple saw the child, they would have done anything to get him. It was love at first sight. You saw him. He was a good find for any family."

"They didn't care about that big ugly birthmark on his arm?"

"I'm not sure they saw it right away. I guess it wasn't a problem."

"Where were they from?"

"The couple lives outside of Mumbai. They seemed rich. He works in a banque or something. She is in advertising. I'm told they both come from prominent families with lots of money."

"Why didn't they just have one of their own and save the money?"

"I guess there is a problem with one of them. They tried, but it just never happened."

"The other three won't buy that hospital excuse for much longer. They'll get clever—they all do."

"Don't worry. If they keep breathing in those fumes, they won't remember much of anything after a few more weeks. If they give us too much trouble, I can always sell the girls to one of the local brothels, and someone will take the boy for something. There are plenty of restaurants in this city that need cheap dishwashers."

"Aren't the girls still a bit young for the brothels?"

"These days, I'm told that the men want them young. With that Mumbai disease infecting people all over the country, they want the little ones because they think they can't catch anything from them. At least the older one is pretty enough, but I'm sure they'll take them both. But don't worry, they'll fetch good money. There will always be buyers. And for the time being, we are earning good money from them here. Finding this family was very lucky."

Mrs Gupta had lied to her all along. She'd known it, on some level, but hearing it said so blatantly was electrifying. Sita tip-toed back to the assembly area, where the guard was still asleep.

"Get up on your feet, we are getting out of here," Sita whispered to her sister and brother who had just finished filling another batch of plastic tubes. They both had watery eyes and a dazed expression from the daily dose of toxic chemicals.

"How can we leave?" asked Chandra, appearing stunned. "What about Ganesh? I thought we couldn't leave here until he returned from the hospital."

"He's not at any hospital," replied Sita, forcefully pulling her brother to his feet. "They sold him to a family in Mumbai. We'll have to go there and find him ourselves. They've been lying to us. If we don't get out of here soon, we will be split up. Do you want that to happen? Now hurry up." Chandra finally sprang to her feet.

As the three of them hastily negotiated their way around the boxes and bottles to the only exit in the building, everyone in the room watched, eyes alert for the first time in weeks. At the far end of a short narrow corridor, there was a large steel door that separated them from their freedom.

"It's locked!" said Chandra as she frantically tried to turn the handle. With both Sita and Chandra pulling together at the same time, they tried their best to force the door open, but it wouldn't budge. Short of having the key, it was no use. "We're trapped in here. What are we going to do? What are we going to do?"

"Hey, what's going on in here?" came a voice from somewhere behind them. The guard had woken and immediately realised that he was short three workers.

There was no way to return to the main assembly room without being severely beaten. This could be her one and only chance to keep the family together. There was no turning back now.

"Quick, under this desk," Sita instructed, pushing her siblings into the small space. The piece of furniture stood beside the door and was used whenever inventory was being taken out of the building. It had several accounting journals and piles of loose papers spread across the rusted metal top.

"But..."

"Shhhh. Just do as I say!"

Not knowing what else to do, Sita anxiously searched the area around her feet. There, on the floor, she found a one-metre-long wooden rod that was used to stir the various chemicals after they had been mixed together in large vats. She picked it up, tightening her fingers around its width to ensure a good grip. Moments before the guard arrived, she stepped back inside into the shadows of the tiny corner and did her best to become one with the wall.

"If I were you, I'd get over here right now," shouted the young guard, full of rage. He had his own bamboo stick in front of him, ready to savagely beat whoever dared to challenge his authority.

When the guard was within striking distance, Sita lifted the wooden rod above her head and swung it hard across his right shoulder, causing him to fall to his knees. Fearing that he might immediately recover, she struck him over and over again, first across the back and then on the head. When she finally came to her senses, he was lying face down on the ground. While he was still breathing, he was completely unconscious.

"Check his pockets for a key," Sita ordered, as Chandra clumsily emerged from the space below the desk. "Hurry up!"

Sita held the wood in front of her, ready to strike anything that got in their way. Ravi took a position behind her.

"I found it," replied Chandra, fumbling with a key chain that had several dangling keys attached.

"Open the door, open the door. Hurry!"

By this time, nearly all of the other children from the assembly area had moved over to the entrance, surprise visible on their wan faces.

"I got it, I got it," Chandra shouted, having located the key that matched the lock. At first, she turned it, but nothing happened. Then, after shaking it up and down a bit, the lock unlatched with a loud click, and the door swung wide open. A burst of sunlight exploded in her face, forcing Sita to shield her eyes even as she ran forward.

"Run down that road!" shouted Sita, pointing straight in front of them toward a street that was lined with carts and fruit and vegetable vendors. "Run!"

In addition to her brother and sister, some of the other children had also made a break for it. Seeing the light of day for the first time in weeks had seemed to spur them on.

With Chandra and Ravi ten steps in front of her, Sita looked back over her shoulder one last time. Mr Singh and Mrs Gupta had arrived and were trying to force their way through the remaining children who were still crowding in front of the open door.

For a split second, Sita and Mrs Gupta made eye contact. Her breath caught in her throat—it was like meeting the gaze of a cobra. If Mrs Gupta ever got her hands on them, she'd kill them.

"Where are we going?" asked Chandra as Sita caught up with them.

"I don't know," she replied, nearly out of breath. "Just keep running. No, wait," she exclaimed, spotting a crowd. "Turn down there. Hurry!"

All three of them turned down a small alley. Entering a massive open bazaar, they stopped running and tried to melt into the sea of people bartering for food, clothes and drink. They had escaped, they were free. It was time to move on, to find Ganesh and to find a way to get back to the life they had once lived.

6

For the remainder of that morning and afternoon, Sita, Chandra and Ravi hid in a small park beside Delhi's Red Fort. The spot was nearly an hour's walk from the factory and well concealed by a grove of Banyan trees; it seemed safe enough, for now. A caravan of travelling performers rested there as well, their wooden wagons displaying colourful paintings of picturesque landscapes and famous landmarks from different parts of India, including the Taj Mahal.

This quasi-secluded spot was also in proximity to a major road leading to the city limits. Not knowing whether to search for her Auntie in Delhi, to go to Mumbai to find Ganesh, or to escape to another place to avoid being caught again by her previous captors, Sita sat and just stared at the road. She needed time to think and to clear her head. The fresh air was helping, and her siblings were also beginning to exhibit more alertness. They had found a water fountain and gulped down some cool water, splashing some on their faces and arms to wash away the chemical stink that clung to them.

An hour went by as she watched cars pass in the distance. She felt hollowed out and empty, not simply from hunger. Since morning, she had learnt that her brother had been sold to strangers like a piece of meat at the market, she had violently beaten a young man with a wooden stick until he fell unconscious to the ground, and she had run blindly for her life with her brother and sister. Now she was hiding in a park like a criminal, five hundred kilometres from home and without anyone to take care of her, with no money, no food and no sense of direction. Somewhere along the way, she had detached from her emotions, as if a vital part of her mind had shut itself down. It frightened her, the idea that she might have lost part of herself.

From the base of a banyan tree, Sita turned toward Chandra and Ravi, who explored their newfound freedom. With no work, no fumes and no fear of being beaten, Ravi ran around in a circle, acting like a child again. From the family of travelling performers, a boy Ravi's age ventured forth. Scrawny and sickly looking, with a grey complexion and drooping eyes, the child walked a baby monkey on a leash. The boy didn't say much, but for hours, he and her brother played together, the boy laughing at nearly everything Ravi had to say.

Chandra, who always needed to find a space she could call her own, sat upon the ropy, above-ground roots of a particularly leggy banyan, untangling her matted hair. Her face was a slide-show of emotions but whenever she began to cry or her mouth pinched in anger, she would groom more vigourously, self-soothing as best she could. Sita felt her pain but had no comfort to offer.

"Sita, I'm hungry," Ravi complained, wandering over and rubbing his blue-stained hands over his stomach for emphasis. "When are we going to get something to eat? I'm starving."

"I don't know." With each problem solved, another took its place. She was failing them.

Ravi's sharp little chin stuck out, as if he were studying the problem. Nodding once, he turned and walked back to locate his new friend.

"Do we have any money?" Chandra inquired, moving to sit next to her sister. "Even that grey factory slop sounds good right now," she admitted, her stomach audibly rumbling.

"Where would I get money from?"

"Then how are we going to eat tonight?"

"I don't know yet!"

"Then let's just go to the police," Chandra pleaded, not for the first time. "We can tell them what happened to our parents back in Pune and how we were kidnapped by that horrible woman and then forced to work like slaves. We can also explain how they took Ganesh away from us. They will help us to find our Auntie, and I'm sure they'll also feed us. Please, Sita. We don't have any choice."

"We can't do that!" Sita shouted, venting a small portion of the rage that was roiling inside her. "How many times do I have to explain this to you, Chandra? Do you want to end up like Mama and Papa? Dead? All of the police in India work closely together. If they find us, they will take us out back of their station and shoot us dead. I told you what I saw in the sitting room at home. That policeman was the one who hurt Mama. No, we have to find a way to locate Auntie Nadia by ourselves. Once we've done that, she can help us to find Ganesh, and then everything will be the way it was before."

"But how will we do that?" asked Chandra with tears streaming down her face. "We don't have an address for her. And until we find her, we have to eat something. We can't just stay here in this park. Where will we sleep? Mrs Gupta is bound to find us. What are we going to do?"

At that moment, Ravi came rushing up with a handful of small rupee bills and coins. With an enormous smile across his face, he held them out in front of Sita and Chandra in triumph as if he had just stumbled upon a hidden treasure.

"Where did you get that money?" asked Sita, surprised to see what he had in his hands.

"I just went up and asked people for it, and they gave it to me," he replied, full of enthusiasm. "I watched my friend do it. Look. I have nearly 12 rupees. See? We can use it to buy some samosas now."

"We are not beggars!" replied Sita, mortified. "Do you hear me? Our parents did not raise us to beg for money. If we need money, we'll earn it somehow. But we will not beg. Never! I don't want you to ever do that again."

Ravi's proud smile crumbled. He gaped at her, hurt.

After grabbing the handful of rupees and tossing them to the ground, she dragged her brother further into the trees, where there were fewer people around. She shouldn't have been so loud, shouldn't have drawn attention. One of the women from the travelling caravan had watched this exchange with interest. Even with the shock of the day, this woman had managed to catch Sita's attention throughout the afternoon. Wearing a colourful flowered skirt with a tight sari top that could barely contain her large breasts, she had walked with her head high amongst the covered wagons, chatting and laughing with her fellow travellers. At times, in a distracted way, Sita had puzzled over what made the woman such an attractive figure. Her body was muscular, with a straight back and strong feminine curves, but her face was not beautiful. When she flashed her broad smile, she seemed to have too many teeth in her mouth, and the brows above her twinkling eyes were thick and unshaped. Yet there was something captivating about her. When her loud laugh occasionally reached Sita's ears, it caused a tiny flicker in her chest.

Looking behind them, Sita was startled to see the woman approaching them.

"Hello, sister, my name is Maya," she waved, then offered a handshake much like a man would do. "What is your name?"

"What do you want with me?" asked Sita. She did not offer her hand in return.

"I want nothing at all, sister. Your son played with my son," replied Maya, not at all deterred. "I just decided to come over and say hello. Your Ravi seems like a very nice boy."

"He's not my son, he's my brother," Sita snarled. "Why would you think he's my son? I'm only fourteen and he's nearly eight."

"Forgive me," replied Maya with a disarming smile. "You seem much older. Where I come from in Rajasthan, our girls marry and bear sons very early in life. So, tell me, what is your name?"

Sita kept silent.

"What is so hard about answering this simple question? Are you afraid that I might bite you?" The woman was frustratingly persistent.

"My name is Sita," she finally admitted.

"And where are you from, Sita?"

"I grew up in Pune."

"I'm told that is a nice place. What about the girl? Does she also belong to you?"

"She's my sister!"

"And your parents? Where are they?"

Sita did not answer the question. After a moment, Maya shrugged, letting this one go.

"Sita from Pune. Why don't you and your family come and share some food with us tonight?"

"Thank you, but no thank you. We can manage by ourselves."

Maya reached down and gently lifted Sita's right hand so that she could better see her fingers. "It takes weeks for this dye to wash off. The smell that goes along with this can ruin a person's mind. It looks like you managed to get out in time. You still have spirit. Most aren't so lucky."

Sita pulled her hand away, hiding it behind her back. She wasn't going to be tricked again by another smiling face. Turning, she began to walk away.

Maya followed close behind, gently grabbing Sita by the elbow.

"What do you want with me?" Sita hissed, pulling her arm back hard as she spun around, ready to slap the woman for grabbing her.

"I want nothing. But you three look as though you could use a hot meal. I know because I have been there myself. Come with me, and you can join our family tonight. The food is good. I have prepared much of it myself. There is no food on this earth better than the cooking from my village. Come and eat. You look hungry. You will be safe."

"We don't want any handouts," replied Sita. What would her mother say, if she found them begging in the streets, if she were still alive...? "I already told you, we can manage on our own," Sita reiterated, a frustrating tremble in her voice.

"Then you can work for your dinner. After we have finished eating, you and your brother and sister can help us to wash the pots and dishes. A fair meal for a fair wage. I will even be happy to pay you for your services." Maya reached into her bra and pulled out a handful of rupees. They looked suspiciously like the ones Sita had thrown to the ground only a minute before. She placed them into Sita's hand, curling her fingers over them.

"Why are you doing this?"

"Your brother showed kindness to my son. Most other children tease him or stay away from him because he is with me and because he has a certain look about him. He is happy today. That makes me happy."

Sita looked over toward Chandra and Ravi, who were watching from a distance. They would all go hungry if something wasn't done very soon.

"Okay, we will eat your food and then work for you," said Sita, reaching out to return the money.

"No, that belongs to you," replied Maya with a sympathetic smile. "Consider it an advance. Always save what little money you have. There will come a time when you might need it."

Sita accepted the rupees.

That night, the family had their first real meal in nearly six weeks. With rice, two types of vegetable curry, daal, pickled mango, naan and sweet yogurt, they ate like kings and queens. As promised, the food was delicious, down to the last bite.

As they ate together in a large communal group, Maya talked about the life that she and her fellow travellers had chosen.

"We own no part of this earth, but at the same time, no part of this earth owns us," she stated with great pride. "We travel on the breath of God. We go wherever the Spirit takes us. We do what we can to make money, and we earn enough to get by."

Maya's cheerful clan included three women, two men, one of whom was her husband, a teenage boy, and three children below the age of seven, a boy and two girls. The younger boy and one of the girls were Maya's own children. All of the group's worldly belongings were packed in the three large wagons; each wagon was pulled by a single white horse. While the others in her group were friendly enough, it was Maya who acted as the spokesperson, telling jokes and stories, putting the family at ease. After completing their meal, Sita and Chandra washed and dried all the pots and dishes, using a barrel of water rolled over by one of the men.

Having spent so many nights in captivity, the warmth offered by these people was a welcome change. It was early July, she had discovered earlier that day, and even after sunset, the breeze was hot. But it was fresh air, and even close to the city lights, the brighter stars were visible. She never wanted to go indoors again unless it was for a long, hot bath. The dish water was tepid and greasy, yet she sloshed it up to her armpits. Every now and then, while they had been eating dinner, she had caught a whiff of the chemicals they'd so recently escaped. The scent was trapped in her thick hair, lingering.

Maya came over and began packing the dishes back into their crates.

"Thank you for the meal," said Sita, finally offering her hand in a gesture of friendship. "I'm grateful for your kindness. We'll be leaving now."

"Where are you rushing off to in such a hurry? If the gods had not wanted us to meet, they would not have brought you to me. I already told my husband that you would stay with us tonight. We have a good fire going and many warm blankets. We can use your help in the morning when we prepare our morning meal. Besides, I am one of the best dancers in all of India, or so I am told," she announced, flashing her toothy smile. "You can't leave until you see me perform."

Ravi and Chandra cast pleading looks her way. The food had been delicious, and Maya seemed genuine. Sita looked back at the camp and to the covered wagons with no locks on them, no ways to trap a person.

"All right, we'll stay. But after we finish with the morning meal, we must be on our way."

"Do as you wish," Maya conceded. "Come, take some blankets, and find a place to lie down among us. There is always more warmth in large numbers."

They hardly needed extra warmth on a night like this, but it was comforting being part of a group. Within a half hour, both Chandra and Ravi and most of the remaining travellers were fast asleep.

Sita, still unable to unwind, sat alone beside the fire. She used a long wooden stick to push small branches that had fallen outside the pit back into the centre again. She wanted to trust Maya and her family, but after what had happened with Mrs Gupta, she couldn't relax. What if when she awoke her sister and brother were gone? She would not be able to withstand such a blow.

"I see you are not tired," said Maya, wrapped in a large black shawl. "May I sit with you?"

"Yes."

The woman settled herself on the ground beside her. On the nearby road, a large truck rumbled past. From the other direction, in the trees, a night bird warbled in the distance.

"You know, Sita, I was not always a dancer wandering from place to place. I once lived in a big house with my mother and father and three sisters in a village not far from Jaipur, the pink city. Everything about that place was beautiful and wondrous."

"What happened?" Sita poked the fire, reluctant to show much interest.

"It's a long story. I don't think you want to hear about someone else's troubles."

The stick in Sita's hand hovered in the air, then quickly continued stirring the fire.

"Go ahead, I don't mind."

"Well, when I was just a young girl, there was a time when the rains hadn't come in over three years. With no water, the wheat and corn didn't grow. So, after we used up all our savings, my father was forced to borrow money from bad men in the city. Months later, when he couldn't pay this money back, they came to our house and tried to take over our land. To stop this from happening, my poor father went to Jaisalmir to borrow money from his older brother. We never saw or heard from him again."

"What happened?" asked Sita, glancing over. Maya was probably younger than her mother, yet there was something about her that seemed older. The woman caught her gaze, her amber flecked eyes compassionate. Those eyes had probably seen just about everything.

"No one knows. His brother gave him the money, but he never made it home. My uncle thinks that someone probably found out he was carrying a large sum of rupees and attacked him. But we were never certain. In the desert, only the circling vultures know when a crime has been committed."

"That's awful. What did you do without the money?"

"After three months had passed, the men from the city returned. When we refused to give them our land, they brought in the police. They hit us with their sticks until we were forced to leave. For a few weeks, our neighbours tried to help by taking us in, but they had their own troubles. To survive, my mother did what she could. She sent my two younger sisters to live with my uncle. That all he could afford to support. Since I was older and stronger, she... she sold me over to a circus. I was around your age, or perhaps a bit younger, when this happened."

"What do you mean she sold you?"

"They gave her money in advance to cover my wages, nearly 4,000 rupees for ten months. Since she knew I'd be fed and I'd be able to earn a living, she handed me over to them."

"Where is your mother now?"

"She lives with her own parents. They are very old now. She takes care of them."

"Why didn't she just take you with her?"

"Her own parents are very poor. They said they couldn't feed another person. They were also afraid that I'd need a big dowry when I got married. Since I was close to the age of marriage, they didn't want to have that additional burden. It would have been too much for them and far too humiliating to have a female with no dowry."

"Are you still in contact with your mother?"

"Yes, I send her money when I can. Not a lot. But when I get some extra, I send it along to her. I have also sent money to my younger sisters over the years."

"But why do you send money to your mother after what she did to you?"

"She is my mother," said Maya simply, as though this was the only explanation needed. But she tightened the shawl around her shoulders, her gaze growing distant.

"Have you seen any of them?"

"I visited with my mother two years ago. She was very happy to see me."

"What about your sisters? Did you see them also?"

"No, they both refuse to see me. They are too embarrassed. I am a dancer, a travelling performer. They said I would bring shame into their homes. They are both married now, with families. Their husbands are religious men." Maya paused for several seconds. "But I understand. I don't want to cause them any trouble, so I stay away."

"But you sent money to them. You helped them. Why would they treat you this way?"

Sleeping a few feet away, Ravi murmured in his sleep, his brow furrowing with dreams. Sita reached over and brushed her hand across his head, watching as the skin smoothed.

"You have a lot to learn about the world, my little friend from Pune. Everyone has their place. Some live high on the pole. And then there are people like us who live on the bottom, right close to the earth. Because we travel around with no place to call our home, people treat us like we are dogs or camels. The police regularly harass us and demand money. When we try to stop to rest, the local people often force us to leave. Sometimes they even throw rocks at us."

"But why?"

"Sometimes, for people to feel big, they have to make others feel small. That is why I approached you today. I could tell that you and your family are not street people. You come from a good family. Your brother showed kindness to my son. It meant a lot to him and to me that Ravi did not look down on him. Because of the way we live, he suffers so."

"I still don't understand how your mother could give away her own daughter to strangers like that," Sita confessed, having never heard of such a thing. "She sounds like an awful person."

"When a person hasn't eaten for several days, they will eventually do anything. And besides, it is not as bad as it sounds. I went willingly. I was so hungry, I didn't care what happened to me, as long as I had something to eat. It was hard at first, but I got used to it. The circus became my new family. That is where I learnt to dance and sing."

The blaze was dying out, the glitter of the hot coals sparkling red in the darkness.

"If you liked it so much, then why did you leave?"

"We had no choice. There wasn't enough money coming in for the owners to keep it going. The troop eventually split. By then, I had married my husband. He was much older than me, but I didn't care. I wanted to be married. I wanted to have a child. Since he had also been with the circus for many years, we were able to take three of the wagons as his payment. It's a hard life but a good one. Lord Ganesh watches over us. He has always provided everything we've needed."

Ganesh. Sita started to sob. For the first time since her parents' murder, the full force of her emotions came bubbling to the surface, like a frozen creek beginning to thaw.

Maya wrapped her shawl around Sita and held her close in her arms.

When the crying finally came to an end, she told Maya everything, starting with her parents' murder.

"And do you know who did this horrible thing to your parents?" Maya asked when the tale was done.

"The person my father convicted that day was Raju Khan. It was one of his brothers who came to the house. Their family runs many of the criminal activities in the Northern slum areas of Mumbai. Have you heard of him before?"

"Yes, his name is well-known. The entire family is notorious and treacherous. They must be looking for you now."

"No, I read an article in the newspaper a week after it happened. We were already in the factory working."

"How did you get a newspaper inside the factory?"

"The paper was wrapped around a shipment of plastic tubes that had arrived one morning. I was the one who was ordered to unpack them. I couldn't believe what I saw. The article read 'Prominent Barrister's Family Killed in Tragic Fire.' There was even a photo of us all."

"That must have been awful."

"It was. Since Chandra didn't know that Mama and Papa had been killed, this is what I used to explain what really happened. For three straight days and nights, we cried. We still haven't told Ravi anything. He is too young."

"What did the paper say?"

"Everyone thought we were killed in the fire. There was little left of the house after the explosions and the blaze that followed. They assumed that our remains had been completely destroyed or scattered throughout the neighbourhood."

"They didn't mention the murder of your parents?"

"No, not once. The paper just talked about the fire."

"That's good."

"What do you mean?" asked Sita, surprised by such an insensitive statement.

"I mean, it's good that they don't know you're alive," replied Maya, sensing her reaction. "This way they won't be looking for you."

"Oh, I see what you mean." Sita looked up at the rising moon, a slim crescent and blinked back a fresh round of tears.

"What about your brother, Ganesh? Did that woman say anything else about where he might be?"

"No. Just that he was with a young couple in Mumbai."

Maya stopped to reflect on all she had just heard. "So what are you going to do now?"

Sita gulped. "I think I really injured the guard when we escaped. Mrs Gupta will be looking for us. Chandra wants us to go to the police, but I don't trust them. I just don't know what to do."

"And your Auntie?"

"She's somewhere in Delhi. But I don't know how to find her." Anxiety caused Sita's voice to rise. "Maya, what should I do?"

"First of all, you have to get out of Delhi for a while. If this Gupta woman wants to find you, it will not be very difficult. All she has to do is ask around for two young girls and a boy with blue-stained hands travelling together. This city has eyes and ears everywhere."

"But what about finding my Auntie?"

"First, leave this area until the stain comes off your hands. After that, you can return to find her. But I wouldn't try to do it before then. People like Mrs Gupta are not forgiving. If she finds you, she might kill you."

"Then should we go to the police?"

"If it were me, I wouldn't. I don't trust the police either. If you go to them and the newspapers find out that you're still alive, the criminal mob that killed your parents will find a way to get you. Mr Khan has links with criminals and politicians everywhere. He's very dangerous."

"Then what am I going to do?"

"Why don't you travel with us for a while? We are heading toward Lucknow. After that, we will go to Kailash and stay until just before the winter months. This place is no good for your family. There are too many bad people around. The high country is beautiful this time of year. You'll like it there. It's my favourite place on this earth."

"But I have to find my brother!"

"Yes, but you can't start looking for him yet." Moonlight silvered Maya's hair as she continued in a low, conspiratorial tone. "Leave Delhi for a month. The dye will wash off, and you'll get your strength back. Maybe you'll earn a little money, which you'll need." She paused. "Ganesh is with people who paid dearly for him. They are surely taking good care of him, perhaps even better than you could at this time."

Sita said nothing to this, hating the truth of it.

"Go to sleep now. If you choose to come along, you can join my family. There is never a shortage of food. The gods have always provided for us all."

Tired from her endless day, Sita lay down. After finding a comfortable position under the blanket, she took one last look up at the stars that adorned the sky, then closed her eyes. Sleep came quickly.

With the rising of the sun came a new day. Sita slept late, waking to find Chandra seated beside her, a bowl of spiced rice porridge cradled in her blue palms. After a full breakfast, Maya and her family left the wagons in the care of the teenage boy and walked towards the city. Sita, Chandra and Ravi followed along as the group picked a spot near an outdoor market to begin their morning performance. The day was still fresh, and those who passed by looked at them, curious, not yet wearied by the long heat of afternoon.

The event started with Maya's husband gathering a handful of people together. A thin man with a drawn face, he wore his long hair combed back with oil, his colourful garb covered in tiny mirrors that sparkled in the sun. Quiet and withdrawn at dinner the night before, he turned dynamic in front of the crowd, drawing in spectators with a fire act.

Maya lit the dumbbell, sticks and balls, throwing them to him one at a time. Effortlessly, he would catch them, juggling more and more items, the height they reached nearly equal to the power lines that ran along the opposite side of the street.

When the juggling was done, he let the items extinguish themselves on the ground, the fire snuffing out as if by magic. Then he told the story of a dragon as he breathed fire at intervals, causing the children in the audience to squeal with delight. Following this, he brought the baby monkey into the centre of the circle and had the creature do flips and rolls, hand clapping, and ball throwing. Delighted, the onlookers tossed coins for the monkey to retrieve.

Then, with a popular Hindi song blaring from a small battery-operated tape player, it was finally Maya's turn in the spotlight. She and the two other women entered the centre of the circle, their costume jewellery and sparkling skirts flashing. With their hips gyrating to every beat, they moved like Bollywood stars. The others did their best to keep up, but it was Maya who owned the crowd. Without the slightest inhibition, she allowed herself to completely let loose—to become one with the music. With her raw sexuality on full display, she was able to enchant the men into staying and paying. Sita was amazed and captivated, both with the dancing and the fact that Maya's husband's face shone with pride. There was no shame or jealousy visible, only adoration.

As the dance went on, the three children walked through the crowd, collecting donations. After getting a nod from Maya, they ran off to a safe place, away from the performance, to count the money. All but forty rupees were given to one of the men for safekeeping. The remaining donations, Sita later learnt, were saved to pay the police in order to ensure that they didn't stop the show or demand more of the earnings.

When it appeared that no more money could be milked from the crowd, the music stopped, and the performers rushed away, hurrying back to the wagons.

"Did you like my dancing?" Maya was still panting heavily, her body covered with beads of sweat.

"It was wonderful. I think you are right; you are the best dancer in all of India. Or at least the best I've ever seen."

"Thank you." Maya accepted the compliment with a satisfied smile, then laughed. "You can't have seen many dancers but thank you all the same."

The man with the money came walking over.

"How much did we earn?" asked Maya.

"Eighty-five rupees. But since the police haven't asked for anything yet, this means we'll probably be able to keep another forty."

"That is enough for now," said Maya, pleased.

"Is that how much you usually earn?" asked Sita. She had spent more on appetisers at a restaurant her family used to regularly frequent.

"Sometimes we collect more, sometimes less. Today was about average. So, have you decided? Are you coming with us?"

"Yes. Do you mind? We will probably only stay a few days. I do not wish for us to be a burden." That small pile of rupees would not go far.

"No, of course I don't mind!" replied Maya. Her amber flecked eyes lit up, and she seemed genuinely pleased. "And next time we dance, you can dance with us."

After packing up the campsite, the horses were hitched to the wagons, and the family began walking down the road. The younger ones sat in the back of the wagon with the others plodding along behind. With no place to go, there was no hurry, and it was important not to tax the animals. To help pass the time, the travellers sang folk songs in a language she did not know, the unfamiliar words dissipating in the heat of the afternoon, one song fading into another. Despite the road dust and blistering feet, her heart was lighter. Hope glimmered in the hazy air as they walked onwards.

7

For the next three weeks, Sita and her family stayed with the caravan. Each day, between two and four performances were staged, this number directly proportionate to the amount of money collected. Usually those who were very poor offered the most donations. With so little entertainment in their lives, they seemed to really appreciate the fleeting escape from reality. Those with a bit more means watched until right before the show ended, leaving when the collection tray was passed around.

Eyes narrowed at the injustice, Sita watched as Maya and her crew were forced to hand over small amounts of their meagre earnings to policemen, thugs and even dishonest fruit vendors who said they were responsible for collecting money whenever a public event took place. To avoid trouble, Maya and the others seldom argued.

As they went from town to town, people sneered at them and gave them a wide berth, as if they were too dirty to rub elbows with. Young men catcalled as if the women of the group were little more than whores. One time, a group of young boys started throwing rocks at Sita as she went around collecting firewood for the evening meal. If it hadn't been for Ravi coming to her rescue, screaming and wielding a large stick, she shuddered to think what might have happened.

When Sita told Maya about it, she shrugged. "The bad things that people may say or do are not a reflection on you—it's a reflection on them. My father used to say this to me when I was a little girl. If you ever go back to your old world again, don't become like them, Sita. Please promise me that."

With a little money she borrowed from Maya, she bought a small notebook and a selection of coloured pencils. When she had free time, she drew fashion sketches of the beautiful Rajasthani style of dress, making a present of them for each of the family members. The younger children fought over them and even the adults seemed touched by the gesture of gratitude.

In between performances, Maya taught Sita to dance. In a short period of time, she was able to pick up many of the more important moves. Chandra declined to join, choosing instead to be by herself.

On one occasion, during the middle of a performance, Maya ran into the crowd and grabbed Sita's hand, pulling her into the centre of the circle. Sita froze. Then the beat took over, her arms undulating like snakes as her hips traced a figure eight. On the balls of her feet, she shuffled forward and back, her arms, feet and hips each keeping a different count. For a moment, it all came together, like juggling. The audience cheered, she smiled, and the balls dropped. She'd lost the rhythm. She ran out of the circle. But that moment, with the dirt beneath her feet, the sun in her hands and the audience balanced on her hips, that moment stayed with her. Her mother would have been ashamed of her, wouldn't have understood. But Maya merely smiled when she hinted at what a high it had been. Still, she relented when Sita asked her not to pull her in again. Maya's understanding was boundless.

Sita hesitated to disclose the odd and terrifying thing that happened to her that morning.

"Sita, what's the matter with you today?" Maya asked. "Come on, you can talk to me. What is it?" They were sitting behind the wagons, waiting for water to boil over the cook fire. They'd stopped early this evening, everyone tired and dusty.

"Well, I woke up this morning and..."

"And what?"

"And there was blood on my clothes and bedding. I think it came out from...from between my legs... and it won't stop! Am I going to die? What will happen to Chandra and Ravi? I can't die, Maya..."

Without warning, Maya began to laugh out loud, slapping her leg several times during this outburst before she was able to regain her composure.

What in the world was funny? Sita stood to leave. "Something is seriously wrong with me, I might be dying and you laugh?"

"Child, stop crying at once. You are fourteen years old, from an educated family and you don't know what a period is?"

Sita pouted slightly. She was loathe to admit she had no idea what Maya was talking about. "No, I guess not. So, what is happening to me? Is it serious? Could this illness be caused from working at that factory? Is there any medicine for it?"

"You're not ill, Sita, and you're not going to die. There is nothing at all wrong with you. You just had your first period. It means that now you will be able to have babies."

"But there was blood, lots of it. And I had terrible pain..."

"Trust me, there's nothing wrong with you. You've just become a woman. Where I am from, we celebrate this moment. You should embrace the change and feel happy about it. It is a good thing, a part of the cycle of life."

Sita offered her a shy smile. Why hadn't her mother told her all of this? Probably if she had not been homeschooled for the last two years, she would have learnt about it from her friends or from their older sisters. Maya must think her very silly.

"I'm happy not to be dying," she said, wiping away the last of her tears.

"And when the time comes, you should explain it to your sister, so she doesn't experience what you just went through."

"Yes, I'll do that."

"Now, Sita, come with me, and let's have something to eat. The night has yet to begin. I will tell you some more magical stories about the places we have seen and the people we have met. But before we do anything, please give me another one of those smiles of yours."

Sita blushed with embarrassment.

"Come on, I want to see those beautiful teeth of yours before I stand up."

Sita finally turned and offered a smile that showed the full intensity of the warmth she felt for her adopted mother, who had also become her friend, her big sister, and her saviour, all in one.

"One more thing," Maya said, standing and offering Sita a hand. "Someday you have to promise that you will share a dance with me in the circle once again. In my village, sisters always dance together. It is one of the ways we honour the love we have for each other. Will you do this for me?"

"I don't think..."

"No excuses, Sita. I am asking you seriously. Will you do this for me?"

"Yes. Okay. Someday I will dance with you again."

"Do you promise?"

"Yes, you have my promise."

"Then this evening when I go to sleep, I will dream of this day."

The little caravan had two more days of travel ahead before reaching Lucknow, and a heavy rain began to fall. Monsoon season was upon them. For two days and nights the floodgates of heaven remained open, turning the narrow roadway into a mud pit. They parked the wagons in a circle beneath a copse of trees and the sodden group did their best to stay dry. Unable to perform any shows, there was little money left to buy supplies. With their food rations low, the adults began to worry.

On the morning of the third day, unlike other times, Maya insisted that the carriages be moved to a small truck stop just outside the city limits. It was an unlikely place for a performance. There were very few people around and the spot seemed completely isolated. That afternoon, in-between the periodic downpours, Sita wandered around the area in search of firewood. As she passed by one of the tea stalls favoured by the truckers, she witnessed something that took her breath away.

Maya, her good friend and mentor, sat on the lap of one of the truckers, her arms wrapped tightly around his neck. He whispered in her ear, and Maya laughed, throwing her head back. He nuzzled her neck, and she said something, her teasing tone evident even at a distance.

Sita stared, stunned. Maya's husband was less than one hundred metres away, yet here she was with another man. At that moment, the goddess-like statue she had created of her friend fell from its pedestal, shattering into a million tiny pieces.

As Maya reached for a glass of liquor that had just been poured, she caught sight of Sita. For a moment their eyes met, then Maya turned away.

The whole thing was so awful, she didn't know how to make sense of it. Hiding in a grove of trees at the side of the road, she contemplated this betrayal. Had everything Maya said been some sort of elaborate deception? She was not a good woman. Maya was something else, something much less.

It was late in the evening when Maya finally made her way back to camp. Staggering from side to side as she walked, it looked as though she was very drunk. The evening meal had already been consumed, and the dishes were being cleaned. Almost everyone sat around the fire. Everything became quiet as she entered the circle.

Maya walked up to her husband and gave him a soft kiss on the lips. He accepted it but without much enthusiasm. Seeing that all their eyes were focused on her, she turned and shouted, "What are you looking at?" She tossed a large wad of rupees onto the ground in front of one of the other women. "As you can see, I worked hard today. Now we will have something to eat tomorrow."

Having made this overt declaration, she turned and staggered away in the direction of one of the wagons. Sita had just finished washing the last set of pots and was sitting alone, away from the fire. As Maya approached, she turned her back to her.

"So, I see my little friend is disappointed with me," Maya declared, her tone antagonistic. "Have I done something that offended you? Is it about me earning money to feed everyone, perhaps?"

The coldness of her presence sent a shiver down Sita's spine.

"I'm talking to you, little rich girl. Why don't you answer me?"

Sita jumped to her feet. "Yes, I'm disappointed with you! That man at the tea stall was kissing you like he was your boyfriend or something. You're married! Your husband is right over there. Married women are not supposed to go off with other men. It's wrong. It's disgusting!"

"Where do you think this food comes from?" Maya spat back. "Do you think our little performances always generate enough money to buy what we need? I do what I have to do to provide enough money to feed us all, including you and your brother and sister."

"What you did was wrong!" replied Sita, full of condemnation and righteous anger. "You can't just go and be with other men. It's shameful."

"Who are you to tell me about right and wrong?" asked Maya, walking up and grabbing Sita's arms. "What do you know about life, about marriage? You didn't even know about a woman's period until I explained it to you several days ago! I love my husband. But he's a lazy man. He does what he can, but it will never be enough with so many mouths to feed. He knew exactly where I was going this afternoon. Yet he let me go." Maya paused to wipe tears from her eyes.

"I do what I have to do to provide for my family. This includes going off with men now and then who pay me good money to be with them. I am a free spirit. I am not contained within my body. Men can do what they want with it. It means nothing to me."

Sita didn't respond. Even if her husband had known, which she didn't believe, Maya was still a whore.

"We are leaving tomorrow to go back to Delhi," Sita said. The words came from the hollowed-out part of her chest which had so recently been filled with love and admiration for the dishevelled woman before her.

"Fine! Go! I don't want to see your face again. You're just a spoiled child. Take your family and leave us. We don't want you anymore. Go, go, go!"

Overwhelmed with hurt and despair, Sita ran off into the night.

"Wait until you get hungry, Sita!" she shouted after her. "Wait until you have nothing in your pocket and nothing left to sell. Then you tell me that what I did was wrong. Just you wait!"

The following morning, after Ravi had finished brushing down the horses, Sita handed them a bit of string.

"Tie up your belongings. We're going to head back to Delhi."

Chandra was still searching one of the wagons for a plastic comb she'd found on the road when Maya stirred. She'd slept a little away from everyone last night, under a tree, with her black shawl covering her face. It was already late; the sun had risen several hours earlier. Finally, she sat up, head in her hands, looking sick. Noticing what they were doing, she lurched to her feet, a confused look on her face.

"What are you doing?"

"I told you, we are leaving to go back to Delhi," replied Sita, tying the string too tight. Did she really think they could just pretend that last night hadn't happened?

"But why?" asked Maya.

Sita stopped what she was doing to stare at her. "You know why!"

Maya winced and touched her head as if it were tender. "Is this because of something I said last night?"

"You know what you said!"

Maya looked strangely fragile.

"No, I don't remember. I'm sorry, Sita. Sometimes I say things when I drink that I don't mean. Please tell me, what did I say to you to cause you to want to leave?"

"It doesn't matter. It's time for us to go back to Delhi, that's all. We've already stayed too long. We should have gone back a long time ago to start searching for my Auntie and for our baby brother." Sita put her hands out with her palms facing upward. "The dye washed off. We don't have to worry about Mrs Gupta or her thugs finding us anymore."

"Sita, don't do this," Maya said, reaching for her but stopping short of touching her. "I thought we were sisters. Why can't you talk to me about what happened?"

"There is nothing to talk about," replied Sita, frustrated both by Maya and her own longing to relent. Having already declared that she, Chandra and Ravi were going to leave, there was no turning back.

"You shouldn't return to Delhi just yet," said Maya, walking over to stand in front of her. "It's still too early. You should take another couple of weeks. Stay with us. Please, I don't want you to leave. Not like this."

"I'm sorry. There is no other choice." Sita moved to the left to circle around Maya.

"But why? Tell me why—oh," Maya stopped in her tracks just as Chandra emerged from the wagon, comb held in her hand, a small victory smile on her face. "It's coming back to me. This is about that man you saw me with."

Sita glared at her but said nothing.

"Oh, Sita, I'm so sorry that I've disappointed you," Maya said, her amber flecked eyes imploring. "I had no choice. We were running out of food. I couldn't let my babies go hungry. Can't you understand that? Why can't you forgive me?"

Something large and painful lodged in her throat. She wanted to cry, to scream. It seemed she stood on top of a hill made of loose stones. One step towards Maya, and she would lose her footing, sliding into the dark valley of awful choices where her friend dwelt.

She turned her back, gathering Ravi and Chandra to her with one imperious gesture, but the little traitors ran first to Maya, throwing their arms around her.

"I love you," she whispered to them, loud enough that Sita could hear. "Take this when you go." Maya handed something to Chandra. Money. "You've earned it."

Sita was torn between the urge to argue and the urge to sob. Maya was still being kind, still looking out for them but it didn't matter. She'd said they were going, and she was angry with Maya—wasn't she? As Ravi whined and Chandra wept, they hurried off down the road, the dry scrim of dirt crackling beneath their feet, giving way to the mud below.

For a long time, Sita listened. But Maya did not call her back.

8

Within a half-hour of leaving the caravan, it began to rain again, first as a slight drizzle, then with the fury of a post-monsoon downpour. A few public buses passed by, each completely crammed with people. With no other form of transportation available, they had no choice but to walk.

"Sita, I'm soaking wet," said Ravi. "Where are we going? This is stupid."

"Why did we leave?" Chandra shouted, overwhelmed with frustration. Her salwar kameez, the sky-blue slitted tunic with matching pants that Maya had procured for her, was drenched with rainwater, the cotton plastered to her thin limbs. "We could have stayed with Maya and her family, they wanted us to stay! Now look at us. We are wet with no place to go. And I'm tired. My feet hurt."

"We couldn't stay with them anymore," Sita insisted, hurrying onward, forcing them to keep up.

"But why?"

"You wouldn't understand. It's grownup stuff."

"Why wouldn't I understand? You're always saying that to me. What happened back there that made us leave? I want to know."

"Never mind. We are going to Delhi, and that is the end of the story. It is time to find Auntie Nadia and Ganesh."

"Why do we always have to listen to what you say?" Chandra challenged. "Why don't we ever get a say in anything?"

"Stop it," Sita shouted. "Just shut up and walk! Do you think I like making all of the decisions? Do you think I want all of this responsibility?"

But Chandra was right; she had made a terrible mistake. With no protection from the rain, little money in her pocket, and no sense of what to do next, the future was once again bleak. Confused by what happened with Maya and wounded by her hurtful statements, she had impulsively decided to leave without giving the matter much thought. Now she was beginning to feel the weight of the consequences.

Another forty minutes passed. The stores, houses and roadside shacks thinned out. With each kilometre travelled, they found themselves venturing into more remote areas of the countryside. Sita hadn't paid much attention to these details when they travelled with the others. There were few houses around and even fewer people. If this type of landscape continued, where would they sleep?

Since she was a child, she'd heard terrible tales of menacing dog packs roaming the night in rural areas, looking for helpless victims to surround and then attack. As they crept forward on the empty, wet road, her ears strained for howls or barks. She gripped Ravi's hand tightly, keeping an eye out for trees they could climb.

From far off came a sound. The cough of an engine, or a rabid wolf? Sita stopped in her tracks. Exhausted, Ravi looked up at her. Chandra realised they'd stopped a moment later and turned back, listless. Her clothes were so wet as to be nearly transparent.

What in the world had she been thinking, dragging them away from the safety of the caravan? It was time to cut her losses and return. She would apologise to Maya and beg that she take them back. What else could she do?

"Have you finally come to your senses?" Chandra asked as Sita began walking in the other direction.

Sita responded by walking more quickly. With any luck, they could get back by nightfall.

"Where are they?" asked Chandra, as they approached the location where the campsite had been several hours before. The caravan was gone.

"Let's go. If we hurry, we can still catch them," said Sita, determined to make things right again.

Several hundred feet up the road, they came to a circle where four roads converged. With the rain still coming down at a steady pace, whatever wagon tracks there might have been had washed away.

"Which way did they go?" asked Chandra, as her eyes frantically scanned the different directions.

"I—I think we should go straight. If we walk fast, I'm sure we can overtake them. They could have just left. Quick, let's go."

"But how do we know they went straight?" replied Chandra. "What if they went left or right? How do we know which direction to go? Why did we leave? Look at where we are now. Nowhere. Worse than nowhere! I can't walk anymore. My feet are sore. Sita, I can't do it. I just can't do it." She plopped down on the ground and sobbed.

"Me either," Ravi confessed, sitting down next to Chandra.

She had brought this upon her brother and sister. What was she going to do? Another impossible situation stared her down. Yet again, their fate seemed completely out of their hands.

"We have to go," said Sita, trying to offer some optimism. "We can't stay here. We will all catch our death of cold. Come on, if we hurry, we can catch them. I know they went straight down this road. I can feel it. Now let's go. We're wasting precious time."

With no other choice, the three of them walked for nearly an hour before coming to another fork in the road.

"That's it. I can't walk any more, Sita," Chandra confessed, this time with conviction. "I have to stop and rest. Please!"

Sita looked around for a tea stall or a shop or anything else that would shelter them from the rain for a short while. The only place she could find was a small vacant guardhouse that stood just in front of the gate of an all-boy's boarding school. The school was of a style she had seen before, with the classrooms on one side and dormitories on the other. Between these two wings was a connecting atrium, where the cafeteria was probably housed. Squashing the thought of food, she eyed the empty guardhouse. The gates around the fenced property were open, the guardhouse just inside.

"Look, we can go inside there for a short while. It looks empty. I'm sure no one will mind if we use it to get out of the rain for a couple of hours."

Once inside the tiny cinder block room, the three of them huddled together on the floor in the far corner. Despite the mild temperature outside, their water-drenched clothes caused them to shiver violently.

"What are you doing in here?" came a booming voice from the entrance of the guardhouse.

Awakened by this unexpected outburst, Sita popped to her feet. Chandra and Ravi were not far behind. Blocking the exit was a young man in his mid-twenties. He wore an oversized navy-blue guard's uniform, and he repeatedly slapped a thin bamboo stick hard against the palm of his hand. He had oily black hair, deep set eyes and an eyebrow that extended from one side of his face to the other. The sight of him immediately reminded Sita of the guard she had beaten back at the factory. The man's dark aura filled the space, pressing against them.

"I'm sorry," said Sita. "It was raining outside, and we needed a place to stay for a short while. We had been walking for hours. We didn't mean any harm. We'll be on our way now."

"You think you can just walk onto private property and go inside whenever you want?" asked the guard.

"I said we'll leave now," said Sita, taking a step forward toward the door.

"I'm afraid it isn't going to be that easy," replied the guard with a devilish smile. "You have broken the law. You trespassed on private property. How do I know you didn't steal something? No, you three are going to have to pay for this." He paused. "Do you have any money?"

"I said we were sorry," replied Sita. "Just move and let us leave. We didn't do any harm. Please. We need to go now." She took another step forward.

As he raised his stick up into the air, both Chandra and Ravi let out a scream. Sita turned her body so that her back was to the man. She then wrapped her arms tightly around her brother and sister's heads to protect them from what appeared to be an impending attack. The first blow struck her shoulder, and she let out a piercing scream.

"What is happening in there?" A second man's voice, harsh and authoritative, stopped the guard in his tracks.

Sita turned around. The guard lowered the stick to his side and took several steps backward. His expression told Sita that he was in serious trouble.

"What are you doing to them?" asked the second man, grabbing the guard's stick aggressively and throwing it to the floor.

He was much older, perhaps fifty, with a full moustache, wire-rim glasses and a head full of silvery grey hair. Under his full-length raincoat, he wore a wrinkled Western-style business suit that looked slept-in. He held a dripping umbrella in his hand which he repeatedly shook to get the excess water to fall off.

"Well? Why were you hitting them? They seem to be merely children."

"I didn't hit them," replied the guard defensively. "I found them inside here. They are thieves. They came in here to steal from the school. They tried to attack me. I was just doing my job. And when..."

"He is lying," Sita shouted, not allowing him to finish his statement. "He started hitting us for no reason. We had been walking for hours in the rain. We were cold and tired and took refuge here. If you hadn't come, he would have beaten us all to death with that stick of his for no reason. I told him we were sorry and that we'd leave. We just needed a place to rest. We didn't do anything wrong. There is nothing here to steal!"

"Nasir, I want you to go to my office and wait for me there," said the stranger. "And I don't want you to move until I arrive. Do you hear me?"

"Yes, sir," replied the guard, slinking away. In the doorway, behind the older man's back, Nasir gave Sita a look that could have seared a hole through a block of wood. His eyes were full of rage, hatred and resentment. How could she have ignored how vulnerable they would be out here on their own? They should never have left the protection of the gypsies!

"I'm sorry," said Sita to the man. "We didn't mean to cause you any trouble. Thank you for saving us from that terrible man. We'll be on our way now."

It was raining even harder than before. The thought of going back outside in these conditions, right before nightfall, was terrifying. But after what had just happened, it was best to get out of the area as fast as they could. She wanted to put some distance between herself and that guard. That look he gave her was permanently etched into her memories. He would surely come searching for them later.

"Wait, don't leave just yet." His harsh tone had softened now that the guard was gone. "Where are you coming from?"

"Delhi," replied Sita, with her eyes looking downward.

"Are you three alone?"

"Yes. Well, no, we were travelling with others, but we got separated. We should probably continue searching for them. It's getting late."

"But it's still raining." The man was examining them, plainly curious. He must have thought they were a strange trio. "You don't have any umbrellas," he continued. "If you'd like, you can stay here until it stops."

"But what about your guard? I'm afraid he'll come back and hit us again."

"Don't you worry about him," replied the man with a warm smile. "He is about to get a thrashing himself for what he did to you. I have warned him many times about abusing his authority. He is sometimes like an untamed dog. I guess that is what makes him such a good watchman. Stay if you'd like. He will cause you no harm. I can promise you that."

"Thank you very much. You're very kind."

The man looked out at the rain and sighed. After taking a few steps toward the door, he stopped and turned around.

"Are you interested in earning some money?" he asked, addressing the question to Sita. "I need someone to do some cleaning—classrooms, offices, kitchens—that type of thing. My name is Mr Sarcar. I am the headmaster at this primary school. We have nearly a hundred students living here during the semesters. Two days ago, one of my regular sweepers and her sister left for their village without any explanation. I was just about to go out in this rain and see if I could find someone to fill in for a few days. But then I stumbled upon you three. Are you interested in the job? I can't pay you much, but we can offer you food and shelter for a few days. Since the school is on break now, you will not have to worry about seeing any of the students. The place is completely empty. But it does need a good cleaning."

"Can we all work?"

"I don't care if you all work together, but the money will be the same: 100 rupees per day for the total job."

"Do you have space for all of us to sleep?"

"I don't think... No, wait. There is a small room behind the kitchen. Nasir sometimes sleeps there. You can use that if you'd like."

"Won't he mind?"

"He is a watchman; he is not supposed to be sleeping here. Besides, he has his own place outside. You can use the space. The room is very small, but if you don't mind sharing it, you can probably stay there without a problem. Please understand that this is not a permanent offer. It is just for a couple of days. When my regular sweeper returns, you'll have to leave again." Mr Sarcar stopped talking as if an unexpected thought had just entered his mind. "By the way, where were you going?"

"Back to Delhi to meet up with my Auntie. She lives there."

"That is 350 kilometres away. How were you planning on getting there?"

"We were going to take a bus, but they were all full."

"I thought you said you were separated from a group of others."

"We were. They must have gotten a bus before it started to rain. But we can catch up with them later. It will not be a problem."

"You aren't in any trouble with the authorities, are you?" asked Mr Sarcar, as if this thought had just occurred to him.

"No, not at all!" Sita hurried to reassure him. "Like I said, we were just going back to Delhi to be with our Auntie. But she is not expecting us right away. We can work here without any problem."

Mr Sarcar studied each of their faces, deliberating.

"Okay, then come with me. There is some food in the kitchen. After you eat, you can get some sleep. You will need it. There is much to be done in the morning. I will take you around myself to show you what is required."

"Thank you again, Mr Sarcar," said Sita, full of gratitude. "You have been very kind."

Ten days passed like a brisk gust of wind. The three of them worked each day from dawn to dusk, cleaning, scrubbing and washing everything in sight. Chalk dust lay on everything, and the wooden desks, in their neat rows, all needed polishing and waxing. The windows, looking out over the cricket fields and badminton nets, were still streaked with spring pollen, having been kept dry all summer by the great overhang of the roof. Sita spent half a day on a ladder, painstakingly scrubbing each pane. Ravi handed her clean rags when she needed them, the two singing whatever song came into his head. Once, he tried to sing one of the gypsy folk songs, but the foreign words eluded him. After a brief, troubled silence, he picked a radio hit. Sita joined in, singing louder than ever, as if her voice could push away the emptiness that had momentarily crept in on them.

While Mr Sarcar repeatedly encouraged the trio to take some time off, they all refused. Sita didn't know what the future had in store for them, but for now, the work kept her doubts and fears at bay. While they all missed Maya and their other travelling companions, they were grateful to have a roof over their heads and two warm meals a day.

Several days before the students were scheduled to return, Mr Sarcar requested that Sita come and see him in his office.

"Please take a seat," he said, reaching his hand out to offer a chair.

She remained standing. "I hope our work has been satisfactory." Their time was up. He would be asking them to leave. In ten days, she had not been able to figure out what to do next.

"Very much so. In fact, that's why I've asked you to come and see me today. I would like to find out if you and your sister might consider staying on here and working for the school. I will pay you a regular salary and allow you to continue using the room. The other staff seem to like you."

Sita thought of the kitchen staff, who had returned the day before. She had scrubbed the filthy black stove top till it shone. Apparently, they'd appreciated it.

"For how long?"

"For as long as you want."

"What...what about the other women who had the job before?"

"I haven't heard from them since they left. Besides, you and your sister do a much better job. Even if they do return, I have no intention of keeping them. They have become lazy over the years. They use any excuse they can find to avoid doing work. It's time for a change."

"And what about Ravi? Can he work also?"

"He is too young to be working. He should be in school. I have noticed that he is a very smart boy. In fact, I can tell that all of you have been educated in some way. While I don't know what's happened to you and I suppose it is none of my business, it is clear to me that you have not grown up on the street or in some small village. Am I right?" His inquiry was polite without insisting on an answer.

Sita didn't respond. Instead, she used the time to think about his kind offer. If they headed off now, the little money they'd earned would be expended quickly, and they'd be left helpless again. On the other hand, it had been nearly five weeks since they had fled New Delhi. With each passing day, it would be more difficult to locate Ganesh.

It was tempting to break down and tell Mr Sarcar everything, but Maya's warning about the mob bosses played through her head. Mr Sarcar would certainly want her to go to the police with her story, something that would place the family in danger once again. He was kind, but she couldn't trust him that far.

"If we stay, would you consider allowing Ravi to attend your school?" asked Sita, not expecting him to agree. The idea just popped into her mind. "Chandra and I will both reduce our salary if you allow us to do this."

"Hmmm. I would..."

"When he was studying, Ravi had excellent marks. In fact, he was always within the top ten percent of his class. He has only missed about two months of school. But I am sure he can make it up quickly. I will help tutor him myself."

"I don't think this would work," Mr Sarcar confessed. "If he were to stay with you, he'd run into trouble with the other boys. I know them. They'd tease him. They are not very forgiving. Status with these boys is everything. It would..."

"Then let him board with the others. No one has to know that we are related. You can just say that he is a new boy who joined over the break. I heard that you have five vacant spots here. Whatever money I earn, I will use it to cover his extra expenses. He will be no trouble. I promise you that."

"How can he pretend not to be related to you? He would see you every day around the campus and in the cafeteria. That would not be fair to you or to him."

"You let me worry about that. We can find a way to spend time together off hours."

"I am not sure this is a good idea. We would..."

"If you do this, I promise you will be satisfied with our work and his performance. Please?"

Mr Sarcar's eyes crinkled behind the wire-rimmed glasses.

"You're a very determined young lady. I guess we can give it a try. But if he isn't able to keep up with the others, then he can't continue. Do you understand?"

"Yes, sir."

"So, you and your sister will stay and work?"

"I have one more request before I decide."

"Another request?" the headmaster laughed.

"Do you mind if Chandra and I borrow books from your library? After we finish reading them, we will return them. This will allow us to continue with our own studies. I noticed that you have a collection of textbooks that go up to class ten."

"Tell me, why are you here, Sita?"

"What do you mean?"

"You and your brother and sister are not cleaners. Like I said before, I can tell you are from a good family somewhere. It's very obvious to me. Now, what happened to you three?"

"Nothing!"

"I don't believe you. Tell me the truth now."

There was a long pause. This time he was expecting an answer.

"We lost our parents in a car crash several months ago," she replied, turning her face away. "We lost everything. That is all there is to say about it."

"There is no other family?"

"No."

"What about that Auntie in Delhi that you mentioned to me that first day?"

"I made that up. We were travelling with some other people, but we somehow got separated from them. But they were not my family. They were just travelling performers."

"Then why lie about having an Auntie?"

"I didn't want you to think that we had no one in this world. I'm sorry I wasn't truthful with you. It will never happen again. I promise."

"But..."

"Please answer my question," she stated, hoping to change the subject. "Can we use the books?"

"Yes, you can," he conceded. "As long as you keep up with your work, I don't care what you do in your spare time. That is your own affair. So, now it is your turn. Do I have an answer from you, or do you have any more demands to put forth?"

"That's all," replied Sita, almost giddy with relief. "Thank you so much."

Sita held her hand out, taking him by surprise. With a small grin, he shook it, sealing their bargain.

As Sita was leaving the room, she suddenly stopped and turned. "Mr Sarcar, what about Nasir? He knows that Ravi is my brother. He will tell the others for sure. He doesn't like us very much."

"What makes you think that?"

"Ever since that day you shouted at him, he has treated us badly. He was also very mad when you took his room away, the one you gave to us. He is always lurking in a corner somewhere, staring at us. He really frightens me."

"That is his job, to watch people. He is a guard. What else has he done?"

"I don't know. He makes rude comments and sometimes goes out of his way to make us do extra work. A couple of times he walked into the dining hall after it had already been cleaned and deliberately tracked mud all around it. He then just stood there and smiled while we cleaned it up. I think he'd tell the other boys just for spite."

"Don't worry about it. I'll have a talk with him. And you tell me if he does anything at all to you or your family. He's been warned many times to stay out of trouble. One of these days he is going to get himself fired."

"Why do you keep him if he causes so much trouble?"

"His father was our security guard for nearly thirty years. He was a good man who served us well. After he had a massive stroke, Nasir took over. He never wanted the job, but his family insisted. I know he drinks. But he has gotten better of late. If it hadn't been for his father, I would have probably replaced him long ago."

"Thank you again, Mr Sarcar. Thank you."

9

Nearly a year passed at the boarding school. The hours were long and the work was demanding, but Sita found the routine of their days comforting. Chandra, too, seemed calmer in this new environment, steadier. After the chaos and the uncertainty of the previous months, they were glad to know what was expected of them and what each morning would present.

Ravi had quickly adapted to the boarding school as well, but Ganesh remained a constant source of self-reproach. A dozen times a day, Sita would remind herself that they should look for him. Then she would picture him with his wealthy new family, a family that had wanted him enough to purchase him. Perhaps he even had a nanny, like their Nilopha, who would dote on him, do anything for him.

Soon, she would tell herself, turning back to the chore at hand. She would look for him and Auntie soon.

After cleaning up the dinner dishes, she and Chandra would study in the library after hours. Mr Sarcar provided them with a key and even borrowed a set of class ten textbooks from a fellow headmaster for Sita. After all, he told them, it was a rare thing for a headmaster to find students who treated learning as a gift rather than a punishment.

When she wasn't studying or working, Sita spent hours drafting letters. She located an up-to-date telephone directory for New Delhi and went through every entry that had the first name Nadia listed. To each person with this name, she wrote the following letter:

Dear Nadia,

If you once had a brother named Prakash Sharma from Pune, please send your contact information to the address down below. I have some very important information about what happened to him and his family in the fire.

Send your address and phone number to Maya, P.O. Box 134688, Jann Station, Lucknow, 12229. I will contact you upon receiving this information.

Sincerely,
A friend of the family

Each week she managed to send about twenty letters. With over 1,600 Nadias listed in the book, the job was daunting, but she couldn't think of any other way to contact her Auntie.

Every Saturday, during her day off, she would go with her sister into town to visit the local post office. An otherwise mundane white building, it had been decorated with bright red columns and trim work, as though it were a temple of correspondence. The replies she received were polite, single-line statements indicating that the writer was not the Nadia she was looking for. Most wished her luck in her search.

In the beginning, Ravi found it very difficult to avoid interacting with his sisters. During the day, he often ran into Chandra or Sita at least once, sometimes twice. Each time, he did something to reveal the fact that he recognised them, and Sita always made a point of scolding him the next time they got together in private. At night, when the others had fallen asleep, Ravi sometimes sneaked out of his dorm and went to visit them. During these times, they shared food together and talked and laughed about everything that was going on around them. Ravi loved to mimic his teachers and make fun of his stuffy classmates.

The school had eleven full-time teachers and five part time employees who cooked, tended to the grounds and provided all-around support to the facility.

Sita and Chandra got along with all of them. In fact, within the first six months, they became very popular with most people, including many of the parents. With one notable exception.

From that first day when Nasir had discovered them sleeping in the guardhouse, he had taken a complete dislike to Sita. Whenever an opportunity presented itself, he would do whatever he could to humiliate her. He was convinced that she and her siblings were perpetrating some kind of hoax on the school and that they would soon be revealed for the little thieves that they were. Until that time, he vowed to make their lives as miserable as possible. Torturing them became his mission.

One Saturday, after a trip to the post office, Sita took a towel and went to the outdoor shower, hidden behind the storage shed. Undressing in the small, curtained foyer, she entered the shower stall, her feet scuffing the cement tiles. The water came out hot but refreshing, and she sang softly to herself as she washed off a week's worth of sweat. Her hair had grown down to her thighs; it took forever to thoroughly wash but she didn't mind. The outdoor shower, with its smell of damp wood and the blue sky overhead, was one of her favourite spots on the school grounds. When at last she turned the water off, it was with a tinge of regret. Towelling off, she opened the door that connected to the curtained foyer. Her clothes were nowhere in sight.

"Nasir," she hissed. The thought of him so close to her when she'd been naked made her shrink back and lock herself in the shower stall. It was late afternoon, the students were mostly home with their families. Still, she waited till the sun went down, then crept back to her room wrapped in a towel, shamed and livid.

The next morning, he crept up behind her as she was leaning over a shelf, dusting the windowsill. He grabbed her breasts and for a moment, she froze in shock. Then she stomped on his foot, making him step back with a curse.

"Have a nice shower?" he smirked, even though his brows were pinched in pain. She hurried to her room before he could try anything else.

Sita was too ashamed to tell Mr Sarcar about this incident, though he punished Nasir for the offences she did relate. Then, for a week or two, the guard would be on best behaviour. But it was only a matter of time. One Friday evening, just before an important holiday break, Nasir staggered into the dining hall while a handful of boys were still finishing their dinner. Sita was clearing a nearby table, her body tensing with his presence.

She watched him scan the room and determine what she already knew: there were no teachers present. Then he walked over to a table that contained several half-empty trays of food and gently pushed one of them onto the floor. Hearing the crash of aluminium against cement, the entire roomful of boys turned to see what had just happened.

"Come over here, girl, and clean up this mess," Nasir demanded, pointing at Sita.

As much as she would have liked to walk away, defying him in front of an audience would only encourage him to do worse. Sita grabbed a broom and a hand rag and quickly picked up the tray off the floor. After wiping up rice and daal, she stood and began to walk away. But before she could take her third step, he pushed a second tray to the floor.

"You missed some," he shouted, his voice echoing through the silent room. For a moment her eyes locked on Ravi, one of the only boys not laughing at her degradation. His gaze was fiery, his jaw clamped shut. Up until this point, Sita had done her best to remain invisible to the boys. But now she stood in a spotlight of humiliation.

For several seconds, she hesitated, staring defiantly at Nasir. The assembled boys watched this standoff with great anticipation. An uneasy quiet prevailed. Her first inclination was to just walk away. Instead, she picked up the second fallen tray and added it to the one she had already collected from the floor.

Knowing that Nasir's little game was not about to end with this, she turned and once again tried to escape. For a third time, the sound of a metal tray hitting the floor shattered the silence. Sita stopped, turned and smiled. But this time, she continued walking.

"Get over here and clean this up!" he shouted, full of rage. When she didn't respond to his command, he marched up to her and grabbed her arm forcefully, twisting her around. "I said pick that up!"

Before his hand could strike her face, an aluminium tray came crashing down against the side of Nasir's head, again and again, clenched in Ravi's fist, the boy's face contorted with rage.

Hearing the commotion from outside the building where they had gathered for a smoke, several of the teachers came rushing inside. It took three of them to tear Ravi away from Nasir. Not knowing what had happened, they dragged him off to the headmaster's office, kicking and screaming. Both Sita and Nasir followed close behind.

"What just happened in the cafeteria?" Mr Sarcar asked both Sita and Nasir. Ravi stood off to one side, crying as he struggled to recover from his fit of rage.

"She and her bastard brother started it," Nasir hissed. "I just walked into the place and they both started hitting me."

"He is lying, sir," replied Sita, pointing her finger at Nasir's face. "He kept dropping plates of food onto the floor. I cleaned up the first two, but when I refused to pick up the third one, he charged over to hit me. Ravi came to my rescue. Neither of us was doing anything wrong. He started it. He has obviously been drinking as well. Ask anyone in that room; they will all tell you what really happened."

Mr Sarcar looked over at the three teachers standing in the back of his office.

"I'm sorry, sir. When the incident took place, none of us were inside the cafeteria," replied one of the instructors, anticipating his question.

"She is a lying whore," Nasir continued. "She was the one who started it. She tried to seduce me last night. When I said no to her unwelcome advances, she got angry. When she saw me today, she just started hitting me. Then her brother joined in. She should be thrown out of this place. She is a no-good whore."

"He's lying," Sita sobbed, feeling like she'd been punched in the gut. No one had ever said anything like that about her before. "He is lying. I would never...we didn't do anything."

"Have you been drinking, Nasir?" asked Mr Sarcar.

"No!"

"Come over here."

"No," he insisted. "I didn't do anything. And I haven't had anything to drink."

"Get over here, Nasir! This very minute!"

He finally did as he was told, standing directly in front of Mr Sarcar. Unable to maintain his balance, his feet continually shuffled around to avoid leaning precariously from side to side.

Mr Sarcar took a sharp sniff then recoiled. "You're fired! Get your belongings and leave the property immediately. I don't want to hear another one of your pathetic lies. Get out. Your father will be ashamed when he learns of this! Leave, right now!"

"I didn't do anything," he replied, stunned. "It is all her fault. She is a dog, a whore, the daughter of a whore. She is the one who is lying. I am not going anywhere. She and her pig family should be the ones leaving. Not me. I was here first. My father worked for you for over thirty years. You can't fire me. All of the trouble started when she arrived."

Mr Sarcar grabbed Nasir by the collar and started dragging him in the direction of the door. "Take him to the gate and see that he doesn't return," he said to the other guard who had just arrived. "And call the police. I want them here so that I can file a formal report."

Hearing Mr Sarcar mention the police, Nasir suddenly backed off, holding his hands up defensively.

"All right, all right, I'll leave. But you're making a big mistake."

As he was walking toward the door, he sidestepped and pushed Ravi down to the floor. Without turning back, he exited the room.

"I'm sorry that you had to endure this treatment, Sita," said Mr Sarcar, returning his attention to her. Ravi stood and ran to his sister, wrapping his arms tightly around her waist as he continued to weep. "I should have fired him years ago. He is no good. I will have to go and see his father about this in the morning. I hope he understands that I did my best to put up with him. But this time he has crossed far over the line."

"Are you going to take him back again?" asked Sita, knowing he had made compromises in the past. "What if his father pleads with you?"

"No." replied Mr Sarcar, with conviction. "That was it. He will never work here again."

Two months passed without incident. With Nasir out of the picture, life was good again. Realising that Sita and Chandra had so much more to offer than just cleaning and sweeping, several of the teachers asked them to help tutor some of the children who had fallen behind. While this kept them away from the library and their own studies, it offered them an added sense of purpose and a little additional money. The recognition and respect also enhanced their self-esteem after the degrading treatment they had suffered at the hands of Nasir.

Following the cafeteria incident, Ravi also went through a metamorphosis. For years, Nasir had been feared by nearly all the students. The way Ravi spontaneously stood up and attacked this villain in support of a helpless cleaning woman turned him into an instant celebrity. The quiet, reserved student now stood tall and developed a swaggering walk, his jutting jaw leading the way. Sita was glad his confidence had grown, but the accompanying cockiness was troubling. Ravi was now often bending and breaking the rules in order to maintain the attention and adoration of the other students, especially the older ones. He liked being special, and being the class troublemaker fulfilled this need. It was a role he adopted with vigour.

One Saturday afternoon, Sita and Chandra walked the three kilometres to town to visit the post office and the local shopping bazaar. They stopped at the post office first, but there were no letters waiting for them. Not too disheartened, they continued on to the bazaar, armed with a list of spices the cook wanted them to pick up.

The spice stall was one of Sita's favourite places to stop. On a long bolt of crimson fabric, the bowls were laid out in neat rows. Curled cinnamon bark, whole chili peppers and mounded bowls of golden turmeric greeted her eye. The smells of cumin, tea leaves and ginger were like a warm embrace each time she entered; the family pantry had once smelled much the same. She haggled in a friendly way with the old woman, who offered a mostly toothless smile upon seeing them. Their errand complete, Sita led Chandra back into the bustling crowd. It was nice to be away from the school, for a change, to see new faces. Loud bartering filled the air, and the bright awnings of the stalls snapped in the wind.

"Sita, look what time it is!" Chandra declared, looking down at her watch. "It's so late! Come on, we'd better go now. I don't like travelling on that road at night. We're bound to get struck by a bus."

"Don't worry, we'll get back in time," Sita responded, looking up at the sky. "We can cut through the fields; it's half the distance. That way, we'll beat the darkness."

"But we'll have to pass through that patch of forest that lines the main road. I really don't like going through there. What if I trip and sprain my ankle?"

"Come on, worrywart. The road will take us an extra twenty minutes. I'm supposed to do a tutoring session this evening. If you want to go by the road, go ahead by yourself, but I'm cutting through the field."

Chandra gave a reluctant nod. "I guess I'll go with you."

They left the bazaar and began walking down a series of raised trails that ran along the paddy fields. The fields were empty at this time of day, the chartreuse leaves of the rice plants glowing in the low light of evening. They kept a brisk pace and soon reached the stretch of forest.

"See, I told you it would be faster," said Sita, with a smile.

"Don't get too far ahead of me," Chandra complained. "I always have trouble with the rocks on this path."

"Don't worry, I'll be right beside you."

They entered the forest path, and within moments, the temperature dropped and dusk surrounded them. The trail's terrain rose sharply, and Chandra stopped. "Sita, my legs are getting tired. Don't go so fast. You promised you'd stay beside me."

"Don't be such a baby. We're almost there. Let's just go."

Sita turned back, her sister's mint green tunic glowing in the low light, her face barely visible. They could hear the nearby road, but everything seemed very far away. Then, in front of Sita, a branch cracked.

"Sita, I think there is someone there."

They both went quiet, holding their breath. Only the chirping of frogs filled the air.

"You've been reading too many of those scary novels lately," Sita chided. They needed to just hurry up and get back. "Now come on. It's getting dark outside. Let's keep going."

A branch cracked, as if stepped on. They both froze. A rustling sound came from the other side of a large patch of bramble bushes. Leaving Chandra several steps behind, Sita slowly edged forward. It was probably a loose cow or a horse foraging in the forest.

She had often seen them leave the road in search of a few exotic leaves to eat in the tall grass.

With her hands, she slowly separated the branches so that she could see what was behind them.

When Sita opened her eyes, she was lying on her back, with her left leg twisted underneath her right one. A variety of vegetation all but shrouded her face and head. For several seconds, she had no idea where she was or how she'd got there. All she knew was that her entire body was infused with an overpowering sensation of pain.

In the distance, she could hear whimpering.

"Chandra?" she called. "Chandra, is that you? I'm coming."

When she attempted to stand, however, she fell back to the damp ground. She tried once more but she could not rise to her feet. Sensing that Chandra was in some kind of danger, she used every ounce of energy she could muster to make a third attempt. This time she succeeded and began hobbling toward the sounds.

In the prevailing darkness, two shadowy silhouettes rolled around on the ground, one planted on top of the other. Recognising Chandra's high-pitched sobs, Sita lurched forward to attack her sister's assailant. She began by grabbing the figure by the hair with one hand, while the other searched for the aggressor's eyes. Enraged by this unexpected counter-assault, the attacker stood and grabbed Sita by the arm. With his fist flying aimlessly, he struck her over and over again in the face and chest.

"You whore— I'll kill you!" She could barely see him, but she knew his voice. Nasir. "And after I finish with your sister, I'll kill her. But you first!"

Even in the dark, Sita could tell that he was drunk. She tried to kick and push him away, but the blows kept raining down on her. For a moment, it was as if she left her own body, observing the action from above.

Then suddenly Nasir stopped throwing punches. He froze, dropped to his knees, stayed in this position for several seconds and then fell face-forward, hitting the ground with a thud. It looked as if his life force had been snatched away from him without warning.

With her left eye nearly swollen shut, Sita looked up. Chandra stood above them, her right hand firmly grasping a large knife. A steady stream of blood dripped down the blade onto her fingers.

Despite her own exhaustion and pain, Sita managed to stand up and pull her sister into her arms. She reached down, took the knife and tossed it into the brush. Chandra showed no emotion, it was as if she were in a deep trance. Tears continued to pour from her eyes, but she made no sound.

"Are you okay?" asked Sita, gently taking her sister's face in her hands. "What happened? What did he do to you?"

Chandra shivered, her expression blank.

"Chandra, Chandra, are you okay?" Sita finally took her sister by the shoulders and shook her violently.

"Sita, Sita, Sita!" she shouted, having regained a sense of awareness. She wrapped her arms around Sita's neck as if seeing her for the first time.

"Are you okay?"

"He, he, he..." Chandra couldn't get the words out and began to hyperventilate, gasping for air.

"Chandra, shhhh. Just slow down and tell me what happened."

She closed her eyes, took a deep slow breath, and began. "After you went down to look in those bushes, Nasir hit you with his fist. You fell to the ground and didn't get up. When I tried to run for help, he came after me. He...he pulled my dress up and then..."

Chandra couldn't finish the statement. Sita didn't need to hear any more. She had read enough modern novels in the library to know exactly what had happened.

"Chandra, we can't stay here," said Sita, trying to keep her sister from losing control again. "We have to leave immediately. Where did the knife come from?"

"Nasir had it. He used it to cut away my under-clothes."

"Did he cut you?"

"No, he placed it on the ground when he was on top of me. Is he dead? What if he isn't dead? What if he comes after us?"

"He's gone. But we have to get out of here. The police will get involved; they'll keep asking questions until they find out who we are. And Nasir's family is going to want someone to blame. They are from this area. They could put us both in jail."

"But he was attacking us," Chandra cried out.

"It doesn't matter. You know the way the legal system works here. His family is well-known in this community, and we are nothing. They will do anything to avoid bringing shame to their name, even if it means putting innocent people in jail. We can't let that happen. We can't get involved with the police. We have to run again, there's no other choice. We'll go back to the school, find Ravi, and leave this place before they find the body. I've saved up our money, it's enough to keep us going for several months. We'll just go to another school. We can start over again. It will be okay."

"What do we do with him?"

"We'll leave him here. They will find him soon enough. Maybe the vultures will get to him first. He doesn't deserve anything better than to have his eyes plucked out and his flesh torn away."

"Sita, I'm bleeding," said Chandra, looking down to the wetness between her legs. A second wave of tears and fear washed over her. "He hurt me. I did..."

"We can't worry about that now. We need to go," Sita replied, fighting back her own tears. If the man weren't already dead, she would surely have killed him for defiling her sister.

"Chandra, I know this will be difficult, but you have to go into the school by yourself. My face is too bruised and swollen, people will ask questions, maybe call the police."

Chandra walked haltingly, Sita holding her hand and leading her back toward the school. When they reached a small stream, she cupped her hands and washed Chandra's face and legs. The moon was rising. In the dim light, she could see that her sister looked strange, bedraggled, but not alarming. But would she be able to hold herself together long enough to get Ravi and the money?

Sita walked her to the gate, explaining over and over, in a lulling repetition, what Chandra must do.

"Go through the gate and to our room. The boys will all be in bed. Gather our things in a sheet and tie it up. The money is under the loose floorboard in a plastic bag. Don't forget the money, Chandra. Then come back to me. If the guard asks what you are doing, tell him you forgot to alter the sheets as Mr Sarcar instructed us to. He's not so bright, the new guard. He won't ask you any questions. Then you will have to go back in once more, wake Ravi and tell him the schoolmaster wants him to pack his things and come to see him. When he's packed, both of you come out here. Okay?"

Chandra made little sign she heard. Sita repeated this once again, trying to keep her panic at bay. When she had finished speaking, Chandra walked through the gate and into the school.

Sita waited down the road behind a crumbling stone wall, praying that Chandra wouldn't fall to pieces just yet. When she heard footsteps, she peeked over the wall. Her sister looked like a ghost in the moonlight. Sita hissed to get her attention, and Chandra turned her head slowly, then made her way over to her sister's hiding spot.

"Did you get the money?"

Chandra handed the plastic bag over and Sita sighed with relief. "The guard wanted to know what I was doing. He'll stop me for sure if I return so quickly. I can't do anymore."

"You have to be strong. Just go inside, get Ravi and return immediately."

"What about the guard?"

"He won't care."

"But…"

"Just go, Chandra, and hurry!"

After handing the bundle over, Chandra turned back toward the school. From her place in the shadows, Sita watched the guard peek out of the guardhouse at Chandra. He merely stared indolently at her and said nothing.

Sita watched her sister walk inside. A minute later, a light turned on in Ravi's dormitory. It was too distant for her to see through the window. In the darkness, guilt crept up on her. Chandra had tried to make her head home earlier, she hadn't wanted to cut through the woods. Sita's eyes stung with tears, but she bit them back. Her eyes were already so swollen she could barely open them. Then, distantly, she heard Ravi and Chandra speaking.

"What are we doing?" Ravi asked angrily. "I thought you weren't supposed to be seen with me. How am I going to go back after this? What will I say?"

"You're not going back. We're leaving this place tonight. We can't stay here anymore. Something very bad has happened."

"What? I like this school. I don't want to go anywhere else. Why do we always have to run?" Ravi stopped in his track, just before the guardhouse. "I'm not leaving here. If you and Sita want to go, then you go. But I'm not leaving. Not this time."

"Shut up and walk, Ravi. I don't have time for your stubbornness now. We stay together, period."

"No. Why do we have to leave anyway?"

"I'll explain it later."

"I'm not leaving just because you say so. I'm not a little kid anymore. I want to know what happened."

"Where are you two going?" asked the guard, emerging from the guardhouse.

"We are leaving this place," replied Chandra, her voice trembling.

"You can't take a student out of this school without notifying the headmaster." The guard repeated this rule by rote, lighting a cigarette.

"I'm his older sister. I can take him wherever I like, whenever I like."

"You, his sister?" The guard laughed. "Get back inside immediately. I don't want to…"

"It's okay, Runi, I'm his sister too," said Sita, coming over to help with the valise Ravi carried.

The guard stopped and stared at the sight of Sita's face. "I'm going to get the headmaster," he said, seeming confused.

"Runi, stop!" said Sita. She reached into her pocket and pulled out a hundred-rupee bill. "You didn't see us leave. Right?"

He looked down at the bill. When he went to grab it, she pulled it away again.

"You didn't see us leave. Do you understand?"

"Deal." He snatched the bill, stuffed it into his pocket and walked off.

Ravi stared at his sister's face. When the girls started walking, he followed, wordless.

10

For nearly three weeks, the Sharma family hid in a cheap hotel situated at a crossroad just outside the northern tip of New Delhi. Fearing that squads of heavily-armed policemen were now out canvassing the region for Nasir's killer, Sita insisted they remain secluded. Between Sita's swollen face and Chandra's new habit of talking to herself, they were sure to draw attention.

Six days after Nasir's death, the newspaper finally reported that a 21-year-old man had been found dead in a patch of forest located in a village ten kilometres outside of Lucknow. The article, which listed Nasir's name and address, said that he had been robbed and stabbed to death. There was no mention of any suspects.

"I'm bored," Ravi complained, rolling onto his back during a commercial break. The black and white tv broadcast a fuzzy image that strained their eyes, but there was nothing else to pass the time. "Why can't I go back to my old school? I really liked it there. Why is it that you do things that always make us have to leave a place?" he asked Sita.

"Are you saying that all of this was my fault?" Sita snapped. "Do you think I wanted to get beaten like this? Do you think I somehow did this to myself on purpose, just to make your life miserable? Don't you say those things to me! Chandra and I worked our fingers down to the bone so that you could go to that school. I didn't see you doing any work back there. What did you contribute to the family? Huh? You did nothing!"

"All I know is that we go someplace and begin to like what we are doing and then you do something stupid that ruins it. It's your fault. First it was Maya and then my school. You..."

"Shut up! I can't take this bickering anymore," said Chandra, finally entering the argument. She tried to stand up but unexpectedly fell to the floor. Both her hands seized her right side as if she were immobilised with pain.

"What's happening, Chandra?" asked Sita, running to her sister's aid.

Chandra moaned. "My stomach hurts something awful."

"When did this start?" asked Sita, reaching up to feel her sister's forehead. It was on fire with fever. "Ravi, go out and get an auto-rickshaw. And hurry!"

"What's wrong with her?" he hesitated, eyes wide, all his schoolboy swagger gone.

"I don't know. Just hurry. She needs a doctor."

Ravi ran out of the hotel room.

"Chandra. Are you alright?"

Her sister drifted in and out of consciousness. Sita had never seen an illness come on so fast.

"Sita, the taxi is outside," Ravi reported, racing into the hotel room, completely out of breath. "What do you want me to do?"

"Help me get her out there."

With Chandra barely able to walk, it took all their strength to get her into the tiny three-wheel taxi. After grabbing her last handful of money, Sita locked the hotel room door and ran over to the waiting vehicle.

"Where to, miss?" asked the driver, looking back at Chandra.

"A hospital! A good hospital. One that is close by. Hurry! Hurry!"

The taxi bounced toward the city centre, causing Chandra to cry out in pain at every pothole. With her sister's head in her lap, Sita did what she could to soothe her. Up front, Ravi sat ruler-straight beside the driver.

"Where are you taking us?" asked Sita. "We need a good hospital!"

"There is a large hospital down this road. It is only three blocks from here," answered the rickshaw driver, totally unaffected by this emergency.

"Do they have good doctors there?" asked Sita, hoping for some additional details.

"Yes. Many people go to this place when they are ill. It is one of the best clinics in the area."

Within five minutes they arrived. It was indeed a substantial hospital. But despite her calls for help, no attendant arrived to help Chandra inside. She and Ravi finally managed to get the sick girl to a plastic sofa in the waiting area.

Looking around, it was obvious that the hospital catered to a middle-class clientele. Sita straightened her sari pleats and finger-combed her hair. They'd never be helped if the staff thought they were poor.

"What is her problem?" the nurse on duty asked, looking suspiciously past Sita at Chandra.

"About thirty minutes ago, she started having severe pain in her right side. When you press on her tummy, she flinches. She also has a very high fever. I have never seen her so weak before. It just came on quickly with absolutely no warning."

"Do you have any money for treatment?" asked the nurse, a dubious look on her broad face.

"Yes."

"Let me see it." Her fingers waggled up and down to demonstrate her impatience.

Sita pulled out the wad of money and held it up for the nurse to see.

"The doctor will cost you 500 rupees. Any medicine you need will cost more. Do you have enough there?" Her tone and manner of speaking was condescending.

"Yes. I have over 650 rupees here. Now may we please see a doctor at once?" Sita decided to adopt the same haughty and rude attitude.

"Give me 500 now, and the doctor will see your sister when he is available."

"It had better be soon then, nurse, because we are not accustomed to waiting," Sita said in her best matronly imitation.

Even though Sita paid up front and demanded service every ten minutes, Chandra still had to wait nearly an hour to be seen. Several prominent, well-off patients arrived and were given preference, even though their maladies seemed very minor. Only after the waiting area was empty did the doctor reluctantly ask Sita to escort Chandra into the curtained examination room.

"What's her name?" asked the young doctor, as he filled out a client record. His long hair kept falling over his eyes, and he repeatedly wiped his running nose with his shirt sleeve, disgusting her. They had been taught from infancy not to do that. For a high-priced hospital, they had an awfully uncouth and dishevelled doctor.

"Chandra Sharma."

"How old is she."

"Fourteen."

"What's wrong with her?" he asked, focusing his attention on the paper in front of him.

"What's wrong with her?" Sita had nearly had enough and was frightened and indignant. "If I knew that, Doctor, I would not be here, would I?" After receiving only a piercing stare from the man, Sita went on. "She has a terrible pain in her stomach. She also has a high fever. This all started very suddenly. I think she is very sick. Please help her."

"Is she pregnant?" asked the doctor.

"No." Sita stopped to think about what happened to Chandra weeks before. "No."

He walked over and began his examination. After taking her blood pressure, listening to her heart with the stethoscope, he then used two fingers to poke around her abdomen. Whenever he touched a particular spot on her right side, she cried out in agony.

"Your sister has acute appendicitis," he replied with confidence, proud of his rapid diagnosis.

"What does that mean?" asked Sita. It sounded bad. And expensive.

"It means that an organ in her belly, her appendix, is severely infected. It could burst so it needs to be removed. She needs an immediate operation, or she will die."

"Can you do the operation here at this hospital?"

"Yes, we can. But do you have the money to pay for it?"

"How much money will it cost?"

"At least 25,000 rupees for the operation alone. But you'll also have to buy the supplies and medicines for the procedure at one of the local pharmacies. That will cost you another 5,000. Maybe more." He looked doubtful.

"I don't have that kind of money!"

"Then I'm afraid you're going to have to go elsewhere," he replied, not surprised. "This is a private hospital. We do not do charity work. You can take her to the public hospital on the other side of the city. They might agree to do the procedure."

"How will I get her there?"

"How did you get to this place?"

"By baby taxi."

"Then I guess that is the best way to leave," replied the doctor as he wrote out a prescription sheet. "When you arrive at the other hospital, show this slip to the attending doctor. He or she will know what to do."

"Will the public hospital charge money to do the operation?" asked Sita.

"Yes. But sometimes they do cases for free. It all depends on if they have a doctor available or not. You'll have to talk to one of the nurses when you arrive. But even if they did the procedure for free, you'd still have to pay for the supplies and medicines. If you don't have the money, I'd go out and get it from a relative or a friend."

"How much will the supplies cost?"

"The same as here: around 4 to 5 thousand rupees."

"What happens if she doesn't get this operation? What if I can't get the money?"

"I'm afraid she'll die from the infection. Her condition is very serious."

"How much time do we have?" asked Sita, as her anxiety level reached a feverish peak.

"It's hard to say. Like I said, she is very ill. She probably needs an operation within the next three or four hours, or she might not survive."

"How long will it take me to get to the other hospital in a taxi?"

"At this time? With traffic? Probably about an hour. You can still make it."

"Can't you do the operation and then I can pay you later?" Sita pleaded. "Please, doctor."

"No, we only accept cash," replied the doctor, as if repeating something he had said a thousand times. "If you can raise the money, we will operate. If not, I'm afraid you'll have to find another place. This is the hospital's policy. If I go against that I could be fired. I'm sorry."

Sita was devastated. They had to do the procedure here. In public hospitals, patients died on the floor waiting for one of the few doctors to come along and tend to them.

As she stood beside the door, praying to the God Ganesh, someone unexpectedly tapped her on the shoulder from behind.

"I heard what the doctor just said to you," whispered one of the uniformed hospital attendants. His eyes kept darting around as if to ensure that no one was watching him. "Maybe I can help. I know how you can get that kind of money in a hurry, perhaps even by this afternoon. There is a woman who lives close by who might pay the bill. But you'll have to work for her for some time to pay it back."

"What kind of work would I have to do?" asked Sita, full of suspicion. Memories of Mrs Gupta and her chemicals were never very far away.

"Go and talk to her first," he replied, without revealing any details. "She'll explain everything to you. She is the only one I know who has that kind of money. She will help you. I know she will. She helps people here all the time."

"Can you take me to her now? We don't have much time."

"Yes, I'm just getting off duty. Come with me."

Sita escorted Chandra back to the waiting area and settled her on the couch. Before leaving the ward, Sita pulled her brother aside. "Ravi, I want you to stay with your sister. Get her some water. I'll be back in a short time."

"Is she going to be okay?" he asked, tears welling up in his eyes.

"Yes, she'll be fine," replied Sita with a forced smile.

"Where are you going?"

"I have to run a quick errand. I'll be back shortly. Wait here."

"Sita, promise me she'll be all right."

"I can't..."

"Promise me, Sita. Promise me."

"Okay, I promise you. Now stay here. I'll be back with some money so we can take good care of Chandra."

The baby taxi pulled up in front of a large white house several kilometres from the hospital in a secluded residential area. When the guard saw Sita's escort, he immediately opened up the gate to allow them both inside.

"Is Madam here now?" he asked, appearing hopeful.

The guard nodded without answering, indicating that they should use the side door.

The house they entered reminded Sita of the one she had grown up in, her parents' old home now in ashes. It had high ceilings, grand doorways and many tall windows. The decor was modern, with many pieces of glass and stainless-steel furniture and several brightly coloured contemporary sofas.

A manservant entered the room, looked at the two visitors and then left without saying anything. Moments later, he returned with a woman in her early fifties who was dressed as though she were going to a fancy society gala. She wore a striking purple silk sari that was highlighted with elaborate gold embroidery. Her silver hair was in a bun coiled on top of her head and held in place with ebony combs. She had the look of someone who had once been stunningly beautiful, but some of this beauty had faded. In addition to massive rings on each of her fingers, she was adorned with gold necklaces and earrings that dangled to her shoulders.

She walked straight to Sita and nodded her head. "My name is Sangeeta Banik. What brings you to my home?"

"I was told by a doctor that you sometimes help people at the hospital," replied Sita, with pleading eyes. "You see my sister is very ill and needs an immediate operation. They want 30,000 rupees or they will let her die! I don't have that kind of money. But if I can't get it, she will die. Please. There is no time to take her to a charity hospital and wait there for their mercy. Can you help? I'll do anything. I can clean, wash, do dishes, laundry. Anything. I am a hard worker. Please, I need your help. I'm desperate."

"How old are you?"

"Almost sixteen."

"Do you have any family?"

"Just my sister and a younger brother."

"No parents or other relatives?"

"My parents were killed. I have an Auntie here in Delhi, but I don't know how to get in touch with her. It is just the three of us."

The woman studied Sita's features closely. "What happened to your face, child? It seems bruised."

"I fell recently," replied Sita, as her hands involuntarily flew up to cover her cheeks.

"Do you know who I am and what I do?"

"No, only that you are kind enough to help people." Sita looked over at the hospital attendant for a hint. He offered none.

"I manage women who entertain men for money. Do you know what that means?"

"No. What do you mean by entertain?" asked Sita. Like the blue chemicals, the memory of Maya sitting on the lap of a strange man was vivid.

"There are many men out there who like to spend time with young, pretty girls like you. It makes them feel younger. They will pay to be with you, lots of money. If you were interested, I might be able to help your sister. But you'd have to agree to do this work for me for a while."

"I still don't understand exactly what you want me to do," Sita admitted honestly.

"You'd have to go to bed with these men. They'd touch you and have you do things to their bodies. For this, you'd be paid. Do you understand what I'm talking about when I say go to bed?"

"No, not really. Does that mean like kissing?"

"Yes. Have you ever heard of having sex before? It is what happens after adults kiss each other and become, um, excited."

Hearing her say this, Sita instinctively took a step backward. While she didn't know what sex was, she knew it was something that young unmarried girls were not supposed to do. The image of Chandra rolling around on the ground with that beast on top of her also flashed behind her eyes. Sex was how women, or girls, became pregnant.

"I'm sorry, I can't do that," Sita confessed. "I have to go."

"What about your sister?"

Sita stopped in her tracks.

"You said yourself she would die without this operation. If you agree, you'd only have to do this work for three or four months. That is all the time it would take to earn the money back. The work is easy, and the men are quite generous. You could do this, pay me back and then go on with your life. While it takes some getting used to, in time you'll forget the experience. You are young and pretty and obviously educated. Do you speak English?"

"Yes."

"Even better. You could easily work in some of the nicest hotels in the city. I'd also provide you with pretty clothes and jewellery. It is up to you. If you stop and think about it, it comes down to a simple choice: let your sister die or come and work for me. I can guarantee you will find no other source of money so quickly. So what do you want to do?"

Despite her desire to run from this place, there was no other choice.

"So, if I work for you, you'll provide all of the money I need for the operation? Today?"

"Yes, the thirty thousand and whatever else you need."

"When would I have to begin work?"

"Soon. In fact, if we agree to this arrangement, you'll have to stay with me in this house for some time. I can't pay this amount and have you run off on me after your sister gets better."

"But I have to go and talk to my sister. And what about my brother? He's still very young. He can't take care of himself."

"Zahid, here, will talk to her and to your brother,' said Sangeeta, pointing toward the hospital attendant. "He will also help out with all of the supplies and food that will be needed. Your brother can stay there at the hospital. Your sister will have to remain there anyway for several days after the operation. During this time, we can get you started here."

"I don't think I can do this."

All at once, Sita began to think about Maya and what she had said. How she went with men to make money to support her family. How she did this because there was no other way. Sita wished Maya was there with her to provide some advice, to help her do the right thing.

For the first time, she understood the meaning of sacrifice. She was about to sell her body to save her sister.

"It is your choice," Sangeeta reminded Sita. "You work or your sister dies. It is entirely up to you."

"Can't I do some other work?" Sita pleaded. "I am a very hard worker. Isn't there anything else? This is a big house. You must need people to keep it clean. I can do that. Please, I..."

"You are wasting my time. Leave me." The woman gestured disgustedly with her hand and turned to walk away. "Just make sure you have enough money for your sister's cremation. This is an obligation of all good Hindus."

"Don't leave. I'll do it." In a mirror, across the hall, she saw her own horrified expression.

"Are you sure?" There was a self-satisfied smile on her painted lips. "Very well. I will provide the money to Zahid. He will take care of all the arrangements."

"Are you sure I can't see my family?"

"I'm sure. They'll be looked after, don't worry. In a short time, I'll send them to you. But for now, you must stay with me. Do you understand? I'm not a fool."

"Yes."

"Let me state it to you another way. If you try to leave before paying me back, I will find you and your entire family, and you will all be killed. Do I make myself clear?"

Sita's heart nearly stopped upon hearing these words. She had just signed a pact with yet another demon.

"Yes, perfectly clear."

11

Two days later, Sangeeta told Sita that she would be having her first encounter with a paying customer. They were in the back of Sangeeta's Padmini. As the car slowed in the heavy traffic, Sita briefly considered jumping out, melting into the crowd.

"It's best for you to get to work quickly, before you have too much time to worry about it. And now that your bruises are gone, I've lined up one of my best customers. He's very excited about you. Innocence, in our industry, is highly desirable and very fleeting." Sangeeta laughed, a coarse sound, then directed her driver to a private beauty parlour.

When they arrived, the owner greeted Sangeeta like an old friend, embracing her and kissing her cheek. The woman wore too much makeup, her eyeliner melting into the age lines around her sharp eyes.

"The usual?" she asked, looking Sita over.

"What else?" Sangeeta said.

The woman's hands were none too gentle as she cleaned, cut and styled Sita's hair in soft, gleaming waves. Sita's fingernails and toenails were trimmed and painted, and her eyebrows were shaped with hot wax, leaving the upper half of her face smarting and raw. Sangeeta then gave her an expensive red sari from an upscale shop, along with a set of gold hoop earrings and a small pendant for around her neck. As Sita changed in the bathroom at the back of the shop, she did not recognise herself in the mirror. A beautiful stranger looked back at her in the flickering light. She felt sorry for herself.

"The clothes and jewellery do not belong to you," Sangeeta reminded her, as the driver nearly clipped a motorbike. "If you damage them, that is more money you owe me."

Sita nodded, not really listening. They were already pulling up in front of the hotel, a five-star gilt palace for the business class who brought money in and out of the immense city. The driver idled at the curb as Sangeeta handed her a pink pill.

"It'll be easier, just take it," Sangeeta said.

Sita was too nervous to argue. As they loitered a few more minutes, her muscles began to relax, her spine softening, until everything almost seemed all right.

At the appointed time, they entered the lobby. Here, in harsh whispers, a detailed explanation of what was to come was offered for the fifth consecutive time.

"Your sister's operation was a complete success. It's time for you to live up to your part of the bargain. When you meet this man, this client, I want you to always be polite," she explained. "He is a very important person in this town, and he has paid a lot of money to be your first lover. I want you to do whatever he says, no matter what. When you are in bed, with your clothes off, he will touch you all over your body. Do not flinch or pull away. The first few times, it may hurt a little bit. There also might be some blood. But this is to be expected. Whatever you do, don't fight him. It will just make the experience worse. If he is disappointed and does not pay, you will be very sorry, I promise you."

Tears rolled down Sita's cheeks. She had no control over them.

"Stop that this instant!" Sangeeta insisted, harshly wiping them away with the end of her scarf.

"I can't do this," Sita confessed. "I thought I could, but I can't."

"You listen to me, young lady," replied Sangeeta, grabbing Sita's hand and squeezing so that her nails bit into Sita's flesh. "If you try to back out of this now, I will personally see that you, your sister and your insolent brother do not live to see another day. You owe me money. I expect you to work to pay this off. If you don't, you will regret the day you were born. Do you understand me? Your sister is alive today because of me. That means her life belongs to me. Don't you ever forget that. I didn't see anyone else lining up to help. Did you? Now we had a deal, and I expect you to live up to it. Do you hear me?"

Sita's head nodded on her limp neck. It was far too late to do anything else. She was about to bring shame to herself and to her family, but there was nothing that could be done about it. She had sold her virtue to save her sister's life. It was the only thing she had to sell, the only thing anyone was willing to buy. She just hoped that one day her family would understand and not judge her as she had judged poor Maya.

A handsome British man in his early fifties entered the hotel. He was tall and dark with thinning, grey hair combed across the right side of his head. He was dressed in a Western business suit. In one hand, he held a newspaper and had a lit cigarette in the other. Seeing Sangeeta waiting in the lobby, he came straight over and whispered something into her ear. She laughed and kissed his cheek affectionately. After catching a quick glimpse of Sita, he offered a smile to show his satisfaction and then walked away toward the lift.

"He is staying in room 218," Sangeeta explained, appearing apprehensive. "I want you to go there now. When you have finished, I want you to call me on this cell phone." A tiny, pocket-size phone was handed over to Sita. "It doesn't matter what time, just call. Wait here in the lobby. My driver will come to pick you up. Now remember all of the things I explained to you. Do you hear me? And don't you dare let me down!"

Sita walked over, pushed the button and waited for the lift. As she entered, joining several couples in party attire, she wondered if they knew what she was about to do. Could they tell that she was about to spoil herself? Was she now marked as rotten goods?

The lift stopped on the second floor. After following the arrows that led to the appropriate room, she stood in front of the door.

For a time, she couldn't bring herself to knock. She had to remind herself that she had to do this for her sister's life, for her brother, and for her family.

With the money having already been spent for the hospital expenses, there was no way out. The debt had to be paid.

She knocked lightly. The door immediately swung open. The man from the lobby had a drink in his hand. He gave her a hungry smile as he looked her over.

After closing the door, he placed the drink and the cigarette down and began to roughly grope her and kiss her face and neck. She tried to turn away, but he held her in place. His kisses were wet, the raunchy stench of alcohol and tobacco nearly gagging her. She'd imagined her first kiss would be so very different from this. He pulled Sita's scarf off and tossed it to the floor, then lifted her arms so her sari top could be removed.

Sangeeta had told her what to expect, but those had only been words. The reality of his fingers and mouth all over her, the stench of his breath and body sweat, left her stunned. She felt vile, dirty.

She desperately wanted to run for the door, to escape. But she had agreed to do this. If she hadn't, her sister would have died. Her limbs felt distant, out of her control, and she was lightheaded. When he pushed her onto the bed, she didn't feel capable of getting back up. The man replied with grunts and moans. The sounds reminded her of a hungry pig with its snout in a trough of slop—raw and animalistic, certainly not the sounds a human being should make.

Her repeated cries began to annoy him.

"Shut up," the man insisted, stopping for a moment. "You're making too much noise. People outside will hear you." When she cried out again, he used the back of his hand to slap her hard across the cheek. "I said stop it!"

His eyes were consumed with a toxic combination of rage, passion and lust. Fearful of what he might do next, Sita did as she was told.

She tried to think of something else—her days as a child in Pune, her old friends, her parents, her brother and sister—none of these images stayed in her mind for more than a second. All she could see, smell and feel was this hot, sweaty creature, dominating her body. It was like a soft knife repeatedly piercing the essence of her soul. She looked into his eyes again. They were void, nothing but lifeless, black marbles.

Suddenly, for reasons Sita could not fathom, he stopped, rolled over and lay on his back, panting and sweating.

Maybe he'd had a heart attack?

She stood up and ran to the bathroom. Alone, she buried her face in her hands and cried quietly. Her virginity was lost forever. She didn't know how she was going to ever face the world again, let alone find a husband who would have her. She was dirty, polluted.

"People will see me and know instantly what I am: a whore," she told herself. "My life is over. Sita is gone."

After scrubbing herself over and over again with soap and water, she dried herself off and then leaned up against the door and waited. With no sound coming from the adjacent room, she assumed that the man had left.

Her clothes were still outside, she exited the bathroom in search of them. But to her surprise, he was still there, sitting in a tan wingback chair. He had poured himself a drink and lit another cigarette.

"What took you so long?" he asked. "I don't have all day. Now come over here. I am ready for you again."

The thought that he might want to repeat this horrible act caught her by surprise. In her mind, the episode was over. Seeing that hungry, vacant look in his eyes again, a wave of despair consumed her.

That afternoon, he brutalised her three times in a five-hour period. After finally showering and changing into his clothes, he walked over and tossed several hundred-rupee notes onto her body. They landed on her sweaty back and stuck to her skin.

She didn't care. She couldn't move. Whatever spirit she had once possessed seemed to have disappeared, abandoning her for happier places. She was just a body into which air entered and in which blood circulated, but there was nothing more. She fell into a deep, blessed sleep and dreamt of nothing.

12

They were headed to the same hotel she'd gone to on her first job, a month ago. Sangeeta was languidly draped across the seat beside her, crushing the stiff folds of her blue organdy ensemble, her head nodding to the sound of Zakir Hussain's tabla drums on the radio. It was September, the air dry and cooling as evening approached. The windows were cracked, and the sounds of people and cars filtered in.

Sita had already taken one of the pink pills, the welcome numbness setting in, when the car came to a halt. At the cross-street, musicians and dancers were visible through the throng that had gathered to watch. The drumbeat was fast, drowning out the car radio and from somewhere came the sound of temple bells. Then a float was carried down the street. Draped in garlands of flowers, a pink and gold statue of Ganesh hovered about the crowd. It was the festival of Ganesh Chaturthi.

Her littlest brother would be walking now, speaking. He would have forgotten them

She held out her hand to Sangeeta. The Madam put another pink pill in it.

With great effort, Sangeeta straightened herself a bit. "Don't take too many of those," she warned. Her glazed eyes stared at the procession, unseeing. Not as many as you? Sita considered asking.

Instead, she said, "Where are Chandra and Ravi now?"

"I already told you, they are in the same hotel as before."

"But how can I believe you? How do I know you haven't sold them to someone, that you don't have them working in some factory?"

To her surprise, Sangeeta looked startled at the suggestion. "You're a good money maker. I know you wouldn't do as well if you were worried about them. We can drive by there tomorrow."

Sita looked for signs of treachery, but Sangeeta seemed in earnest.

"Have they asked about me? What do you tell them I'm doing?"

Sangeeta's eyes closed, for a moment Sita thought she'd fallen asleep. Half a minute later she opened them again, answering the question as if no time had passed.

"I don't tell them anything. But Zahid has told them you have a good job in the city, working at a shop."

"They need to go to school." The second pill was kicking in, her voice came to her as if from far away.

"That can easily be arranged. I will pay for it, and you can pay me back."

This debt she owed Sangeeta was not written down. Everything she ate and wore was added to it; it was a hole that grew deeper each day.

"Please have them start school soon," Sita said.

Sangeeta merely nodded, a flicker of a smile stealing across her face.

When they finally pulled up to the now familiar hotel, Sita looked up at the balconies that lined the upper floors. In her fantasy, she knocked on the door, smiled as the man let her in, then walked straight to the balcony and jumped. A moment of flight, followed by the quick violence of the sidewalk. Then nothing.

But Chandra and Ravi needed her, chained her to this world. As she sauntered past the doorman into the glaringly bright lobby, resentment towards them washed over her.

Sangeeta did not accompany her inside. Slowly, the Madam was allowing her more freedom. The room number had been given to her in the car. She walked upstairs and knocked. A repeat customer opened the door, his hairy potbelly peeking out of his unbuttoned shirt. She entered the room, smiled at him. Then, pouring herself a drink, she sat on the bed.

"Remind me of your name?" the man asked, sitting down beside her.

She drank quickly, the rum like a sea of calm she was floating away on.

"Wasn't it Chara? Or Krisha?"

She thought a moment. "Mayana," she answered. Yes, that would be better. "Call me Mayana."

Let Mayana lie with this man.

Sita would just go away for a while.

The next day, Zahid and the driver both accompanied Sita to the hotel where Chandra and Ravi were staying.

"Sita, you're back!" said Ravi, opening the door to the hotel room. He jumped forward to embrace his sister. "Chandra, Sita is back!"

For some reason, he looked much older to her than before, as if the short time apart had aged him. Or perhaps her own aging had jaded her eyes.

Chandra was lying in the bed with a pair of sheets covering much of her body. Five weeks after her operation, she still looked weak and frail. When Chandra peered up at Sita, she initially offered a welcome smile but then turned away in anger.

"Chandra, what is the matter?" asked Sita, surprised. "You aren't happy to see me?"

There was no answer.

"Chandra, why won't you talk to me?"

Chandra rolled over and glared at her. "Where have you been? I nearly died in that hospital, and you never once came to see me!"

"I couldn't come," Sita confessed. "I needed to get money so that we could pay for your operation. I was..."

"That is no excuse," she replied, not allowing her sister to finish. "You just abandoned us. I will never forgive you for that. Never!"

"What are you talking about? You nearly died. I had to come up with the money to pay for your operation or they wouldn't have done it. They wanted over 30,000 rupees. I...I had to..."

Chandra looked her sister up and down.

"Where did you get those clothes and that jewellery? It doesn't look as if you are working all that hard to me."

Sita was stunned. She desperately wanted to tell her sister what had happened to her, to explain what she was forced to do to save her life. But she just couldn't find the words. She was afraid she'd be shunned if the truth ever came to light. She remembered how shocked she'd been at Maya's behaviour, and she didn't want to see that kind of disappointment in Chandra's eyes.

"I needed you, and you weren't there," Chandra repeated. "Between what happened with Nasir and my time in the hospital, it's been awful. How could you abandon us at a time like this?"

"I'm sorry, Chandra, there was no other choice. I'm doing the best I can. I couldn't..."

"So, what are we going to do now?" asked Ravi, hoping to change the subject. "Are we running away again?"

"We're not going anywhere, Ravi. I have arranged for both of you to attend boarding schools right here in this area. The schools are located quite nearby, only a few kilometres apart. Zahid will go with you to get you settled."

"Boarding schools? What are you talking about?" Chandra finally sat up, her hair matted, eyes red and puffy. "I don't want to go to another boarding school. I don't want to work in one of those places again."

"You're not going to work. You're going to attend classes."

"No, I'm not," replied Chandra.

"You have no choice. You and your brother are going, and that is the end of it."

"And where are you going to be, Miss High and Mighty?"

"I have to stay here in the city and work. I have a job now. It pays well. The money I make will cover your school fees and expenses, as it covered your hospital bill. You both need to get a good education. Without anyone to help us, it is our only way out of this life."

"But we don't want to be split up anymore, Sita," said Ravi. He looked pale, like he had hardly set foot outdoors since she'd last seen him. "Why can't we find a school like before where we can all stay together? We did it once already. We can do it again."

"We can't do that. Things have changed. I owe a big debt that must be paid off. I will have to work, and you two will have to go to school. That is just the way it must be."

"But why? What debt?"

"Just because!" Sita insisted, not willing to offer any more explanation. "Now I'm not going to say this again, there is no other choice. You are both going off to school, and that is final."

"I'm not going, Sita!" Chandra declared with defiance. "I will not go. And you can't make me do this. In fact, I'm not listening to you anymore. You abandoned us in our time of need. Who are you to tell us what to do?"

Enraged, Sita walked over and grabbed Chandra by the wrist and squeezed it tightly. For the first time in her life, she completely lost control of herself. Perhaps it was the lack of appreciation on her sister's part for her sacrifice. Or perhaps it was a sense of frustration that had been building for weeks. Whatever it was, it rose to the surface and boiled over.

"You will go to this school, you will get good grades and you will finish your education," Sita hissed. "Do you hear me?"

Chandra stared at her, frightened. Beside them, Ravi looked similarly stunned.

"On Monday morning, Zahid will take you both to your schools," Sita continued. "It has all been arranged. He will buy your books, some new clothes and whatever other supplies you require. Don't you dare disobey me on this! Whatever you need in the weeks and months to come, he will be the one to supply it for you. Do you understand me?"

There was no reply, only tense silence.

With tears streaming down her face, Sita turned and marched out of the room, slamming the door.

As she drove off to her next hotel appointment, the rage subsided, leaving her empty inside. Someday they'd find out what she was doing and really turn on her. It would be better not to see them, to simply disappear from their lives. She would work, send them money and live out her life the best she could. There was no other way to maintain what little pride and dignity she had left. Seeing the disappointment in their eyes would kill her.

Sangeeta opened Sita's bedroom door without knocking. It was early morning, but the Madam was fully dressed, her makeup thick enough for the stage. "Well, as much as I enjoyed your company," Sangeeta's ironic smile indicated this was not the case, "it is time for you to move in with the other girls."

Sita had heard Sangeeta scheduling customers for her other girls, she'd seen the ledger book with thirteen names running down the side, but she had yet to meet any of them.

"Where am I moving to?" At first, the door to her room had been locked behind her every night. Since having the Madam enrol her siblings in school, however, it had been left unlocked. Sangeeta knew she wasn't going anywhere. Apparently, she was confident enough to put her on a longer leash.

The older woman set an embroidered travel bag on the bed. In her other hand, she held a glass of whisky. "An apartment nearby. My little harem occupies one entire floor. You'll share with two other girls. If you stay long enough, you can have your own apartment and entertain customers there."

Mechanically, Sita began folding her clothes into the bag as Sangeeta looked out the narrow, barred window onto the street. It was early for drinking, but perhaps the Madam hadn't slept. Sometimes, faintly, she could hear knocking on the door late in the night and a whisper of the Madam's coarse laugh echoing up to the top floor even as the sky turned grey.

"You'll need to see one customer a day, six days a week. I'll handle all the money, and we'll split the tips." She said this as if she were being generous.

"Who will I board with?" Sita asked, though it made no difference.

"Amisha is from Nepal; she's been with me three years. Kajal is from Bangladesh; her family left her with me two years ago." Sangeeta finished her drink, then walked to the small mirror and checked her appearance, smoothing the hair that had come loose from her signature coif. Perhaps she had been entertaining a man all night. "Don't worry, they all speak English, so you'll at least be able to communicate that way. All my dark-skinned beauties speak English," she added, with a self-satisfied smirk.

Sita's bag was packed, and she made the narrow bed while she waited for Sangeeta to say they were leaving. Not for the first time, she wondered just how many desperate girls had found themselves sleeping beneath this thin cotton blanket, the magenta flowers fading until they were pale pink.

"As long as you make regular payments and continue to attract customers, you can work for me. If you get pregnant or gain weight, you'll be out on the street." Sangeeta gave her a shrewd look. "You may think I'm a wicked witch, but you don't know how good you have it. My business is high end. This ladder has many rungs, and you don't want to climb down them. On the street, your pimps will beat you, the money will be terrible. Your customers will be worse." She laughed, recognising the dubious look on Sita's face. "Oh yes, they can be much worse! I've built up a clientele over the years. If they damage my girls, I tell them to get lost. You don't know how good you have it," she repeated, with a bitterness in her voice that at last made Sita stop tucking in the sheets. She'd never stopped to wonder about Sangeeta's story.

"Businessmen and politicians have something to lose. Their reputation is important, so I have leverage over them. You don't want to meet customers who have nothing to lose. And they trust me to make sure you are healthy. Once a month you need to get a shot of antibiotics, and every three months you must have the Depo-Provera shot."

Sita nodded. She'd been through the process once. If it would keep her from becoming pregnant or contracting a sexually transmitted disease then she hardly needed convincing.

A month later, after seeing Amisha thrown out onto the street by Sangeeta's bodyguard, Sita began applying herself to learning her trade. She quizzed the more established whores about their techniques and began to build up her own clientele. The men were disgusting, loathsome, yet there was some satisfaction in fooling them, in making them think she desired them, found them attractive.

Another fourteen months found her well-established among a set of regular customers who repeatedly asked for her by name. Now seventeen, her body had fully developed. She was curvaceous, and her large brown eyes and intelligence seemed to captivate them. If she wanted to keep money coming in sufficient quantity to maintain herself as well as Chandra and Ravi, she needed to excel. Each day, as she lit incense at a small shrine to Lakshmi that graced a little alcove outside the kitchenette, she prayed for the strength to be successful at this career she would never have chosen. With the morning sunlight filtering through the smoke, it seemed, at times, that the goddess heard her. Her depression loosened its hold on her, though it continued to trail her through her day.

One of the many regrets that haunted her was the reaction she had had to Maya being with that truck driver. She wished she could talk to her again and explain that she now understood what happened that day at the truck stop, the sacrifice Maya had made for all of them.

Whenever Sita needed money to cover school costs or other expenses, she approached Sangeeta, and it was offered freely. But when she repeatedly asked how much longer she'd have to do this work to pay off her debt, Sangeeta kept telling her it would be another couple of months. It was the same ruse that Mrs Gupta had used in the sweat shop. The debt would never be paid off.

Despite the fact that she had ample free time, Sita seldom visited her sister and brother. While they begged her to come, she would always find half a dozen excuses to explain why this wasn't possible. When they asked what kind of work she was doing, she always explained that she was a salesperson in a small clothing boutique. Satisfied with this answer, they selfishly didn't bother to ask for any other details.

One afternoon, Sangeeta rapped on the apartment door earlier than usual. Sita was the only one home, but the other girls had left their half of the tips out on the counter, as was their custom. Sangeeta entered, looking particularly peaked after having her hair freshly dyed black.

"Amita's sick. I need you to cover one of her regular customers."

Sita glared at her. As well as she'd gotten at hiding her emotions from her customers, something about the Madam often unleashed them.

"I already have an appointment."

"This is a very important man," replied Sangeeta, waving away her objections like they were smoke. "Someone who is really connected."

"You say that about all of the men we are with."

"This one is different. He is not someone you say no to. Just cancel your other appointment and go to see him. This is very important, Sita. He is not the type of person you want on your bad side."

"But what if he likes me better than Amita? This will just create tension between us. You know how it is with these kinds of arrangements. They always go wrong somehow."

"Then don't allow this to happen. You know how to play the game. So go and play it," she said, grabbing the tips from the counter.

Begrudgingly, Sita arrived at the hotel at the appointed time. After knocking, a man in his mid-sixties answered the door. Despite what Sangeeta had said, nothing in his appearance suggested that he was important. He was thin with a crooked back and a bad leg. He hardly looked physically capable of the activities he'd hired her for.

"Who are you?" asked the man, surprised.

"My name is Sita Sharma. Sangeeta sent me over."

"Where is my Amita? I was expecting her to come."

"She couldn't make it today. I was asked to fill in for her. I promise you will not be disappointed, sir."

The man didn't say anything for a long time. He seemed irritated that his usual routine had been broken.

"Can I come inside?"

"I wanted Amita," he declared, moving out of the way to allow Sita to enter. "I specifically asked for her."

"Like I said, she couldn't come today. She is not feeling well, otherwise I'm certain she would not miss an appointment with such an important man as you. So, you are stuck with me." Sita offered a warm smile in hopes that this would change his mind about her.

"Very well. Have a seat on the couch."

Sita did as she was told.

"Are you thirsty?" he asked, slowly walking over to the mini-bar to mix a drink.

"Yes, I'll have a rum and soda," she replied with confidence.

"Rum? At your age?"

"Yes, please."

"Ice?"

"Yes."

The man poured two drinks and brought one over to Sita. She took a large sip and then placed it on the table within easy reach.

"Do you know who I am?" he asked.

"I have no idea, sir, except that you are very important to Sangeeta. She implored me to take very good care of you, which I shall do." Again, she offered a smile, hoping to relax the old man.

There was another pause in the conversation.

"Where are you from, Sita?"

"Pune."

"How long have you been with Sangeeta?"

"Nearly two years."

"How come I haven't seen you before?"

"Perhaps Amita has been keeping you all to herself," she flirted.

There was another moment of silence. Sita picked up her drink and stirred the ice with her finger.

"Why are you here?" asked the man, out of curiosity.

"What do you mean?"

"Why are you in this business? You don't seem like one of the usual girls, and you certainly don't act like one."

"I don't know what you mean. What makes me any different from the others?"

"Well, most of the girls that Sangeeta sends to me are trying to act sophisticated, but they still have one foot in the village or the slums. But you look like the kind of girl my daughter would bring home from school. I doubt you have ever even been in a slum."

Sita did not answer. She had no idea how to respond to such a comment.

"Is this about money?" asked the old man.

"Isn't everything about money?" she replied with practiced indifference.

"So let me see if I got this right. You needed money and Sangeeta provided it for you?"

"Yes."

"What for?"

Sita remained quiet. He had no right to her personal life. Somehow his questions felt even more invasive than the sex that would surely follow.

"Did you have a father who gambled his fortune away?" he continued. "Or was he just a drunk?"

Riled, she answered, "It's not like that. My father was a great public prosecutor, an educated and brilliant man. He never took a sip of alcohol in his entire life, and he never would have gambled."

"Then what is it? I'm curious. Where are your parents?"

Ignoring the question about her parents, she answered, "If you must know, it was my sister. She needed an operation two years ago. She was dying from appendicitis. I had no choice. I needed thirty thousand rupees or she wouldn't have made it. Sangeeta offered to give me the money if I agreed to work for her. So, I did. Like I said, I had no other choice. But that was a long time ago. It is of no consequence. I am here today to ..."

"You don't have parents anywhere?"

"No, they were both killed. Sir, could we just ..."

"Killed? How?"

"They were murdered," Sita stated, surprised to hear herself make this confession. He was the first person she had mentioned this to since she'd first disclosed it to Maya. It just slipped out. For a moment, a wave of anger passed through her body. She often felt irritated with her parents for having left her the way they did.

"Murdered? Who did this to them?"

"I can't say."

"Tell me."

"I can't."

"Was it a robbery? Did they do something that got someone angry? You can tell me. I know about these things."

"Are you a policeman?" asked Sita with a contemptuous sneer.

"No, far from it. In fact, I guess you could say I am on the opposite side of the fence."

"You are a criminal?" Somehow that thought appealed to her. At least they were on the same level.

"Let's just say I'm a businessman and leave it at that," he responded with a slight chuckle. "Were your parents killed by the mob?"

"Why do you ask that?" Sita barked. "Look, sir, whoever you are, can't we just get to ..." She stood and began taking off her shoes and jacket.

"Sita, sit back down. I was just noting your reaction to my questions. You seem to harbour a lot of anger toward both the police and the mob. Am I right about this?"

Sita turned her body away and looked toward the room's only window. She had said too much, and now she was regretting it. He was far too probing and intuitive.

"You are from Pune, and your parents were murdered? You wouldn't happen to be related to Prakash Sharma, the barrister, would you?"

Sita gasped, turning toward this strange man in astonishment, her mouth wide open.

"Hah! You are from that family, aren't you?" he replied with a self-satisfied grin.

"How did you know that?"

"It is my business to read people. Your reactions answered all of my questions. Let's just say you would never make a very good card player."

Sita stood up and began walking toward the door. She needed air. She had to get out of that room. She had somehow stumbled into a conversation that was making her very afraid. She may have just signed her own death warrant and that of Chandra and Ravi as well.

"Don't worry, your secret is safe with me." The man took a small sip of his scotch. "Many believed that Mr

Sharma's children weren't killed in that fire. But since no one ever came forward to claim the estate, we all wondered what really happened. Are the four of you still together? Are the others alive too?"

"I don't want to talk about this anymore. I have already said far too much. Who are you anyway?"

"Me? My name is Masud Kumar. Delhi is my home. Let's just say I happen to know the person who had your father killed. In the past, we were associates. Now, we no longer do business together."

"You know that man?" asked Sita, curious about this provocative comment but more frightened than ever.

"Yes. In the early days, we were friends. But as time passed, he became overly greedy and selfish. His ambition has driven him to take over most of the criminal enterprises in Mumbai. He is one of the most powerful men in that city now. But he has gone mad. He has forgotten his friends. And now, he has mostly enemies. Including myself."

"Please, you can't tell anyone that you know who I am. It would put me and my family in great danger. That's why I've remained silent, why we fled. They'll surely come after us if they know we're still alive."

"I understand. I won't say anything but only if you promise to tell me everything that happened to you."

"I can't!" Flustered, she looked about, wondering again if she should just go.

"Don't worry, I will not betray your secrets." There was a certain gravity to his words. Despite herself, she believed him. Besides, it hardly seemed she had a choice.

"Do you promise?"

"Yes."

"Can you be trusted to keep this promise?"

"With my life."

She studied his face. In the last two years, she'd learnt how to read men. He was in earnest, or he was a very good liar. In either case, it seemed too late to hide the truth. For the next two hours, she recounted her family's story. She described the victory party, the night her parents were killed, the train ride, the sweatshop, and everything else. Mr Kumar listened without asking a single question. He just nodded his head, sipped his whisky and took it all in. He seemed to have completely forgotten about the evening's promise of sex with a young woman.

"That is an incredible story," he confessed after she had finished. "Sounds like you have all been through a great deal."

"Yes, it has been a very trying time, nearly four years. But we have survived." She lifted her chin in a gesture of pride.

"So how much do you owe Sangeeta?" asked Mr Kumar.

"I calculated nearly 100,000 rupees. This includes the money I borrowed for the operation and for sending my brother and sister to boarding schools. No matter how hard I work, the debt seems to mount faster than I can pay it off."

"Does she give you any money?"

"Just enough to pay for incidental expenses. She provides me with my clothes and make up which is also added to my debt."

"And you say you've been working with her for around two years?"

"Yes. Nearly every day I am with at least one customer, sometimes two."

"Did she ever say when your debt would be repaid?"

"No, she just repeatedly says I have to keep working. But I know she is lying to me."

"Yes, she is cheating you," said Mr Kumar with another laugh. "In that period of time, you have paid back the amount owed at least twenty times already. Do you know how much it costs me to be with you today?"

"No, I am not involved in the money side of the business."

"It cost 3,000 rupees. If you've worked 720 days at that rate, then she's made over 2,000,000 rupees from you. But that is all part of the sex trade. There are those who give and those who take."

Sita stared at him. She'd had no idea that people paid that much money for sex.

Mr Kumar stood and excused himself, then walked into the adjacent room to make a phone call. He returned several minutes later.

"Do you have a cell phone?"

"Yes."

"Do you have the numbers written down somewhere?"

"Yes."

"Give the phone to me. It belongs to Sangeeta."

Sita handed it over.

"You are now free," he declared with a smile.

"What...what do you mean by that?"

"I called Sangeeta and told her that I thought you had earned enough to buy your way out of debt. After a bit of persuasion, she agreed with me. You no longer work for her."

"Then who do I work for?"

"Well, I guess you now work for me."

"You have bought me?" asked Sita, horrified. Had she just traded one slave owner for another?

"No, it is not like that."

"Then please explain what it is like. Do you not now own me?"

"You are now a free agent. No one owns you, not me or anyone else. You can go out and do whatever you'd like."

"But you just said I had to work for you."

"Yes, once a year, you have to come to me and personally hand over 100 rupees, from your hand to mine."

"Why are you asking for so little?"

"Because I do not want your money. I just want to make sure I know where you are in case I need to talk to you someday."

"Are you serious?" She was excited, hopeful for the first time in years. But was he playing a cruel joke on her? Had she misread him that badly?

"Yes, Sita, I am serious. You are free to go. Free to be with your family."

The reality of being free suddenly hit home. "But what will I do now? I still have to work to keep my brother and sister in school. No one wants to hire a whore to do any other kind of work. I won't be able to afford to keep my brother and sister where they are."

"Then start your own business. You must have some regular clients. You can let them know that if they want to see you, they can contact you directly."

"But what about Sangeeta? She'll be very angry."

"You still don't understand who I am, do you? I control much of Delhi and the surrounding area. If I ask someone to do something, they will never go against my will. I'm a very powerful man. Despite my appearance," he cast a disparaging look at his bad leg, "I am feared by many. She will not cause you any trouble. In fact, none of the others will either. All you have to do is say you work for me, and that will always be enough to keep you safe."

"Are you going to sleep with me now?"

"No, I'm no longer in the mood."

"Tell me, why are you doing this for me?"

"Because I might someday need a favour from you."

"What kind of favour?"

"I don't know yet, but the day might come. That is why I want you to see me once a year. You have to promise me you will do this, no matter what."

"But how will I know when the time comes?"

"If something comes up, I will call you."

"But you took my phone."

"Then go out and buy one." Mr Kumar reached into his pocket and handed Sita a handful of one-thousand-rupee bills. "When you have it, give me your number. Here is mine." He wrote his number onto a small piece of paper and handed it over to Sita.

Sita looked from the money to Mr Kumar, then threw her arms around his neck. "I can't thank you enough. My family can't thank you enough."

"Based on what you've told me, you've suffered enough. You can pay me back someday, when the time comes. Deal?"

"Yes, of course, deal."

With the money given to her, she bought a new phone, found an apartment, and then began contacting several of her regular customers. She informed them that they could call her directly, without going through Sangeeta. This way, she was able to control who she saw and when. She also took referrals from regular customers. With no middleman, the amount of money she was making jumped tenfold.

On the few occasions when pimps approached her to link up with them, all she had to do was mention Mr Kumar's name, and they went running.

While she hated the work and spent much of the time feeling badly about herself, she knew of no other way to support herself. She also needed money to maintain the school fees. Once again, even though she was technically free, she felt trapped with no way out.

13

Before exiting the taxi, Sita looked down at the road to make sure she wasn't about to step into a large puddle of muddy water. With the relentless rain that had persisted throughout the night, she didn't want to soil her newly purchased shoes.

"Would you wait for me?" asked Sita, offering a hopeful smile to the taxi driver. "I'll pay you extra."

"How long?" he grumbled.

"No more than an hour."

"Well, it's not like I'll get another fare this far outside of town. Fine."

The signboard prominently posted in front of her read -asters' *English Medium Boarding School.* Following years of neglect, the "M" had faded away, without anyone bothering to repaint it. This was only one of many things that had gone unattended to over the years.

Having received another urgent phone call from the school administration, Sita was once again summoned to attend a meeting with the Vice Chancellor concerning Ravi's unruly behaviour. Ever since he began attending boarding schools in the Delhi area, he seemed to get into trouble on a regular basis. Expelled from two other places, this was the school of last resort. The only reason they hadn't expelled him so far was that the admission rate had declined by over thirty percent. They couldn't afford to lose yet another student. With stiff competition from rival institutions that were much better funded and equipped, enrolment had dropped for the third consecutive year in a row.

Since placing Ravi at the Masters' School, this was the fourth time Sita had been called upon to make the ten-kilometre journey to talk to the administrator. The first time, Ravi got into a fight with two other boys, resulting in one of them going to the hospital with a broken nose. A second time, he was caught breaking into the school cafeteria with an accomplice. For his third offence, he was caught selling cigarettes to some of the younger students. At each meeting, the administrator threatened to throw him out. But Sita was always able to reverse the decision with a combination of charm and a small under-the-table donation to the school. Ravi had become such an angry, rebellious child. She didn't understand him, and she certainly couldn't control him.

Before entering the compound, Sita smoothed the wrinkles that had formed on her sari. Looking fresh after a cramped taxi ride was always a challenge. Like everyone, the administrator would judge her by her appearance.

"Excuse me, I have an appointment with the Vice Chancellor," said Sita, walking over to the reception desk. "Could you please tell me where I'm supposed to go? I see you've changed your offices around."

"You can wait inside that room over there. When he finishes with his 1:45 appointment, you'll be next." The receptionist pointed with her pencil, never looking up.

The waiting area contained two newly purchased, blue overstuffed chairs and a large tan couch. There was fresh paint on the walls, and the curtains no longer looked old and tattered. Perhaps they were making an attempt to compete with the new schools. A small coffee table, which was positioned between the seats, had a display of "Bollywood" movie magazines fanned out across the top. Unlike the three-year old samples that had been there on her previous visits, these magazines were new editions. Sita picked one up and took a seat.

A few minutes later, a man in his late twenties entered the room and sat on the couch just beside her. Wearing a pair of sandals, blue slacks and a white button-down shirt, he was, at first glance, unremarkable.

But every now and then, he'd look up to catch a quick glimpse of her, making her paranoid that he'd been a customer in the past or that he had recognised her from her work. Irritated, she did her best to ignore him. It was one thing to be gawked at while she was working. It was quite another thing when she was on her own time.

Having finished flipping through the pages of the magazine, she placed it back on the table. As she went for another, the man reached for the same one.

"I'm sorry," said Sita, politely. "You go ahead."

"No, you take it," he replied in earnest. "I'm not really in the mood to read. I just want this meeting to be over."

She offered a superficial smile and began browsing through the pages, altering her position to turn away from this stranger.

"I'm Krishna Dutta, Binod's father," said the man. Apparently, he wasn't one for subtle cues.

"Nice to meet you," replied Sita. She kept her eyes on the magazine, hoping that might get through to him.

"Do you have a student attending this school?"

"Yes, my younger brother is in class six," she answered with great reluctance.

"My son is only in class two. He stays here at the school. He's usually a good boy, but ever since his mother died, trouble seems to follow him around like a shadow."

There was a long period of silence.

"What's your brother's name?" asked Krishna, still not taking the hint.

"Ravi," replied Sita, irritated with all the small talk and questions.

"I like that name. In fact, I almost named my son Ravi after he was born. Do you have any children of your own?"

"Why are you so interested in the details of my life?" Sita snapped, finally losing her temper. "Can't you see that I'm reading?" With so much on her mind, the last thing she wanted was to be interrogated by some elementary school parent.

"I'm terribly sorry," Krishna apologised. "I didn't mean to offend you. I was just making conversation. Please, please forgive me."

He looked mortified, and she was instantly remorseful. Why was she so touchy, so defensive? She looked at him then, really looked at him, for the first time. He had light, hazel eyes and straight brows, a slender face and hair that needed a trim. The top button on his shirt was missing, and there was a small ink stain on his sleeve. He'd just said his wife had died. He was overwhelmed, clearly. Why hadn't she seen that right away? Not for the first time, she wondered about the more insidious repercussions of her work. Her empathy was like a slumbering animal inside her, slow to wake up these days.

"No, I'm sorry. I shouldn't have snapped at you that way. It's just that I'm not very happy to be here myself. I'm sorry."

"No, you were right to say what you did. I was prying into your personal affairs. That was impolite of me. Once again, please forgive me." His tone seemed sincere.

A period of silence lasted for several minutes before Sita finally spoke. "No, I do not have any."

"Excuse me?" asked Krishna.

"You asked me if I had any children, and I do not. I have never been married."

"I see," he replied. His hazel eyes rested on her a moment longer, looking for a cue.

"Do you have any other children?" asked Sita.

"No, only the one. As I mentioned, my wife died. It happened about two years ago. We never had a chance to... well, you know, have a second child."

"I'm sorry about your loss."

He stood and began nervously pacing back and forth. He was tall, his long legs dividing the room into two steps. "I'm still not used to coming to this school and doing all of these parent things. My wife used to take care of these matters herself. Ever since her death, it's been hard for me to manage him. I sometimes feel like a bird swimming around in the water when it comes to parenting. In my line of work, it's also not very easy to find the time for him."

"What type of work do you do?

"I run my own business, a small printing press in Delhi. We print stickers, flyers and newspapers, that type of thing. And what about you?"

"I work...I work in a retail clothing shop," Sita lied. This is what had been listed in her application to the school for Ravi's admission.

"That sounds like a good job."

"Yes, it is."

At that moment, two parents left the administrator's office. Their sour expressions said it hadn't gone well. She doubted her own meeting would be much better.

"Well, it was nice to meet you, Miss Sharma," said Krishna. "I hope your meeting goes well."

"It was nice to meet you too, Mr Dutta. I also hope all goes well with your son."

There was something about the sincerity of the man's manner that was refreshing. She was used to being around people who were rude and self-centred. It was nice to know that not all men in India were this way.

As expected, Ravi had once again gotten into trouble. This time, he threw a stone through one of the classroom windows after getting into an argument with another boy. For nearly thirty minutes, the administrator threatened to expel him. But in the end, Ravi was given one more chance. When yet another four-thousand-rupee compensation was offered and accepted, order was again restored.

The taxi dropped her near the Imperial Hotel, but she had several hours before she needed to meet her next client. The afternoon weighed on her, the awkward interaction with Krishna Dutta playing over and over in her mind. She wandered down to Connaught Circle to see what distractions the shops might offer.

For a moment, as she crossed a busy street in a throng of pedestrians, her mind flashed back to the fashion drawings she used to make. It had been a long time since she'd done anything like that, though she could pass hours sorting through fabrics in a shop. Each colour and texture represented a small world of possibility, the clean elegance of the folds oddly calming.

A "Help Wanted" sign in the window of one of her favourite stores stopped her in her tracks. The store specialised in upscale saris and salwar kameez for women of means. The shelves were festooned with a rainbow of silk and chiffon, satin and beaded lace, velvet and light wool blends.

Sita approached the woman behind the counter. "Excuse me. I understand that you are looking for someone to work in your store. Are you the person I should be talking to about this?"

The middle-aged woman was dressed in a stunning yellow silk sari. She had beautiful brown eyes and long, straight hair that was artfully twisted into a bun on top of her head. With a smile that never seemed to leave her face, she greeted Sita in a very warm and friendly manner.

"Yes, I am the proprietor," she stated proudly, as her eyes looked Sita over. "Are you considering applying for this job?"

"Perhaps," Sita replied, hesitantly. "What would I need to do?"

The woman picked up an application form. "You will need to fill this out. Have you ever done this kind of work before?"

"No, I haven't worked now for several years. I am new to this city. But I am very good with people, and I love fashion. I love drawing sketches of dresses and reading about all the new trends. You have a lovely inventory. I am sure business must be brisk."

"I wish it was, but this business is very competitive. And let me warn you from the very beginning that the base pay is not very much. If you are expecting to make a lot of money in this line of work, you should go elsewhere. I have had other college-types come in and ask about the job. But when I explained that their income would be based on commissions, they immediately walked out."

"I'm afraid I'm not one of those college-types," replied Sita, flattered that someone would mistake her for a college graduate. "I was never able to get that far in my studies. I'm also not worried about the money. I just want to find a good job, one I can feel proud of."

"Very well," replied the owner with another warm smile. "Then fill out the form, and let's talk, you and I. Okay? By the way, my name is Mrs Shrestha."

"Pleased to meet you. My name is Sita, Sita Sharma."

Sita filled the form out and handed it back to the woman. It was probably a waste of time. She had no experience. She couldn't even provide a reference.

The interview lasted for more than thirty minutes. Not wishing to share any of her past, Sita fabricated an elaborate story about how her parents died when she was young and how her Auntie raised her. She also mentioned again that she used to spend hours reading Hindi movie magazines and drawing sketches of original dress designs. She didn't bring up anything about her brother or sister.

"Well, thank you very much for a lively discussion," stated Mrs Shrestha, shaking Sita's hand affectionately.

"Thank you," replied Sita, pleased with her afternoon diversion. "I guess I'll be off now."

"Don't you want to know if you got the job?" asked Mrs Shrestha, surprised.

"Excuse me?" The thought that this woman would actually take her seriously had never once crossed her mind. "Yes, I would like to know."

"I'd like to try you out. I will take you on for one month. Your hours will be from 10:00 a.m. to 6:00

p.m., five days a week. If you work overtime, you'll be paid extra. If this works out, you'll have the job on a permanent basis. Now it is up to you. After hearing the terms and conditions I mentioned earlier, are you interested?"

The offer came as a complete shock. "Yes. Yes, I would be interested!"

"So, when can you begin?"

"I can begin right now. Well, I mean after I run one small errand. Do you mind?"

"Not at all. But if you'd like, you can start fresh tomorrow. There is no real rush."

"No. I want to start now. Today!"

Sita walked out of the store, wide-eyed. Just like that, her life had changed. What had even possessed her to apply for that job? It was as if some outside force took control of her and made it happen. Whatever the reason, the gods had smiled upon her, and she was grateful. A day that had begun with dread was turning into something hopeful.

After walking several blocks, she stepped into an alleyway and looked around. Finding what she was looking for, she picked up a heavy brick, placed her mobile phone on the cement, and smashed it into pieces with a single blow. For good measure, she hit it two or three more times. She then picked up the many pieces and threw them into a trashcan.

The phone was the only link she had with her clients. Without this connection, she was once again free, no longer tied to her degrading customers by a digital chain. She would get a new phone and let Mr Kumar have the number. Everyone else could get lost.

Smiling to herself, she returned to the store, ready to start a new life.

Sita quickly became indispensable at Impressions, the name of the dress shop. Her enthusiasm for fashion led her to spend time educating the customers on fabrics, accessories and colour combinations rather than just trying to sell to them. The result was that they bought more and left satisfied. Within the first three weeks, sales had increased by nearly fifteen percent. Two weeks later, they increased another ten percent.

In addition to selling clothes, she also began to take on some of the day-to-day administrative responsibilities. Mrs Shrestha was a hopeless manager, seldom paying vendors on time and never really knowing if she was profitable or not. As Sita continued demonstrating her willingness to take on new challenges, the entire management responsibility was eventually offered to her.

She began by developing a simple vouchering system to streamline the finances. She then created a logging system to track inventory. After reading that computers were essential tools to manage any business, she talked Mrs Shrestha into buying a second-hand one for the store. Not knowing anything about these machines, she pulled it out of the box and began reading the instructions. Before long, she taught herself to use the various programmes for managing every aspect of the shop.

To help create a competitive edge, Sita convinced Mrs Shrestha that she should begin advertising in the newspapers. Creating the layouts herself, Sita was able to come up with a series of attractive ads that resulted in more and more customers visiting the store.

Realising that many of her patrons were interested in learning more about the clothing industry, Sita also held a series of seminars inside the store. The speakers included struggling fashion designers who spoke about their clothes and trends in the business. These events served three useful purposes: they brought new customers into the shop, taught people what they needed to know to keep up with the trends, and provided exposure for designers to showcase their own work. Although the initial attendance numbers were small, as word soon got out, as many as forty people crammed into the tiny store to listen to each lecture.

Having done all she could to promote the clothing side of the business, Sita then turned her attention to other items. She convinced Mrs Shrestha to expand her inventory to include fashion accessories such as shoes, beads, necklaces, belts and other jewellery. They even began handing out a small attractive brass pin that had the name of the store on it for their special customers. Her reasoning was that, rather than just selling a dress, they should be selling an entire look. Within eight months, with business booming and sales up by nearly 50 percent, Mrs Shrestha was forced to find a much larger showroom and hire two more girls to help with the sales. Nearly every day, she'd walk up to Sita and say that hiring her was the best business decision she'd ever made.

Sita tried not to look too pleased with herself when Mrs Shrestha said this, but it was hard. She loved the work and things were going really well. Ravi was behaving himself and Chandra had been more welcoming on her last few visits. Finally, it felt as if her life was coming together.

"We have a big problem," said Mrs Shrestha, rushing up to Sita as she entered the shop one sweltering July morning. "I just received a call from the printer. They didn't print up our posters for the August 5th event."

"But I spoke to them just two days ago!" Sita protested, setting aside the pricing gun that she was trying to refill. "They promised they would finish by this morning."

"Their press broke down; they can't do it before Friday. What are we going to do? We should have those posters up by today. This is a complete disaster."

Sita raced over to the office, pulled the Business Directory off the shelf and wrote down the addresses of the three nearest printing companies.

"I'll be back in an hour or so. Wish me luck!" she replied, grabbing a sample of the material to be printed. She stopped briefly to check her reflection in the large, gilt mirror that leaned against the wall. Her salwar kameez was a mint green chiffon, the leggings capri-length, the sleeves filmy. She looked fresh despite the heat. Her real challenge at Impressions was not spending all her paychecks on new clothes. With a satisfied nod, she rushed out into the midday crowd.

After visiting two of the shops with no success, she entered the third one feeling desperate.

"Hello, can I help you?" The clerk, a young, slender man with taped glasses, sat behind a desk.

"I need forty copies of this poster printed up." Sita handed over the prototype.

"When do you need them?"

"Well, that's the problem. I need them by tomorrow morning. Another printer has let me down, and I'm hoping you will save me." She gave him her best flirtatious smile and crossed her fingers.

"I'm afraid that's not possible," replied the clerk with a sympathetic smile. "We need at least three or four days for something like this. I'm sorry. These things can't be..."

"Miss Sharma?" asked a voice from across the room. "Is that you?"

Sita looked around to see who had called out her name. To her surprise it was Mr Dutta, the man she had met at the school eight months earlier. He looked more put together than the last time she'd seen him, his clothing neat and his hair trimmed. His hazel eyes caught the light from the window as he smiled at her. For a moment, they were luminous.

"Hello, Mr Dutta. That's right, you told me you ran a printing business," she said, oddly pleased to see him. While he hadn't been responsible for the change in her life that day they'd met, he was somehow entwined with it. Perhaps, without their conversation, things would not have happened the way they did.

"What can we do for you?" he asked, walking up to the counter to see what his assistant was holding in his hands. "You need this printed?" He spoke loudly, the sound of the press in the backroom echoing around the concrete building. It was a grey place. He looked at her as though she were a flower in a sidewalk crack.

"Our usual printer had trouble with his press. I'm really in a bind. Everyone is telling me it can't be completed in less than a few days. Is there anything else that can be done? Anything at all? I am willing to pay more if..."

"You will have it by nine o'clock tomorrow morning," he replied quickly. "I will see to it myself. Just tell me where I should have the flyers delivered?"

He took the poster from his assistant and held it carefully, with just his fingertips. His assistant began filling out the order form, only the trace of an amused smile on his lips.

"Thank you for taking this trouble. I really, really do appreciate it!"

"I just need an address," he reminded her.

"I am working at the dress shop named Impressions. It is..."

"Ah, I know it. I've seen the ads in the papers many times. As promised, 9:00 a.m. sharp. All right? Is there anything else?"

Sita shook his hand, his warm palm holding hers for just an extra second. His eyes again caught the light—there were spokes of green and gold in them, like a sunburst. Thanking him one more time, she hurried outside, more flustered than she'd felt in a long time.

Ten minutes before the appointed hour, Mr Dutta's presence was announced by the tinkling of bells over the door. Sita came out of the backroom, where she'd been counting the register. He smiled at her, the forty posters draped across his arm.

"Here they are," he said, handing the pile over to Sita. She carefully inspected the one on top.

"They came out more beautifully than I had hoped. Thank you so much!"

"So your shop is doing a lecture on fashion." He nodded toward the poster which announced as much.

"Yes, we're inviting a prominent designer to come in this week."

"Is this open to anyone?" he asked, cocking an eyebrow in a shy, hopeful way.

She laughed. "Are you interested in women's fashion?"

"Not really. But I was hoping you'd go to dinner with me after the presentation."

Sita's stomach clenched, and she took a deep breath. Foolishly, perhaps, she hadn't been expecting this. Her first inclination was to refuse. After all, she valued little above her privacy. But he had made a great effort on her behalf, and there was something about him.

"Yes, I'd like that." The words had come out of her without a conscious decision having been made.

"Wonderful. Then I'll see you on Friday." If he'd noticed her tepid enthusiasm, he didn't show it.

He left, looking elated, before she could change her mind. She smiled to herself, hoping she hadn't made a huge mistake.

That Friday, immediately following the designer's presentation, Mr Dutta took Sita out to dinner as promised. All through the talk, he had stood against the wall in the packed room, not far from her, their eyes catching every now and then. She hadn't heard much of what the presenter had said. She'd tried to stall afterward, saying she needed to help clean up but Mrs Shrestha shooed her out, saying she'd take care of it herself.

They took a taxi, the evening air warm and carefree and completely at odds with how she felt. She was terrified. During the taxi ride, he talked a little about the presentation. He may have caught more of it than she had. When this subject dwindled, he spoke about his business, often pausing, giving her an opportunity to interject or change the subject.

The restaurant he'd chosen was small but clean, and the smells coming from the kitchen were aromatic and enticing. The overhead lights were dim, the candle on their table casted a flickering light across his face as he smiled at her.

She was glad for the low lights; her cheeks felt warm. After all the men she'd known, why should she feel so uncomfortable now? How strange it was to think that, after all those men, this was her first real date.

He talked more about his work, then asked about Impressions. She said little, hardly able to eat her Chole Bhature. Even at the shop, she felt like an impostor. One day, her past would surely raise its ugly head, and she'd have to run away again. She had nightmares about this; she kept a bag packed and ready for the eventuality. The sense of being a fraud was even worse here with him. If he knew about her past, he would be appalled, disgusted. She sipped her wine, tapping her foot under the table, anxious for the meal to be over.

Yet Mr Dutta, or Krishna as he asked her to call him, was kind and considerate. He did his best to coax Sita into talking about herself, though she offered very few details. To fill the awkward moments of silence, he went on about his business, his family and his childhood in the village—whatever seemed to pop into his mind. He fussed over her wine glass, kept offering her bits of bread and olives and appeared completely taken with her, seemingly with no ego or artifice.

Unlike most men Sita had been with, when he spoke about himself, he did it without bragging or boasting. In fact, she suspected he downplayed his accomplishments. Near the end of the dinner, he described what had happened to his wife. Diagnosed with breast cancer, she had died three months later. It was clear that he was still devastated by this loss, but he declared that he was young, with a young son, and it was time to move on.

"I really enjoyed our time together," said Krishna, as they left the restaurant. "I hope I didn't talk too much. When I get nervous, I tend to go on and on about things." A long silence prevailed. "Do you think we can do this again?" he asked, sheepishly.

She wasn't sure how to respond. The crescent moon, visible above the skyline, offered no clues. She liked him, but she couldn't offer him what he was seeking. Besides, as soon as he found out about her past, he would want nothing to do with her.

"I had a wonderful time tonight, Krishna. Honestly. But I don't think we should continue meeting like this."

"But why?" he asked, totally devastated by this response.

"I'm not looking for a relationship now. There are things that have happened in my life—things that I cannot speak about. I can't do this. I just can't."

"I don't care about your past," he pleaded, in an attempt to change her mind. "I really like you. Even from that first day we met. Won't you please reconsider?"

"I'm sorry, I cannot. Thank you again for a lovely evening. And thank you for helping to print those posters. You really did save my life."

With this, Sita flagged down a baby taxi, leaving Krishna standing alone. Although the driver went slowly enough, the wind whipped through the doorless cab, tugging at her dress and hair, adding to her sense of restless agitation. She could not soil his clean life with the dirt from her past. He was a good man and did not deserve to be tainted with her problems. One day she would have to flee, and anyone in her life would be harmed. She couldn't do that to another innocent person.

14

The following Monday, a large bouquet of flowers was hand-delivered to the dress shop by a messenger. The note read: "Dear Sita, I saw these flowers and thought of you. Please reconsider. Forget about us having another dinner. I'd even settle for lunch. In fact, I'll go even further—how about a parata at a roadside stand? Warm regards, Krishna".

"I see you have a secret admirer," said Mrs Shrestha after coming over to smell one of the roses. Her guileless smile betrayed her keen interest to learn more. "Was it that man from the printing shop? He seems very nice."

"Yes, but he is just sending these flowers to thank me for doing business with his company," she replied, feigning indifference.

Mrs Shrestha laughed at this. "I think he has more on his mind than that," she replied, teasing. "As much as I love having you here, there is more to life than work, you know."

Sita offered a tight smile and found some inventory to unpack on the other side of the shop.

The next day, a second bouquet arrived. The note read: "Dear Sita, At 12:00 sharp, I will be at the same restaurant I took you to on Friday night. Please come. I just want to spend some time with you. I have no expectations. If you'd like, we can meet as friends. If you don't agree, I may have to continue sending you flowers every day until you do. With my meagre salary, this might put me into the poor house. Please come. This time it is your turn to save my life. Warmest regards, Krishna".

That afternoon, Sita went to the restaurant hoping to talk Krishna out of his fruitless attempts to win her over. But after seeing his face and his expression of pure joy, she forgot all about her mission. Instead, she sat down and shared another meal. Three hours passed in a heartbeat. Something had changed.

Over the next three months, Sita and Krishna met regularly. On her lunch breaks he would bring takeout, and they'd eat in the nearby park. On the weekends, they would go to the movies and see the latest Bollywood releases. Krishna had a pleasant tenor voice; he would often sing songs from the movies as he walked her home, to her embarrassment and delight.

In Lodi Gardens, they walked along paths that passed by fifteenth century tombs, children playing badminton and families picnicking. As they reached the pond full of geese, she let him take her hand for the first time. But when they were seated in a shady bower, tucked away from the crowd, and he leaned in to kiss her, she offered her cheek instead. He said nothing, only squeezed her hand. They continued walking. It was clear he was in love with her.

She tried to tell herself that she didn't feel the same. His singing was goofy, his fashion sense terrible. On the bus, he would talk for half an hour to anyone who'd sat nearby. He let his employees get away with murder.

However, on each date, it grew harder and harder to leave him, to say goodnight and watch him walk away. From time to time she imagined waking up to his brilliant smile, the warmth and security of his embrace. In her weakest moments, she longed for his touch, his kiss and his body against hers. Then she would chastise herself and get busy rearranging the newest stock. It was ridiculous to want such normal things. She was not worthy of them.

It was a Thursday afternoon, and the Chinese restaurant was nearly empty. Sita and Krishna sat at their favourite table by the window. Having finished their green tea, it was time to return to their respective workplaces.

"Oh, one more thing, Sita. Happy birthday," said Krishna. He'd been carrying a jute bag when he arrived, and now he unrolled the top and pulled from it a bouquet of red roses, only slightly squashed, and a small package wrapped in colourful paper. "Go ahead and open it."

"How did you know it was my birthday?" Sita asked, astonished.

"You told me once, a long time ago," replied Krishna with a loving smile. "I remembered the date. Go ahead, open it."

Sita gingerly unwrapped the package and took out a small jewellery box. Inside was a pair of simple sapphire earrings.

"I know they are not very large stones, but I do hope you like them. They are your favourite colour blue. Right?"

"They are beautiful, Krishna. I don't know what to say. I'm totally speechless." She blinked hard. When was the last time someone had given her something, unbidden and without a cost to her?

Overwhelmed, she leaned forward, planting a kiss on his cheek. Before she could pull away, he cupped her face in his hands and kissed her on the lips. For a moment, she allowed it to happen. Then, as if awakening from a deep hypnotic sleep, she jerked away.

"I'm sorry, I can't do this," she stated, standing up. With every fibre of her being, she wanted to kiss him, to hold him in her arms, to tell him how she truly felt about him, but she just couldn't allow this to happen. It would not be fair to him. He knew nothing of who she really was. The more compelled she felt to act on these feelings, the more she realised that she needed to pull away, to run for her life. To run for *his* life.

"What's the matter?" asked Krishna. His wounded expression was a knife to her heart. "I love you, Sita, and I think you feel the same way about me. What is wrong with us taking the next step?"

"I can't!" she replied, with tears again welling up in her eyes.

"Why are you so frightened of getting close to me?" he asked, finally demanding an explanation. "What could have possibly happened to you that makes you so frightened of me? Don't you understand? There is nothing you could ever say to me that would change the way I feel about you. Nothing! You have to trust me. I love you. I adore you. I..."

"Stop, stop, stop," Sita insisted, covering her ears. She felt the old familiar panic pushing her to run. "I can't talk about it. You'd never understand. I...I can't. I think we should stop seeing each other. You don't really know me. You have this image of me, but that's not who I am. I have a past. I have been through so much in my life. I did everything I could to protect my family. I had no choice. I was the oldest. There was no one else who could help us. It was my responsibility. I couldn't let my sister die. She was so sick. They said she'd die. I had to do something..." Sita stopped herself when she realised she was rambling incoherently. "I have to leave now." She turned and headed straight for the door, already thinking about her packed bag and where she could go next.

Krishna jumped to his feet and ran after Sita, placing his hand gently on her shoulder to prevent her from leaving. She made a feeble attempt to pull away, but she couldn't find the strength to resist. She remained where she was standing. The urge to run had evaporated with his touch.

"Sita, I love you," Krishna stated with total conviction. "I have never felt this way about another person before. Not even with my first wife, who I thought I adored. When I am with you, I feel as if my life is complete. Please do not ever suggest that we not spend our lives together. I would die a thousand deaths without you. For whatever reason, we are together now. I don't know how or why it happened. But at this point, you have become as important to my life as the air I breathe. Your blood runs through my veins. We share the same heartbeat. I cannot imagine a life without you. I want to marry you. Yes, marry me. Will you be my wife?"

Sita's heart began to race. The thought that she'd ever get married had long since been abandoned, along with so many other dreams. The fact that this wonderful man felt that she was worthy of his love, worthy of happiness, was a shock. She'd become so cold and unfeeling over the years, her heart covered by a callus. As if given a hard rap, the callus cracked, and memories bled through: the hours she used to spend talking to her parents about anything and everything, the annual holidays that the entire family spent together on Mount Abu, her days as a young student. How wonderful life had been then. There was so much promise, so much excitement, so much laughter and so much anticipation. But now she had to face her own tainted karma, to be true to her own fate. That path had been left behind at a fork in the road, never to be revisited.

"Sita, let me make a promise to you," Krishna pleaded. "From this point on, I will never again bring up the issue of your past. It is dead to me. I don't care about that at all. Can't we look forward? Can't you find a way to close that chapter and to start fresh? Like I have said over and over again, there is nothing you or anyone else could say to me that would change the way I feel about you. Nothing. I can promise you that!"

She could confess everything to him, let him know the truth about her once and for all. Perhaps his love would stand up to the test. More than likely, he would turn away, ashamed of his feelings for her. She had been spoiled beyond redemption. It was better to leave now and hold onto the memories of what she'd had with Krishna. She couldn't risk seeing the disappointment in his eyes when he eventually learnt the truth she had kept from him.

Sita gently lifted Krishna's hand off of her arm and turned and walked away. Once again, life had cheated her of happiness.

Nine days passed with no word from Krishna. He didn't phone, he didn't call, he didn't send flowers to her work. Without his presence, her days were dark, and she passed through them mechanically. She couldn't believe he had given up on her. But she'd said it was over, hadn't she? What had she expected?

It was time to move on. But his absence left a tremendous void. At night, in her third-floor apartment, sleep eluded her. Anxious and distraught, she listened to the faint sounds of her neighbours through the walls, to the gurgling of a small plug-in fountain that she had bought on a whim. The ceramic Ganesh statue perched on a rock above a small pool, trumpeting water from his trunk.

At the store, it had not sounded so much like sobbing.

At work, she was moody and distracted. Once, she left a customer in the middle of a fitting to change the radio station. A song Krishna had sung to her was playing, and in seconds she would have been weeping. She returned to find Mrs Shrestha and the customer exchanging a knowing look, sympathetic but amused.

"He will come around," the customer told her. She was a regular, an older woman. "I had many days of heartbreak before I married my Amir."

Sita dredged up a smile. It must look so simple to them all, just a lovers' quarrel. But beneath that façade of normalcy, her whole rotten history lay hidden like black mud, ready to squelch up through the cracks and cover everything with one misstep.

On the tenth day, her depression turned to complete despair. She'd been a fool to think she could live without him. Calling out of work sick for the first time, she took a taxi to Krishna's shop. The streets were as busy as ever, people going about their business as if the world had not turned upside-down. Why he had given up on her so easily when he'd always fought for her? Why did he finally quit? She needed to look him in the eyes, so she could know if he'd found out about her.

"I would like to return something that Mr Dutta left with me," Sita said to the clerk in a matter-of-fact tone. The shop looked the same as the last time she'd been there, but the office door was closed. The clerk slid the newspaper he'd been reading out of sight and straightened up. His glasses were still taped; he pushed them up his nose, trying to look alert as she handed over the box that contained the blue earrings.

"Mr Dutta isn't here," replied the clerk, leaving the box on the counter. "His father passed away early last week. The family is very traditional. They'll grieve the entire thirteen days."

A brief wave of vertigo washed over her as her world realigned itself. He'd had to leave. A family emergency and here she was thinking only of herself...

"I was supposed to deliver a letter to you," the clerk continued, looking sheepish. "I misplaced your address, I'm so sorry," he said, pulling an envelope out from beneath the counter.

He took a step back, busying himself with sweeping the other end of the counter as she tore open the letter.

Dearest Sita,

An hour after I left you, I received word that my father had expired. Because I had to rush over to my mother's home, I couldn't call. Please forgive me. Happy birthday again. I am sorry that it didn't go as I had planned.

Since my family is very religious, I must follow all of the rituals associated with my father's death. This will take up to two weeks. Upon my return, I will call you immediately.

I am so sorry that I tried to push you against your will. While I meant what I said about wanting to marry you, I will not bring it up again.

Please know how much I love you!

Krishna.

P.S. And happy birthday again!! The world was blessed indeed with your birth.

"Do you have a piece of paper?" asked Sita, folding up the note and placing it into her bag.

The clerk handed her a sheet of white paper.

Dear Krishna,

I am so sorry to learn that your father has passed away. I did not receive word until just now (Monday). Please offer my condolences to your family.

Thank you again for the earrings and the wonderful birthday surprise. It was so thoughtful. I am also so very sorry that I ran off the way I did. Please forgive me. While I probably shouldn't say this, I am going to say it anyway. I do miss you a great deal.

With love, Sita

Sita took the earring box back and left the store. The best thing for him would be for her to get out of his life. But she couldn't.

Another two months passed during which Sita did her best to stay busy. She spent time with Ravi, impressed with his growth and developing maturity. She visited Chandra, brought her garments from the store that pleased her, and masked her own sallow complexion.

Krishna finally returned, and he and Sita began to get together again at their favourite meeting spots. But something had changed. It began with Sita allowing Krishna to hold her hand under the table and then progressed to exchanging lingering goodbye kisses. A few weeks later, they began meeting at Sita's apartment. She was terrified at this change in their relationship. But at the same time, she realised that there was no way she could deny her feelings. She was madly in love with him and he with her. They had become giddy teenagers again, laughing, touching, telling silly jokes and learning to know each other's souls.

The first time they made love, something Sita avoided as long as she possibly could, she did her best to seem inexperienced. While she knew very well how to provide pleasure to a man, she made an effort to appear awkward and innocent. Krishna couldn't have been more patient or gentle in his touch. The tenderness went beyond anything Sita had ever experienced. For the first time, she associated love with pleasure – something that had never happened with any other man, even the rare customer who showed her kindness.

With each passing day, the love and affection they shared continued to grow. Instead of returning home to his mother's house, Krishna began to spend nights at Sita's apartment.

"Sita, I want to ask you to do something," said Krishna, wrapping his arms around her naked body under the sheets.

"What is it?"

"Marry me! Don't answer now. Just think about it. We are living like husband and wife anyway. Why not take the next step? I want to grow old with you. I never want you to leave my side. Please, think about it."

She did not respond at first. She had spent weeks thinking about this possibility, knowing that it would one day come up again. She knew what she wanted to say.

"I will marry you but only under the following conditions."

Krishna sat up in the bed, clearly surprised. "Anything you want."

"First, we are not going to have a big wedding. No families or friends, just you and me." Sita watched his face and waited to see his reaction. There was none. "Second, I do not want to live in your mother's home. If we marry, I want to stay in the city. Third, I want to continue working. I like my work; it makes me feel good. I also like the independence it offers me. Finally, but most importantly, you have to promise me that you will stay with me forever and beyond. No matter what happens, you have to be there for me, by my side. If you have any question in your mind about this, then this is the time to reconsider. I will try to put my past behind me but only if you agree to these terms."

"How can I marry without my family?" he murmured, as if talking to himself. "And living in the city? My mother will..." He stopped in mid-sentence. "I agree. You have me until the end of time. And you have my promise. I will always be there for you. Always!"

"Are you sure? This last condition is most important to me. You must promise me you will never, under any circumstance, leave my side, no matter what."

"I promise. I promise. I promise."

"Then let us marry."

To solidify their decision, they made love again, this time with a passion and ferocity that had never occurred before. It was as though they could not get close enough to one another and fought to become one.

The marriage ceremony took place in a small Hindu temple outside the city limits. As agreed, there were no family, no friends, and no celebration, just two people in love who wanted to take the next step together. Beneath an arch carved with lotus flowers, standing on a carpet of rose petals and marigolds, they said their vows. There was little fanfare, but they had dressed for the occasion, in matching gold-embroidered satin costumes. Krishna looked so handsome, the colour bringing out the gold and green spokes in his eyes.

Immediately after the marriage, the newlyweds went to the school to introduce Sita to Binod and to explain to him that she was now his stepmother. They had called ahead, and Binod had been allowed to skip class and wait for them in his dormitory. The room had four bunk beds, and although the school was air conditioned, the upstairs rooms were quite warm, the smell of unwashed laundry ripening in the still air. Sita ran her hands down the beautiful marriage gown and wished she'd changed first. She felt ridiculous, wearing this here. Binod did not bother to get up from the bed when they arrived. His uniform blue shorts and white collared shirt were too small on him; he'd grown several inches since she'd last seen him. They had never been introduced, but she'd had Ravi point the boy out to her on a previous visit. Now he stared at them with dark, round eyes, so unlike his father's. Perhaps he had his mother's eyes, she thought with discomfort.

While Krishna would surely be jealous of all the men she'd been with, should he ever find out, she felt more entitled to envy. She had never loved any of those men. But he had loved his first wife enough to marry her, to create a child with her. Binod stared at her with those disquieting eyes as Krishna introduced her as his new wife. Then, quite discouragingly, the boy abruptly turned around and faced the wall.

"Binod, I know it will take some getting used to, having a new mother—" she tried.

"You're not my mother!" he shouted.

"Of course not," she soothed. "But we are family now, and I think we will have so much fun together! When you are next home—"

"I'll just stay here next weekend," he muttered.

Sita looked at Krishna. He shrugged, helpless.

"I'm sorry you feel this way, Binod," he said quietly. "I hope you'll change your mind and give Sita a chance."

Somehow, she had managed not to give much thought to how Binod would react. Krishna's mother she had thought about, worried about. She'd thought a little boy would be easy to love, to convince to love her.

"He'll come around," Krishna said once they were out in the hall. They walked to the other end of the dormitory, to Ravi's room. But when they opened the door, he wasn't there. To kill the time, Sita looked through his drawers. She tried to keep him constantly supplied with fresh clothes and undergarments and was wondering what he might need. But in his sock drawer she found a pack of cigarettes, along with a pipe for smoking hashish. She slammed the drawer before Krishna saw it. Another day, she'd deal with that.

Ravi sauntered in, taller than her now, and stopped in his tracks at the sight of their outfits.

"You married him? Without asking me? I'm the man of the family! You couldn't even invite me to the ceremony?"

Krishna reached out, a placating gesture, but Ravi simply snarled and left the room.

"I—" Krishna began, looking as stunned by Ravi's rejection as she had been by Binod's.

"He'll come around," she assured him. Knowing Ravi, he wouldn't.

Deflated, they left the building, hurrying past the administration offices before anyone could waylay them with more complaints about the boys. Their cab was still waiting, the Pakistani driver snoring even after they opened the door.

Krishna politely tapped him on the shoulder, then helped her into the cab. He looked like a prince in his golden wedding clothes. She smiled at him, determined not to let this ruin their day. He smiled back at her and kissed her cheek as the cab took off.

"Are you sure you don't want to spend our honeymoon in some fancy hotel?" he asked.

The mere suggestion made her heart rate double. There were so many people who could recognise her, so many ways that things could go wrong. She hadn't even let him put a wedding notice in the paper.

"I'm sure our apartment will be romantic enough," she said, giving him a meaningful look.

He pulled her close and didn't mention it again.

The next day, Sita called Chandra to let her know about the marriage. But Chandra seemed indifferent, as though she couldn't be bothered to care about anything concerning Sita.

"That's nice," she said, as though perhaps there was a television in the room she was watching at the same time. "Send me a picture, when you get a chance," she added. Sita suspected, if she did send one, it would end up in the back of a drawer, out of sight.

"Sure," she said, trying to keep the anger out of her voice. "When I get a chance."

The honeymoon passed and still Krishna had not told his mother. Sita let it go, at first; she was not overly eager to meet her mother-in-law. When two weeks had gone by, she put her foot down.

"You have to call her and tell her." They were both home from work, and she'd pulled the telephone over to where he sat on the sofa and set it down beside him. "I know it's going to be uncomfortable, but there will be times when we have to get together with your family. I must start trying to develop some kind of relationship with her, with all of them."

He looked slightly ill as he picked up the receiver and let it dangle.

"As bad as Binod and Ravi reacted, my mother will be much worse."

"Best just to get it over with," she said, then went into the bedroom and shut the door, not wanting to overhear. Over an hour later, looking utterly dejected, he opened the bedroom door.

"She wants us to come to tea next weekend."

"Not dinner?" Sita said, indignation fighting relief. Tea would be a briefer meeting, but it was also an insult.

"She's very angry."

It was only Tuesday. She had so much time to dread the meeting. "Tea then."

The taxi pulled up in front of the house. For several minutes, Sita fought back a panic attack. The thought of stepping inside his mother's house made it hard to breathe.

"You have to meet them sometime," said Krishna, hoping to coax her out. "Come on. Today is the day. We can't put it off any longer. You were the one who made me set this up. My mother doesn't bite – well, not much."

Sita looked at the modest plaster-walled house with the cracked clay rooftiles. From inside those small windows, they were probably being watched.

"I just don't know if I can face yet another set of disappointed eyes."

Krishna sighed. "She's never been satisfied with anything I do. Don't worry, she'll get used to the idea in time. You have to understand, she really loved my first wife. They were very close. When Tara died, she was heartbroken. It's just difficult for her to accept that I would marry again, let alone someone she's never met. My mother is old, and she has had a long, hard life. She is also a very simple, very religious person, and she is very proud. To her, family and family honour are everything. The fact that I made this decision by myself without consulting her is what's bothering her most. It's not really about you. Don't worry, after she gets to know you the way I have, she will warm up. I promise."

"Well, here I go," said Sita, stepping out of the taxi and preparing herself for what was sure to be an uncomfortable ordeal.

On entering the house, Sita was escorted straight to the sitting room. Standing along the wall were at least a dozen men and women of different ages. After all of these aunts, uncles, cousins and siblings were introduced, Sita was asked to sit down.

They were all humble village folks, simple in their dress, speech and manner of expressing themselves. The house was also filled with photos of days gone by, some even old daguerreotypes. The entire environment was foreign to her. She'd never spent any time in a village. The expensive silk sari she'd worn to make a favourable impression was totally out of place here. She wished Krishna had advised her to dress more plainly. These people would think she was a peacock.

"Please have some tea," said Krishna's mother, as she nervously poured. Her hands shook. She was a tiny woman dressed in a simple blue cotton sari. While the effects of age had begun to shrink her body, she made every attempt to stand tall with her back straight. There was dignity in everything she did, but she was unable to conceal what she was thinking and feeling; everything was clearly reflected in her coal-black eyes. "We have biscuits too," she added proudly.

"Thank you," replied Sita, picking one up and taking a small bite. It was stale. She placed it down on the saucer where it remained. Her mother-in-law's nostrils flared at this.

There was a long period of silence.

"Mama, Sita works at a very nice dress shop in the city," said Krishna, trying to initiate a conversation. There was no response. "In many ways, she runs the entire business. Since joining there, the shop has really blossomed. She can even use the computer."

"Are you planning to continue working now that you are a married woman?" asked the mother, with suspicious eyes. There was no small talk with this one, just direct questions that needed to be answered.

"Yes, I was planning on continuing. Your son and I talked about it. He and I agreed that it wouldn't be a problem."

"How will you get back and forth to work from here?" asked the mother, surprised by this statement.

Realising that the old woman hadn't yet been told that they would be sharing an apartment in the city, Sita turned toward Krishna, but he looked away.

"We will both be staying in my apartment near the centre of town," Sita replied, irritated that Krishna had forced her to be the one to answer this all-important question. "It is large enough for the two of us and very close by to our businesses."

"And who will help me around the house?" asked his mother, addressing this question to her son. "I am old now. With your father gone, I will need help around here."

"I'm sorry, Mama. I forgot to mention that I will no longer be staying in this house. Please forgive me. With my business growing and me spending more and more time there, it is much easier if I have a place nearby. Don't worry, I can send you some money so that you can hire someone to help out around here. This will not be a problem."

"You want me to have a stranger working inside my own home? Someone who isn't a part of my family? Is this what you are suggesting?"

"Many people do it. You'll get used to it. All you..."

"I don't want anyone in my house. I will do the work myself. Even with my bad back and knees, I will clean my own floors. You go off. You live in your city with this... this woman. Leave us. We do not need you. We will make out just fine."

Krishna's mother stood up and marched out of the room. Sita didn't know what to say or do. In minutes, the woman had turned her back into a helpless child, chastised and powerless.

Leaving Sita all by herself with the other relatives, Krishna followed his mother to the next room.

Off in the distance, she could hear her husband, and his mother shouting at one another. Despite everyone's attempt to show a good face and pretend not to be hearing any of it, it was clear that the entire room was catching every word.

Moments later, Krishna came out, grabbed Sita's hand and together they left his childhood home. So began her family life with her new in-laws. Sita wondered again if their love would be enough to overcome the forces aligned against them.

15

Eight wondrous months of marriage passed during which Sita and Krishna's love continued to grow and blossom. There were no visits to his mother's home, but he sent the promised money, which was never returned. He continued to hope that his mother would relent and see the error of her ways. At least once a week, they both took time off from their busy schedules to meet for lunch, usually at their favourite Chinese restaurant.

On one of these occasions, Sita arrived at Krishna's shop twenty minutes early. Having never taken the time to acquaint herself with her husband's business, she wandered around the back area, looking at the various machines that occupied the main workshop. Each minute, miles of paper passed through these complicated mechanical devices that miraculously put words and images to print. With the big presses churning out thousands of newspapers and election posters every hour, the noise in the background was deafening.

"I never realised it was so loud," Sita shouted, as Krishna entered the space. "You're going to go deaf if you spend too much time back here." She continued strolling about the space, inspecting.

"I'm mostly in the office these days. But I appreciate the concern." He smiled at his wife. "So, what do you think of my printing presses? They're all very old, but they still get the job done."

"I think they are..." Sita stopped, leaning over to pick something up. "Where did you get this?" She held up a small plastic container, filled with a dark blue dye.

"I get them from a supplier located in old Delhi," Krishna replied, giving her a puzzled look. "We use them to supplement our regular ink. This product is very concentrated; it helps us to cut costs."

"Where is this shop?" Sita demanded.

"I don't know. I have the address somewhere in my office. I have never been there before. They always deliver to us directly when our stocks run low. They have the best price in the area, no one else...are you alright? What's the matter?"

"Where is this address?" Sita shouted above the sound of the machines.

"Sita, what is the matter with you?"

She was trembling with anger. He reached out a hand to calm her, but she shrugged it off. "I want the address now!" she demanded, then turned and marched off in the direction of his office.

Krishna followed her with the air of one waiting for calmer winds to prevail. After opening his cabinet, he pulled out a file with "Gupta Industries" typed across the top right corner. He handed it over to Sita who studied it carefully.

"We need to go to this place," Sita insisted, folding up a piece of paper from the file and placing it into her purse.

"Now?"

"Yes, now!"

"What is the matter with you, Sita? Why are you so concerned about some insignificant product I use in my business?"

"Just trust me and take me there. Please, don't ask any more questions. I just need to see this place."

His brows were reaching for his hairline, but he ushered her out the door and found them a taxi.

The vehicle weaved in and out of a labyrinth of tiny roads that carried them deeper and deeper into the bowels of the old section of town. Sita said nothing, even though Krishna was clearly confused and a little shocked by her behaviour. He'd never seen her enraged; hopefully, he never would again. But for now, she eyed the buildings, hardly blinking. Explanations could come later. Maybe.

"Stop," Sita shouted. The large metal door of the building was still familiar to her. Her heart pounded remembering how they'd wrestled with the lock, the seconds ticking down before the noise would draw attention.

"Do you know this place?" asked Krishna, curious.

Sita didn't answer. She climbed out of the taxi and stood for a long time just staring at the non-descript entrance. There was no number or sign to indicate the horrors that went on behind the anonymous door. Krishna was staring at her, a worried expression on his face.

"Do you have your cell phone?" she asked, reaching her hand out.

"Yes. Who do you want me to call?"

"Do you have any friends in the Delhi police force?"

"Yes. I know someone."

"Is he high up in the ranks?"

"Yes, he has some status within the force."

"Do you trust him?"

"Of course. We went to school together. I've known him since I was a child."

"Please call and report that there is a shop here that uses children as slaves. If he comes now with a small squad of officers, he will find at least ten or twelve young people working here. Because of the toxic fumes inside the place, they will be dazed and disoriented and perhaps under the influence of drugs that they are fed. They need help, and we are going to give it to them."

"I can't do that, Sita. What if they don't find anything? I'll look ridiculous. What business is it of ours? And besides, how do you know these things? You are making wild allegations..."

"Krishna, I want you to trust me," replied Sita, taking a deep breath and trying to calm herself. "Please just call and ask him to come. I promise you he will find what I just described. Please. I know what I'm talking about."

"But..."

Sita put her finger over his mouth to prevent him from saying another word. He almost looked frightened of her. Nodding, he relented.

An hour later, a small police van pulled up beside the taxi with several officers inside. Sita stood a few yards behind Krishna. She didn't want to have anything to do with the police. At her urging, Krishna agreed to keep her completely out of all of this.

"Krishna, it's good to see you," said Siddhartha, his policeman friend. He was an exceptionally tall man with a thin, lanky body and a waxed moustache that extended out several inches on either side of his face like handlebars. "What's going on here?"

"Well, it's hard to explain. I was told that this place has child workers who are imprisoned by the owner. Could you check it out for me?"

"Since when are you interested in saving the world?" asked his friend with a sarcastic smile.

"Just do me a favour and look into it, will you?" Krishna pleaded, gently pushing his friend with his hand. "Be a good guy."

"Are you sure about this information?"

"Yes, I'm pretty sure. When a friend of mine found out that I buy from this place, she told me all about what happens inside. I was a bit shocked at first, but then realised that if it is true, someone needs to stop it. It's not right to have kids working with these chemicals. They are very dangerous if inhaled."

"I still don't understand. Why would you care what they do inside there?"

"I have a son of my own. I don't want this kind of thing to happen to others. Could you check it out for me?"

"Yeah, I guess. Perhaps I will get my picture in the paper. Be a big hero, huh?"

Having assembled his men into a squad, the officer walked to the door and banged on it hard several times. When there was no answer, he turned to his friend. Krishna made a gesture to egg him on.

Next, several of the men were ordered to knock the door down. To achieve this feat, they each took turns kicking the door, one after another. Finally, after the hinges gave way and it swung open, they all ran inside with their guns drawn.

Ten minutes passed as Sita and Krishna nervously waited. When the officers finally exited the building, they were shepherding a group of eleven children appearing to range in age from five to eleven. As they emerged from the building with their blue-stained hands and pale skin, most of them had to cover their eyes against the harsh sunlight. A few minutes later, two adults were brought out in handcuffs: one was Mrs Gupta and the other was one of her young security guards. Judging from the blood coming from his nose, it looked as though he'd put up a fight.

"You were right," said Siddhartha, walking up to greet Krishna. "Those kids were living and working in that place like animals. All the exits were blocked. The stench inside there was deadly. It's difficult to believe people can be so cruel."

"Who is the woman?" asked Krishna, curious.

"She seems to be the one who runs the place. Judging from the condition of the children in there, she's a real monster."

As Mrs Gupta was being placed into the police van, Sita walked up to her. For several moments, the woman looked directly at her, and their eyes made contact. But from her blank expression, it was clear that she did not recognise Sita. Rendered completely speechless by her untamed anger, Sita could only glare at her as the policeman shut the door.

After the children and those arrested had been taken away in squealing police vans, Krishna turned to his wife with an expectant look across his face. But how could she tell him about her time as one of those children? From this one loose thread, her whole story might unravel. She kissed him on the cheek, grateful that he'd done as she asked, unquestioning. Then she climbed into the back of the car and never said another word about the incident.

Ten months later, as she relaxed on the hand-me-down sofa that she had recovered in blue velvet, a mug of sweetened mint tea on the rattan table close by, Sita sat bolt upright. It was morning, her day off, and Krishna was in the shower. The monsoon rains had started, and the light filtering through her hand-made curtains was a silvery yellow. She'd been reading the paper, enjoying the peaceful morning, when she came across the article. Mrs Gupta had been convicted of child endangerment, kidnapping, trafficking and a host of other charges. She read it again, a wide smile spreading across her face. How nice it was when the legal system worked and a criminal actually went to jail for her crimes! She read it a third time, then set the paper aside, her smile dimming. She only wished the same could have been true when her father tried the case that resulted in his own murder. The memory of that night was still an open wound, one that might never heal.

Restless now, she went into the bedroom and began to make the bed, smoothing the cotton sheets and the blanket that was stitched with lotus flowers. It bothered her that she hadn't said something to Mrs Gupta that day. She had desperately wanted to tell the woman how evil she was, to scream that what she'd done to them made her a monster. But the words simply would not form. It was as though the memories, the hatred and the fear she had lived with for so long had paralysed her tongue.

Never again, she swore to herself. Never again would she allow herself to remain silent under such circumstances. She would somehow manage to speak the truth.

16

Sita was first aware of the rattle of the ceiling fan. She lay on her side, the breeze tickling her nose with a loose strand of hair. It was still dark, the apartment building quiet in a way that said it must be early morning. In the other room, Krishna was speaking on the phone.

He entered the bedroom a moment later, grief stricken.

"My sister Nandita and her husband Vihaan were killed, in a car accident."

He was too stunned to cry. She rose from the bed, folded him in her arms.

"I'll leave now, for my mother's. I'll call you later."

She choked back her own fear at the thought of entering his mother's house again.

"Shouldn't I come with you?"

He pulled back, kissed her gently. "I'd like you to, but my mother…"

For a moment, this seemed the most awful part of everything she'd been through. She couldn't be with the man she loved when he needed her most.

"I'll call you later," he said. Then, throwing on clothes, he hurried out the door.

Feeling useless and irritable, she paced beside the phone for hours. Finally, it rang.

"How is your mother doing?" she asked, after determining that he'd arrived safely.

"She's hardly talking to me," replied Krishna, sounding tired. "I have never seen her so upset before. First Father, now Nandita and her husband…" he gave a heavy sigh. "All she does is moan and weep."

"Do you want me to come out there right now?"

"No, wait until after the two cremations are over. If you can come this evening, that would be much better. Mama is still not very happy with us. She hasn't got over my decision to marry you without her consent. And then there is the fact that I moved in with you instead of staying at her home. My mother is very stubborn, but, Sita, she means well."

"Maybe I shouldn't come at all."

"No, you have to come. If you don't show up, this would just add to her feelings against you. She would add heartless to your list of transgressions. You don't have to stay very long. You can make an entrance and then just leave after an hour or so. Just keep the taxi waiting there."

"When are you planning to return home?"

"Probably not for a couple of days, my dear. I need to be here with my family. There are lots of details that must be sorted out. You know how it is."

"Stay as long as you have to." There was a long pause. "You know, I really miss you. I couldn't sleep a wink after you left without your body next to mine."

"I know how you feel. I feel the same way."

"Are you doing all right, darling?"

"Not really. This is still a huge shock to us all. One never thinks that such a thing can happen in one's own family, especially people so young and full of life. I still can't believe they are both gone. I just spoke to my sister two days ago."

"Does anyone know what caused the accident?"

"Apparently a truck that was trying to pass on the wrong side forced them off the road. The car struck a tree head on. They both died instantly."

"Who is going to take care of their young daughter?"

"We need to talk about that sometime in the next few days," replied Krishna with some reluctance. "Actually, they are suggesting that I take her."

"What? Are you serious?"

"Mama does not want her to go to Vihaan's family. She's afraid she'd never see her again because they live near Chennai on the coast and have a shipping business that keeps them travelling. There is tension with them as well. My mother has this way of alienating everyone somehow. I know I shouldn't be saying this about her, but it's true. As I said, she's stubborn and set in her ways. There's no changing her now."

Sita did not respond. She was not thrilled with the thought of raising someone else's child when she was trying to get pregnant herself, but this was not the right time to discuss it. She did not want to further upset Krishna or appear cold-hearted.

"We can talk about this later. I'll see you tonight. I'll bring you a valise with fresh clothing and some toiletries."

"Yes, thank you, and please be careful. Hire a good driver, all right? I love you."

"Me too."

After a busy day of dealing with many of her own business matters, visiting Krishna's shop to make sure everything was running well in his absence, and packing his bags, Sita arrived at the house a little before six o'clock. Unlike the last time she had been to her mother-in-law's home, she wore a sombre conservative sari in the hope that she could come across as being less cosmopolitan. Upon entering the house, she immediately began looking for Krishna amongst the crowd of relatives and neighbours. She felt like a kitten in a lion's cage.

She did not recognise anyone from that first, awful visit. It was as if she'd walked into a stranger's home by mistake. Then, as she was reentering the foyer area in her continued search for her husband, a familiar face turned her to stone. The man was a high-ranking civil servant who worked in the Home Ministry, a leading figure in one of the religious-based parties. His deep-set eyes locked on her from behind his thick-rimmed glasses. He pushed a lock of greasy hair behind his ear as he stared at her, puzzled.

She'd been on three dates with this man, but when he requested a fourth, she refused. He had a terrible temper and once slapped her face when she hadn't done exactly what he wanted. Furious at her rejection, he would often call her up and say terrible things over the phone. It had become so uncomfortable that she'd been forced to change her phone number. And now here he was, in her husband's childhood home, staring at her like he was trying to recall how he knew her.

Suddenly, recognition sparked in his eyes. Seeing Sita at such a sombre event, his pious expression instantly soured. "What are you doing here?" he whispered, using a disapproving tone and wagging his finger in her face. "This is not a place for someone like you. Now get out of here. Right now!"

Sita couldn't move; she was paralysed.

"What are you waiting for?" he added. "Get out!"

"I can't just leave," replied Sita, her head lowered. "The woman who was killed is a relative of mine."

"You are related to this good family?" he asked, appearing shocked.

"Yes."

"How?"

"My husband is Krishna, the brother of the woman who died," Sita confessed.

"When did you get married to him?"

"Nearly two years ago."

"Does he know what you are?" asked the man, unable to hide his total outrage.

"What I am?" Sita asked, finally regaining a bit of composure. "You mean what I was?"

"Don't you try to play games with me. Does he know you're a common whore who once worked for Masud Kumar?"

"I never told him anything about my past. He doesn't care. That was a long time ago. Are you going to say something to the family? Please don't say anything. I beg you." Sita tried to study his expression.

"What do you think I'm going to do? These are decent people."

In his own narrow mind, it was clear that she had seduced and deceived a good man, probably in a desperate attempt to buy back her respectability. But for him, once fallen, forever fallen. Without saying another word, he marched off to one of the other rooms, never considering his hypocritical attitude or his own complicity in her crimes.

Sita stood still, not knowing what to do. How could he bring such news with two deaths in the family? At a time of grief, it would bring shame and embarrassment to the entire family. And how would knowing a prostitute sit with his wife?

Not knowing what to expect, Sita decided she had to escape. As she looked around for her shawl, which she had draped onto one of the chairs, she turned to find Krishna's mother rushing into the foyer area with a large broom in her hands. She was followed by a handful of other relatives and friends, including the man who had been Sita's former customer.

From the crazed look in the old woman's eyes, Sita could tell that her secret was finally out.

"Get out of my house, you whore!" shouted her mother-in-law as she swung the broom at Sita's head, missing by mere inches. "Leave this place. You dare to come here? You have brought shame to my son and to my family. Get out of here at once before you defile the memories of my dear daughter and her husband!" The old woman was hysterical, flailing away with the broom and screaming.

Sita ran out the door and through the yard to the taxi that was waiting for her as instructed. As others followed her outside, they picked up stones from the ground and began throwing them in her direction.

While she was climbing into the car, Sita looked back one final time only to find Krishna standing beside the front door, doing nothing to defend her. He just stood there, passive, as this attack against her unfolded. Hadn't he vowed that nothing in her past mattered? He obviously had not meant a word of it.

Hoping to avoid damage to his vehicle, the taxi driver sped away in a cloud of dust.

Sita laid down in the back seat and sobbed, covering her head with her shawl. Never in her life had she been so humiliated. Her past had finally caught up with her. Krishna and his entire family now knew her secret.

17

For four long days, Sita sat alone in her apartment, waiting for Krishna to come back to her. But he never returned home, nor did he call. Despite all she had been through over the years, this was by far the lowest point in her life. She had invested all of her hope for redemption and love in him, and he had turned against her. She sat in the bottom of a deep emotional well of unforgiveness and feared she might drown in her own tears.

By now, Krishna had become everything to her: husband, friend, soulmate and lover. She cherished him with all her heart. The thought that she might have hurt him with the news of her past was more than she could endure.

More than anything else, she felt ashamed and embarrassed. All she wanted was a chance to sit down with him and clarify the whole story: explain what happened to her parents and her family and describe how she was forced to become a prostitute to save her sister's life. She wanted to reveal all of the secrets she had harboured in her heart for so long. She couldn't understand why she had waited, why she hadn't confessed these things to him earlier. It would have been infinitely easier if he had found out from her instead of the cruel way he had.

As the hours passed and turned into days, her feelings wavered between love and anger.

"He promised, he swore he'd never leave my side no matter what," she repeated to herself, recalling his vow to her. "And yet he let me go from his mother's house under those awful circumstances, and he hasn't even had the decency to come and see me." Always, in the middle of her rage, she would ultimately remember her devotion to him and then come crashing down again. Her life had been so good since marrying Krishna that she couldn't believe it could be ending. She had nowhere left to run.

By the end of the fifth day, Sita finally came to terms with her new situation. If he had planned to come home, he would have shown up by now. She was yesterday's trash.

She needed a drink.

There was no alcohol to be found in the apartment, so she took a shower, dressed and headed for one of the five-star hotels she had frequented in years past. A double scotch whisky might help, a little.

Sita sat alone on a barstool, stirring her second drink with her index finger. With each passing moment, Krishna's betrayal weighed more heavily on her thoughts. The alcohol did not reduce these feelings; it instead seemed to fuel them from slow burning embers to a raging inferno. There was no escaping the immense suffering he had brought upon her, and her heart was quickly turning into a lump of coal. Then she heard a voice behind her.

"Sita, is that you?"

The stranger was a tall, handsome man. With his smart Western-style suit, expensive gold watch and highly polished Italian leather shoes, he seemed to belong in the plush hotel's surroundings. Sita tried to focus on him.

"It's me, Raju," he stated. "I haven't seen you for almost two years, perhaps longer?"

"Yes, Raju. I'm sorry, of course I remember you," replied Sita, slurring her words. Kind and gentle, he had once been one of her favourite regular customers.

"What have you been doing with yourself?" he asked with keen interest.

"Me? I am just passing my life away, like everyone else."

"Are you waiting for someone? I mean, are you free tonight? I have some time and well..."

Sita looked into his hopeful eyes. His offer was clear: he was asking if he could have her body for the evening. She suddenly remembered what it was like to prostitute herself, the posturing for business, the negotiations and the game-playing that she had mastered during that period of her life. At that moment, it seemed so natural to her. Without any effort, it all came flooding back as if she had never left the game.

While her first inclination was to say "no" outright, and to explain that she was now married, she didn't. She couldn't force the words to pass her lips. Another wave of betrayal came over her. Her husband had abandoned her.

"I am free now," replied Sita, extending her hand for him to take. "Do you have a room here?"

"Yes."

"Then let's go." She gave him her best flirtatious smile, picked up her purse and once again fled one life for another.

An hour later, Sita returned to the lobby. The two additional Scotches she'd had with Raju had finally taken the edge off her misery. The outside world had faded away; there was only the polished white hallway and the grand wooden bar at the end of it. Steadying herself on the brass railing that ran along it, she heaved herself onto a stool. To her left, a few seats over, a group of businessmen seemed to be celebrating. To her right, an older couple was having a quiet drink.

Raju—how strange to see him again. How disappointing, really. The sex had been mechanical, leaving her as empty as when they'd begun. She'd let him buy the drinks, but she wouldn't take his money. Drinks were better than money anyway.

"I would like another Scotch," Sita told the bartender, waving her hand for his attention. The bar was not busy, yet he had not come over to take her order. She had a suspicion he was avoiding her.

"I don't think you should do that, madam," he replied quietly, finally standing in front of her.

"I said I want another Scotch!" she repeated in a scolding voice, slapping the bar top. "Who are you to tell me what to do? It's my money. If I want to buy a drink, then I have the right to buy a drink."

To avoid any further confrontation, the bartender did as he was told and brought Sita her drink.

The clink of ice cubes was a pleasing counterpoint to the classical music. She swirled the drink looking around the room. At a corner table, a man sat alone. Every now and then, he'd look up to catch a glimpse of her. He wasn't so bad-looking himself. Older, but with a kind face. She slid off the stool and wobbled over to his table. If everyone was going to treat her like a whore, perhaps she should own the role.

"Hello, my name is Sita," she stated with her hand extended.

"Hello," replied the man, offering a weak, unenthusiastic handshake in return.

"What is your name?"

"My name? Ramesh."

"Are you here on business, Ramesh?"

"Yes. And yourself?"

"Yes, I am selling myself. That is my business. I sell my body for money. Are you interested?"

He stared at her, his jaw hanging open.

"I'm afraid that I'm a married man," he replied in an apologetic manner.

"What does that have to do with anything?" asked Sita, angrily. "Most men who spend time with me are married. I myself am married. It means nothing. Marriage means nothing."

"I'm sorry, you must be confusing me with someone else. I don't go for that kind of thing."

"Don't you think I'm pretty?"

"Yes, you're very attractive. It's just…"

"What is it?"

"If you'll excuse me, I have another engagement," replied the man, standing up and rushing over to the bartender to pay his tab. Sita noticed them talking, and at one point they both looked over in her direction.

The rejection smarted. Had she forgotten how to even whore properly? She downed the rest of her scotch, then staggered over to the bar for another drink. The bartender was on the phone talking to someone. The man from the corner table had already left.

"I need a double Scotch," she demanded, banging the glass down hard.

The bartender did not answer. He turned and smiled and then continued with his phone conversation.

"I said pour me another Scotch. You can talk and pour at the same time, can't you?"

The man hung up the phone. "I'm afraid I cannot serve you any more alcohol, madam. By the way, are you a guest of this hotel?"

"That is none of your business," Sita hissed.

"Then you are not a guest, is that so?" replied the bartender, still maintaining a polite demeanour.

"I don't have to answer that."

One of the hotel managers and a security guard arrived at the bar and immediately approached Sita. With a simple nod of his head, the bartender confirmed that his suspicions were correct: she was not a guest.

"Madam, I am going to have to ask you to leave this place," said the manager sternly. "And we do not want you to ever return here again. Do you understand me? This is a respectable hotel. We do not tolerate prostitution or your kind of behaviour."

"What are you talking about?" asked Sita, her voice shrill. "I can come into this place for a drink if I want. You can't do this to me."

"Yes, we can. One of our guests just complained that you made an obscene advance toward him. This is not some common brothel. Now get out of here this minute before I call the police and have you arrested and sent to jail where you belong."

"That man is a liar. I did not approach him for sex. He was the one who approached me. Why don't you go and arrest him?"

"I am only going to say this one more time," insisted the manager. "You either leave quietly now, or I am going to have you physically removed. The choice is yours."

The security guard took a step forward. There was nothing she could do. She was being thrown out for prostituting herself. If only her mother-in-law could see her now.

"I will not leave this place until I'm ready. You can't make me leave. If you try this, I will go straight to this hotel's director."

"Be my guest," replied the manager with confidence. "He will say the same thing to you. Your kind is not welcome here in this hotel. Now please leave."

"My kind?" asked Sita, becoming furious. "My kind? How do you think I became this way? Do you think I just woke up one day and decided to give my body over to strangers because I like being groped by filthy men just like you? Is that what you think? You did this to me. All you men did this to me. You don't care about us women. You don't care who I am, what my problems are or what I want out of life. You just want to sleep with us—to use us. It doesn't matter if I want to or not. That doesn't come into your mind, does it? I am what I am because of all of you. You all just use and use and use...all of you." She stabbed her finger accusingly at each of them.

The security guard came up and gently grabbed Sita's arm. She pulled away and staggered toward the door. Her face was hot with humiliation, but she was not going to be escorted out of this place like a common criminal. She held her back straight and her head high as she entered the lobby and made her way out the front door.

18

Sita slowly opened her eyes. The light was painful, and her head throbbed. She had no idea where she was.

Propping herself up on her elbows, she looked around. She was in an alleyway, lying on a collection of cardboard boxes, directly beside a heap of trash. It was morning. A small delivery van parked several feet away prevented her from being seen from the main road. The location was completely unknown to her.

Appalled, she rose to her feet, her head swimming. Looking down, she realised that her expensive sari had been soiled with a combination of what appeared to be vomit and dirt. Her hair was matted and tangled, and her mouth tasted foul.

As hard as she tried to remember what had happened the night before, most of the details eluded her. She recalled being in her apartment, going to the hotel for a drink and even spending time with Raju in his room. The image of them having sex sent a wave of horror through her. What had she done? She recalled being thrown out of the hotel but nothing after that. Where she had spent the night and how she had ended up in the alleyway was a complete mystery. She felt physically sick, dirty and disgusting. All she wanted was to go home, wash and climb into bed.

Desperate to escape from this living nightmare, she searched the alley for her handbag. But it was gone. Without it, she had no money to take a taxi home.

Blinking back tears, she did what she could to clean herself up. Using some packing paper, she tried to wipe her clothing. This did not seem to make much of a difference. To keep the flies from landing on the soiled fabric, her hand was constantly in motion.

The main sidewalk was already filled with people who had begun their morning routine. She couldn't recognise a thing; the location completely escaped her.

"Excuse me, sir, could you tell me where I am?" asked Sita, after approaching a man who was in the process of tying his shoelace.

He looked up, completed this task and then walked away, ignoring her question. Sita approached another man with a very similar outcome.

She caught her reflection in a shop window; she looked homeless, crazed. No wonder people were afraid of her. For someone who always took pains to appear refined, the embarrassment of being in public like this was excruciating. For the first time in her life, she understood what it felt like to be invisible – no one wanted to have anything to do with her. Frantic to get back to her apartment, Sita decided to try another approach.

"Excuse me, could I just talk to you for a moment?" asked Sita, approaching two middle-aged women on the street. They appeared to be waiting for someone to pick them up. "Something terrible happened to me last night and I seem to have lost my purse. Do you by any chance have some money that I could borrow for taxi fare? I promise, I can pay you back immediately after I return home. I just need to get back to my apartment. If you give me your address, I will bring the money right over. I promise."

The two women impatiently looked through their purses. Simultaneously, they both pulled out twenty-rupee notes and handed them to Sita. The expressions on their face said it all: they had nothing but pity and disgust for her.

"Can you tell me your address and I will return this money?" asked Sita, as tears rolled down her face. The two women ignored the question as if it were somehow silly and irrelevant. Who in their right mind would expect a street person to return money?

After they walked away, she looked down at the two bills in her hand. She had just begged for money, something she had sworn she would never do. She recalled the day Ravi had done the same thing at the park beside the Red Fort and how she had left the bills on the grass. She had still had a little dignity then. But that was all gone, the last vestige of her self-respect dissolved in scotch last night. She'd slept with another man, awoken in an alley covered in vomit and begged for money.

For years she'd been a fallen woman. There had been so much further to fall.

The dizzying shame and humiliation of the last day exceeded anything she had ever experienced in her life. Other circumstances could be attributed to events beyond her control; she had merely been reacting to them or in survival mode. This time, everything she had done was her own fault. She suddenly appreciated how wretched and pathetic she had become. The disgrace and disappointment was more than she could bear; she hated everything about herself. There was no way to erase this poisonous karma, she simply had to put an end to it all. She had vaguely considered ending her life before but had dismissed the notion when her brother and sister were depending on her. Now no one would care whether she lived or died.

Acting quickly, before she could talk herself out of it, Sita dropped the money to the ground as though it were burning her fingers and ran headlong into the middle of a three-lane street packed with speeding traffic. Several cars skidded to an abrupt stop to avoid hitting her. She looked at the drivers, silently pleading with them to end her misery. When it seemed as though her wish would not be carried out, she looked up at the sky and raised her hands in the air. "Take me!" she shouted again and again at the top of her lungs, addressing the gods. "Take me!"

"Get out of the road, lady," shouted a taxi driver as he did his best to enter the only lane that was moving. Horns blared as angry motorists cursed her presence in the middle of the road.

Sita looked into their crazed eyes, seeing only hatred reflected. "They are right to curse me. I am evil," she whimpered sadly.

Realising that there was little chance of being struck on this side of the road, Sita crossed over the dividing line and tried desperately to get hit by jumping in front of cars on the opposite side. Once again, all of the vehicles somehow managed to brake or swerve just in time.

A crowd began to form on each side of the road to watch. Dimly, she was aware of them, standing by and watching the spectacle unfold. Some even clapped and cheered her on, urging her toward her death. No one tried to stop her.

"Get out of the road," shouted a pair of police officers that finally ran toward her. A lone concerned bystander had summoned them to the scene.

"She's mad," shouted someone. "She's trying to get herself killed!"

Realising that they were coming after her, Sita turned and began racing down the middle of the street to escape. Even after one of her shoes fell off, she continued running as fast as she could. Upon arriving at a second major intersection, she turned her head to see if they were gaining ground—they were.

Just as she turned back, a small van struck her from the side. She flew through the air, landing hard on the pavement. Vehicles swerved around her as she lay still, a puddle of blood forming beneath her head.

She sensed a large crowd forming around her; they seemed to all agree that she was dead. Then her world went totally silent. She floated in space and time. The shame, humiliation and betrayal were replaced by a sense of peace. She willed death to hurry and take her the rest of the way.

PART TWO:

"REBIRTH"

19

Sita awoke to discover a world of white. She was in a hospital bed with her arms strapped tightly to a set of handrails. A deep sadness washed over her; she was still alive. Lying in this sterile room, strapped to a bed, was somehow worse than death could possibly be.

"Doctor, your patient seems to be waking up."

Sita turned her head toward the voice, finding a nurse speaking into an intercom phone. After relaying this message, the woman walked away, her crisp skirt rustling.

"Well, I see my patient is finally coming back to life," said an attractive female doctor who entered the room. "My name is Dr. Hussein. I'm here to take good care of you."

The doctor looked as if she might have just graduated from university. Her eager, bird-like features knew nothing of shame or debasement. Wearing a white lab coat, a pink linen blouse and a beige pair of baggy scrub pants, she appeared a successful, modern woman. Sita tried to turn onto her side but was held back by the restraints. The only way to show her displeasure was to turn her face toward the wall. Coming back to life indeed. Not if she had anything to say about it.

"I'm sorry, we had to keep those on during periods when you were left alone," Dr. Hussein continued. "Whenever someone tries to take their own life, we are forced to take these precautions. I'm sure you understand. Do you promise you will not try to hurt yourself again?"

Sita nodded but kept her face turned away.

"Okay, I will take them off for now, but only if you remain calm." The young doctor removed the restraints and rubbed Sita's wrists where the leather had chaffed them. "So, how are you feeling? Do you know where you are now?"

Sita did not respond.

"Do you understand what I'm saying to you?" asked the doctor. Holding Sita's chin steady, she shone a small penlight into her eyes. Sita wrenched her chin free and turned onto her side.

"You know, you're a very lucky woman," said Dr. Hussein. Sita could hear the scratch of pen on paper. "With the exception of a slight concussion and some blood loss, it looks as though there are only a few minor injuries. Not a single broken bone, no internal bleeding, and no significant lacerations. Based on what I heard from those who witnessed the accident, you should have been much more seriously hurt. Perhaps even killed."

"Where am I?" asked Sita, her voice hoarse and throaty. She suddenly realised that she was incredibly thirsty.

"You are at Saint Vincent Hospital in Delhi. Would you like something to drink?"

"Yes, water please."

The doctor pressed a button to raise the bed, then held a glass with a straw close to Sita's mouth.

"How did I get here?" asked Sita, sipping the cool water. She didn't want it to taste so good. Every small pleasure seemed like a chance for her body to betray her new purpose.

"The police brought you in, and a good thing too. You didn't have any identification with you, but after they checked around, they found someone who knew who you were. They then brought you here quickly."

"Who was it that said they knew me?"

"I can't say for sure." For the first time, the doctor averted her eyes.

"How long have I been here?"

"For nearly three days. When you arrived, you were unconscious. On a few occasions, you briefly woke up. You seemed delirious, mumbling to yourself. But now you seem to be much better. I think you'll be fine after a few more days of rest and rehydration."

Sita reached up to touch her head, finding a large bandage wrapped completely around it. The right side of her head felt very tender to the touch.

"We had to shave some of your beautiful hair away to put in a row of stitches. But don't worry; it will grow back soon enough." She met Sita's eyes again and smiled, woman to woman. Sita looked away. The doctor thought she cared about her hair?

She tried to sit up to take another drink, but the pain was too intense. Any movement involving her muscles was excruciating. She settled back against the pillow and allowed the doctor to hold the straw for her again.

"I will be back in just a few minutes to check on you. I will also ask the nurse to get you something for the pain. Try not to move too much until you receive this medication. It will only bring you more discomfort. After what you've been through, your body needs some time to heal."

Alone in the room, Sita examined the many wires and tubes attached to her. She had an I.V. in her arm and a tube in her nose, presumably for oxygen. Perhaps, by removing one of them, she might be able to cause harm to herself. She would wait until the doctor and nurse had left her alone for the night. Then she would finish the job the vehicles had been unable to.

There was a light rap on the door. Sita did not respond. A second, firmer knock followed. Once again, Sita made no attempt to acknowledge it. Couldn't they just leave her alone to die?

The door opened. Mrs Shrestha, her boss, held a large bouquet of fresh flowers in her hands. Sita couldn't imagine how the woman had found her. She had not spoken to her since the death of Krishna's sister, when she had told her she would be away for a while due to a family emergency.

"May I come in, Sita?" asked her friend, politely. She wore a sari so blue it was almost purple, a soothing colour, and the orange tiger lilies accented it perfectly. Sita almost smiled at the sight, but a stabbing pain checked that impulse. She turned away towards the wall, too embarrassed and ashamed to face her colleague. Mrs Shrestha had probably learnt the truth about her too.

"The doctor tells me that you are doing much better now," said Mrs Shrestha. She spoke soothingly, as if to a small child. "I'm so lucky that I'm here when you're awake. I have been back and forth at least a dozen times over the past few days."

"How did you find me here?" asked Sita, her voice muffled by the pillow. If she could have fled, she would have. Humiliation compounded her pain.

"The police found the shop pin you always wear on your chest and called Impressions. They asked if I knew a person who fit your description. When I found out what happened to you, I immediately told them to bring you to this hospital. I have a brother-in-law who works as a doctor here, so I know the care is exceptional. I have been so worried about you."

"And what did they tell you about what happened?"

"They said that you ran into the middle of some heavy traffic and tried to kill yourself. Is this true, Sita? I have been hoping that report was wrong. It did not sound like you."

"Yes, I wanted to die. I still want to die."

"Why would you want to do such a thing?" asked Mrs Shrestha, walking over to grab Sita's hand. She gently pulled the pillow away from her friend's head.

"I can't explain. It's too complicated. You'd never understand."

"But I do understand."

"There is no way you could know all of the details."

"I know enough," replied Mrs Shrestha with a sympathetic smile. "I do not care what happened to you over the years. It makes absolutely no difference to me."

"I have heard that before, from Krishna. People say such things, but they don't mean them. You don't know what you're talking about!" Sita snapped. "If you did, if you knew the real me, you'd feel much differently."

"Listen, Sita. After I found out you were in the hospital, I called your husband, Krishna. We had a very long talk together. He eventually told me what happened at his mother's home."

"What...what did he say about me?" She looked up in horror, wanting to know and yet dreading it.

"I know what they say you did for a living before you came to my shop. And I know how they ran you out of the house because of this. But this doesn't make any difference to me. You are a dear friend and a partner in my business. You had a bad experience. So what? I want you to come back to the store when you've recovered. I am lost without you. Everyone is asking where you are. We all miss you terribly."

"But I was a prostitute," Sita declared, so her friend could make no mistake. "I sold myself for money. Doesn't that change the way you see me? It certainly changed my husband's view of me."

"Stop saying that," Mrs Shrestha insisted, using her hand to stroke Sita's forehead. "It doesn't change the way I feel about you, Sita. Nothing could change that. I suspect you did what you did for the sake of your brother and sister. But the details are not at all important to me. It doesn't matter how or why you entered into that trade. All I care about is the Sita that I know, my friend, my sister and my coworker, found her way out and became a wonderful partner to me."

"But what if someone comes into your shop and recognises me? That has happened twice in the last week, once at Krishna's mother's house and then again..."

"So what? They always say the world is a small place. No matter. I am proud of you, Sita. If I defined myself by all of the bad things that happened throughout my own life, I would go totally crazy. The past is dead. It's time to move on. If someone were to ever recognise you in my shop and say anything bad against you in my presence, I'd throw them right out with my own hands. You're a dear friend. You've always been honest, supportive and helpful to me. What I now know about you changes nothing in my mind."

"But I lied to you about many things."

"Perhaps. But those were not malicious lies. They were meant to cover up something that you did not feel you could share. We all have things like this in our past. Don't be so hard on yourself." The older woman winked. "You might be surprised to know some of my own secrets."

Sita couldn't help but smile. She didn't know what to say. Up until this point, she had been convinced that everyone would react the same way Krishna and his family had. It had never occurred to her that people might be understanding and empathetic.

"I only wish that Krishna felt the same way," said Sita, almost whispering.

"He will come around in time," replied Mrs Shrestha. "He told me he'd visit you at the hospital. In fact, he may have already done so."

"I will believe that when I see it. I hadn't heard from him for over a week before I came here. I told him before we got married that I had a troubled past. While I never went into any of the details, he kept saying over and over again that it didn't matter to him. He even promised to always stay by my side, no matter what happened. And yet he abandoned me that day, like a rat scurrying off a sinking ship. He never even gave me a chance to explain what really happened."

"Give him time, Sita. He is confused. Men are very simple creatures when it comes to such things. He doesn't know how to make sense of this unexpected news. His mother, it seems, has a great deal of influence over him still."

"But I told you, he knew I had something bad happen to me."

"Yes, but he never would have imagined it was something like this. He said he'd come to visit you. When he does, you can explain everything. I know he will understand."

"I'm not sure I ever want to see him again. I'm so hurt and so angry with him. I still want to die. My feelings have not changed about this."

"Don't say such things, Sita!" Mrs Shrestha insisted. "You have so much to live for."

"Like what? My brother and sister hardly speak to me anymore. And I know they will turn on me when they hear the news, even though everything I have done has been to support and protect them. Medical care and schools ... And as for my husband, he has abandoned me. No, I have nothing now, and I deserve no less."

"What about me? You thought I'd feel differently about you, and what happened? You have a job waiting for you, and you have many people who love you, Sita. All of the customers keep asking where you are. They want to know when you are coming back."

"They wouldn't feel that way if they knew what I was."

"And what do you think you are?"

"I'm a whore."

"Sita, I am going to say this one more time. You're nothing of the kind. You have to find a way to forgive yourself for whatever happened in your past. In life, we're all given second chances. That is the beauty of life. We can constantly improve ourselves, reinvent ourselves and move on. You are a lovely, intelligent, capable young woman. You have so much to offer this world. Please stop focusing on what you think is wrong about yourself and begin giving yourself credit for what is honestly good and right. There is so much of that."

Sita didn't say anything for a long time.

Finally, she sighed and said softly, "I think I need to get some rest."

"All right, then I will go now, Sita. But I will return this evening. Please think about what I said. I love you. You are so dear to me." Mrs Shrestha leaned over and gave Sita a long hug.

As Mrs Shrestha was leaving the room, Sita whispered, "I love you too."

The following morning, there was another knock on the door. Sita opened her eyes. Krishna stood in the entry, holding a small bouquet of white roses, her favourite flower. He gently placed them on the table next to the tiger lilies, staring at her with a look she couldn't interpret. Was he still angry? Did he despise her? For that matter, did she despise him? The only emotion clearly present in his eyes was sadness.

Moments passed, with only silence permeating the small white room.

Just seeing him there, the overwhelming urge to hold him, to kiss him, to be with him was so strong, she wanted to leap out of bed and fly into his arms. Something inside her cracked open, the love she felt for him poured out. She saw it in his eyes too, but he held it back. His love for her was guarded now. There was a spark of anger as well.

Once again, she wished she had succeeded in ending her life. If she had died on that busy street, she would not be faced with Krishna's accusing eyes and further rejection.

"How are you feeling, Sita?" Krishna finally asked, his voice distant and strained. His eyes were now focused on the floor.

"How do you think I feel?" Sita replied angrily. "Hurt, and not just by the car."

"I...I am sorry about everything."

"What happened to you? Your family viciously attacks me, and you just watch like a complete bystander? You did nothing! You said not one word in my defence." Tears streamed down her face.

"I'm sorry," he stammered. "I didn't know what to do when..."

"You're ashamed of me, embarrassed that I'm your wife! You knew I had a past. I told you many, many times. Yes, I sold myself. Yes, I was a prostitute. I did this to save my sister. She was dying, and we needed money for her operation. It was the only way I could help. It was that or her death. I chose to save her life. What would you have done if it were one of your own?"

"I didn't know. I..."

"You can't look at me, can you?"

Krishna turned and stared directly at Sita for several seconds, but then looked away.

"Get out of here, you weakling!" she ordered. "I don't ever want to see you again."

"Sita, don't say this to me," he replied, finally walking close enough to take her hand in his. "I'm so sorry for what happened. I just froze when I heard the news. I wanted to help you, but I couldn't move." There was a long pause. "You're right, I have been weak. But I still love you very much, Sita."

"You *still* love me? If you loved me so much, why didn't you come to our apartment? Where were you? I died a thousand deaths waiting for you. I needed you so much. Never in my life have I needed a person more. Don't you know how much I love you? Don't you know how hard this has been for me? I cannot undo the things that have happened to me."

"I'm so sorry."

Some errant instinct made her long to comfort him, but she held herself back. Her chest hurt, and she struggled to breathe.

"I'm afraid that being sorry is not enough. I tried to kill myself. I only wish I had been successful. You can't even look at me without turning your eyes away. What does your 'feeling sorry' do for us and our marriage? Knowing what happened to me in a previous life has poisoned you against me. I can sense it in your voice. If I were able to see your heart, I'm sure I'd see it there as well."

"You have to give me time. I need to sort this out. I..."

"My love for you has always been unconditional. I have never even asked you about your past or past lovers. Love is not based on 'sorting something out.' If you feel this way, then we have nothing left. I slept with men for money. I did it not because I wanted to, but because I had to. There is no changing this reality. If this bothers you now, then you will always be bothered by this, Krishna. It will always be something that stands between us. We can never be more than a tainted, watered-down version of what we once were."

Sita stopped talking. Whether she had convinced Krishna or not, she had convinced herself.

"I want you to leave now."

"When can I visit you again?" asked Krishna. "We have so much more ..."

"Never," she screamed. "I want you out of my life."

"But why, Sita? We are man and wife."

"Man and wife? You betrayed the bargain we had."

"What bargain?"

"What bargain?" She sat bolt upright, her head pounding at the motion. "You promised that you'd stay by my side, no matter what! For me, this was the most fundamental basis of our marriage. I needed that security. It was something I had not had since my parents were murdered. And what did you do? You allowed me to walk away. You allowed your family to say terrible things to me, things that were cruel and hurtful. And after all of this had happened, you did not even bother to come and see how I was. I cannot give my love to you again. In fact, I have stopped loving altogether. I will close my heart to anyone and everyone. Now leave." She crossed her arms over her chest to emphasise her point.

"I only wanted a little time..."

"Now you have plenty of time. Leave!" she demanded, turning on her side to face the wall.

Krishna tried again to plead his case, but he received no response. He bent to kiss her cold wet cheek and reluctantly left the room.

Sita slept the rest of the day, too depressed and defeated to open her eyes. The following day Mrs Shrestha came again, this time with samples from their vendors to distract her. And Dr. Hussein stopped in the following evening, though Sita had been certain it was her day off. Despite herself, she was feeling better. The storm of depression and humiliation was subsiding. In its place, a thundercloud of anger was forming.

But while this rumbled away inside her, she was not sure who it should strike. Krishna? Chandra? Who had seeded this cloud? It seemed the anger had always been inside her, only now she was able to see it clearly, to hear it. As her days in the hospital turned to a week, her thoughts kept returning to one person in particular: Mr Khan, her father and mother's assassin. It was he who had stolen her parents away, extinguished her youthful dreams and cheated her out of her happiness. It was he who had caused her life to take so many tragic turns. Taking away her beloved Krishna seemed to be the final blow that cracked the shell containing her fury.

Armed with righteous anger, Sita concluded a simple truth—her life was over. All good that could possibly come from it was spoiled by this one event that took place so many years ago, altering the course of her life forever. In some ways, her destiny had been sealed by that one act of double murder. The more she thought about it, the more she realised that the only way to undo this destiny was to go back and get rid of the source of all of her pain and suffering: Mr Khan. Only his death, his blood, could wash away the evil that had permeated her life. He must pay for what he had done. Until he did, she could not hope to go on with her life, she could not hope for change.

Three days later, Sita was released from the hospital. Mrs Shrestha had brought her a new sari to wear, but the cloth hung on her. She'd lost a lot of weight, her skin looked sallow, the circles under her eyes nearly black. Her hair, part it how she might, would not cover the shaven area of her head. Mrs Shrestha patted her shoulder, caressed her hair.

"You'll be looking like yourself soon enough," she assured Sita. "And don't worry about the medical bill. I'll handle it."

Sita, lost in thought, came back to the moment. "Absolutely not. I will pay it. I just need to go to the banque."

Mrs Shrestha looked her over, then decided not to argue.

After completing this task and insisting to Mrs Shrestha that she could get herself safely home, she walked up to a barber who cut hair on the street and asked if he'd shave her head.

"No. Absolutely not. What will your family say? They will think you have gone mad. They will blame me for doing this." As he spoke, he stepped behind the simple wooden bench on which his customers sat and on which the battery-operated hair trimmers were laid. Did he think she was going to attack him?

He shooed her with both hands, and, when this didn't work, he began gathering up his tools as if to make her think he was packing up for the day.

"There is no family. Here," she held out a hundred-rupee bill. His lips pursed in a moment of serious deliberation. Then he nodded, took the bill, and sat her down. After placing a bandage on her stitches with a careful hand, he set about cutting her hair as quickly as he could. When he was done, he offered her a small hand mirror. A grim smile stole across her face. She looked fierce, like some sort of warrior.

As a final gesture of defiance, she went to a local bazaar and purchased three 120-rupee saris, all made from simple white cotton. These were the traditional outfits worn by Hindu widows.

She went home. The balconies that lined her apartment building looked the same as they had a week and a half ago. Laundry waved on the slight breeze. Her immediate neighbour's potted plants still looked green and lush, despite the heat. In the stairwell, she could still hear the old woman singing in the first-floor apartment as she cooked.

Upstairs, her apartment smelled awful. The furniture, once welcoming, seemed soulless and inanimate. The wedding photos mocked her. The Ganesh fountain had run dry and now made an awful sound as the pump regurgitated air. She unplugged it, then changed into her new white cotton sari, carefully folding the one Mrs Shrestha had given her. If all went well, maybe one day she could wear it again. In a new life.

The trash was rotten and fly-infested. She emptied the contents of the fridge into the bin, then carried it out to the alley. On her way back, she encountered her next-door neighbour in the hallway with her little boy. The woman stared as Sita kept her eyes straight ahead. Only as Sita opened the door to disappear into her own space was the silence broken. The little boy spoke, as the door was closing, "Mama, you did not tell me that a goddess had moved in next door."

20

Mr Kumar was sitting alone in his study, quietly reading the newspaper when Sita followed his bearer into the room. The space around him was filled with an impressive collection of elaborately carved traditional Northern Indian furniture and antique miniature paintings.

"Excuse me, sir," stated the bearer politely. "This woman keeps insisting that she see you personally. No one else would do. I told her you were busy, but she walked right in!"

Mr Kumar looked up from what he was doing. His glasses hung down at the end of his nose as he peered above the frames.

"Sita. Of course, come in," he said, nodding to the bearer that he should leave them. He neatly folded the paper and placed it aside on the desk.

"So, what happened to you?" he asked with a warm smile. "Did you find religion or something? You look like a nun."

"It's a very long story," replied Sita, hoping to avoid a lengthy explanation.

"I heard you got married some time ago. Congratulations. I guess you no longer work for me."

"Yes, I did marry, but it didn't work out. My past got in the way."

"I'm sorry your husband wasn't more understanding," he replied. "So what can I do for you? Do you need money?"

"No." She paused, and he waited patiently. "I need a gun."

"A what?" He cupped his ear with his hand, as if he might have misheard her.

"A little gun, one that will fit into a handbag."

"What do you want with one of those?" he asked, surprised.

"I have decided to go to Mumbai and kill M.S. Khan. Once he is dead, I will then go after the others if I can."

"What others?"

"The other men who helped him to kill my parents."

"And why, Sita, do you want to do something like this after all these years?" He leaned forward, revealing how much more his crooked back had twisted since she'd last seen him. His black eyes were solemn, the skin around them like crepe paper. His hair, still thick, had gone entirely steel grey.

"They ruined my life. Because of Mr Khan, my parents are dead, my youngest brother Ganesh was taken away from me, and the rest of my family has suffered great hardship. Now my husband has left me. Everything bad that has ever happened to me and my family happened because of Mr Khan. He has to face some justice for what he did to all of us." Sita paused before asking her next question. "Would you be angry with me if I were to do this to him? I know that you were once friendly with this man."

"It would make no difference to me. But you will never be able to get close enough to him to take a shot. He is always heavily guarded by many bodyguards. I can assure you that you will die if you try to carry out this plan of yours."

"I don't care. My life means nothing to me anymore."

"You should forget about him. He is getting older. Like us all, he will not live forever. Life is taking its own toll on him, believe me. He is not a happy man."

"He may not be happy, but he is breathing. That is intolerable to me. I cannot forget about him. Two weeks ago, I tried to kill myself. I failed. When I was lying in the hospital bed, I decided the only thing left to do was to even the score with this man, to see that he never does to anyone else what he has done to us. This would finally give my pathetic, ruined life a purpose."

"Like I said, you will never be able to get close enough to him."

"I must try. Will you help me?"

"No, I can't, Sita. I have always liked you. I don't want you to do something that will bring about your death. This idea of yours is foolish. We can never even scores, my dear. We can only live our lives the best we can and enjoy what days we have."

Sita stood and began to walk out of the room.

"Where are you going?" asked Mr Kumar, surprised by her abrupt departure.

"If you won't provide me with what I need, I will just go onto the street and find someone who will," replied Sita. "If I can't get a gun there, then I will use a knife or a rock or anything else I can find."

"Sita, come over here and sit down next to me," said Mr Kumar in a fatherly tone. "Please, just for a few minutes."

Sita reluctantly did as she was told.

"How old are you now?"

"I'm nearly twenty-one years old."

"When did your parents die? Six years ago? Eight years? My memory is not what it used to be."

"Seven years ago."

"That's a long time. Can you read?"

"Yes."

"Can you write?"

"Yes."

"Have you ever had a legitimate job before, something other than sex work?"

"Yes."

"Then why are you doing this? You have your whole life ahead of you. You can't transform the past. There is nothing you can do to change all of the bad things he has done over the years. No one can. Even if he were in his grave, your past would still be your past. And like I said, Mr Khan is getting older. In time, he will give up the business. Then someone else will take his place. It's just the way life is. You cannot kill everyone."

"My father died trying to put that man in jail. My father was a good man, a committed man, a man of principles. All of that was taken away from him, and from me. Look at me now. I am nothing. I am less than nothing. The only way I can add any meaning to my life is to see that this person is finally brought to justice. Since it will never happen in the courts, I will play by his rules."

"Sita, forget it. Even if you succeed in somehow killing him, they will shoot you on the spot. You would be throwing your life away."

"My life has already been thrown away. So will you help me?"

"I don't..."

"Please? I'm going to do this whether you help me or not. Please do me this one favour. I beg you."

Mr Kumar waited for a long time before answering, turning his chair toward the window and steepling his fingers thoughtfully. He finally stood and picked up two pieces of paper from his desk. He wrote something on one of them and handed them both to Sita.

"Write your address on the blank sheet and give it to me. You will have what you need by tomorrow afternoon. When you arrive in Mumbai, call the number on the other sheet and tell them who you are. They will provide you with a time and a date when you might be able to carry out your plan. This will at least give you a fighting chance."

"How much do I owe you?"

"Nothing. Consider it a favour from me. You can do me one someday if you ever return. And I will hold you to this."

"Thank you," said Sita, walking over and kissing the old man on the cheek.

"You know that I am not much different from Mr Khan," he confessed, as he walked over to pour himself a drink. "I'm sure that there are a few Sitas out there who feel the same way about me. Am I going to someday be on your list of people to be taken down, should you succeed in eliminating Khan?"

"No, you are not like him at all."

"I'm not sure about that, Sita. If I had been him, I might have done the same thing to your father. The world I live in has its own set of rules. We all live and die by them. Up until now, I have been very lucky."

"Then I guess it is a good thing that you are not him," replied Sita, with a smile. "Or else, it would be you I am going after. Don't worry. You have helped me out several times in my life. I don't care what you are or have been in the past, I will always consider you a dear friend."

"Do I have your word on that?"

"Yes, you have my word. And unlike my husband, I keep my word."

The following afternoon, Sita received a box tied with string. Inside she found a layer of Bengali sweets. Beneath them, the gun lay nestled in packing strips. It was delivered to her apartment by a messenger who also handed over a note urging her to reconsider. Within the lower compartment of the box, her friend had included a small container of twenty bullets and a set of instructions on how to safely load, aim and fire the pistol.

With her menacing new gun in hand, Sita packed up a small bag and prepared for her long journey southwest from Delhi to coastal Mumbai. She had to leave quickly, before she lost her nerve.

Before leaving, she sat down and wrote a series of letters to those who had been important to her in her life. She thanked Mrs Shrestha for being such a good friend and for standing by her side. To her brother and sister, she wrote long, extended letters describing everything that had happened to her after Chandra had become ill. She told them in plain language how she was forced to sell her body to get money for the operation and how not telling them had affected their relationships. She also repeatedly told them how much she loved them both. For her husband, Krishna, she prepared a detailed accounting of everything that happened to her from the moment her parents had been killed to the present day. She described the factory they were forced to work in, the one that he helped to shut down. She detailed the time she spent with Maya and the travellers, the job at the school, their escape after Nasir raped Chandra and then all of the details concerning her entry into prostitution. In an attempt to be honest and transparent about everything, she even described that she had slept with Raju at the hotel two weeks before. This was to be their final communication, and she wanted to leave nothing unsaid.

The final note was sent to Mr Sarcar at the boys' school. In this message, she thanked him for offering her a job and for allowing Ravi to attend classes there. She apologised for not saying goodbye to him when they'd slipped away into the night. Since she didn't want to get Chandra into any trouble, she did not mention the incident with Nasir. She felt she didn't have a right to do that without Chandra's permission. It was her story to be told or kept secret.

For some, these letters were meant to set the record straight and to allow Sita a chance to express her deep love and affection. For others, they were meant to express how grateful she was for their help. Since she was convinced that she would not survive her assassination of Mr Khan, she wanted to leave with a clear conscience. This last attempt at honesty helped free her mind to concentrate on her upcoming mission.

Having completed this task, she dressed in her white sari and went straight to the train station. As she began this final journey, the sounds and smells of the train brought back many memories of their late-night escape from Pune. She could feel that the ending of her life was near. This time, she was more than ready.

21

Upon arriving in Mumbai, feeling surprisingly rested and calm, Sita took out the contact number given to her and made the call.

"Hello, is Mohammad there?"

"Speaking."

"My name is Sita. I was told by Mr Kumar to call you upon arriving in Mumbai.

"Where are you staying?"

"The Rose Garden Inn. Do you know where that is?"

"Yes."

There was a long pause.

"What do I need to do?" Sita inquired.

"Nothing. Just wait for me to get back to you. I will call in a couple of days. Just be patient."

The phone went dead with no pleasantries.

Not knowing when the call from her contact might come, Sita seldom left the room. The hotel was old and crumbling, built around a courtyard with neglected, half-dead plants. There was no air conditioning, and the open windows brought in the conversations of those passing by. She lay in bed, on the rayon bedspread printed with elephants, and used the time to think about her life. While much of the week before had been spent focusing on her feelings of anger, betrayal and hatred, here, beneath the rattan blades of the ceiling fan, she recalled the good things that happened in her life. She recalled long forgotten childhood memories, the period of freedom she had spent with Maya and the various adventures and mishaps that had taken place while she was working at the school. She even recalled some of her customers who had been kind to her over the years and how many of them seemed more interested in the affection and intelligent conversation that she offered than the sex.

Despite these warm memories, she was resolved to kill Mr Khan. Of all the things she had ever done in her life, this act would be the most important. It would be a watershed moment, one that would wash clean a lot of the stains on her life. She needed to do this for her parents, for Ganesh and for all those whose lives had been destroyed by his hand.

Nearly a week passed by with no word from her supposed contact. A thousand times Sita reached for the phone, then stopped herself. He'd told her to be patient. She just hoped that her friend hadn't tricked her and was just waiting for her to cool her heels so she would forget about her mission.

On the eighth day, there was a knock at the door. When she opened it, the doorman handed her a small envelope, bowed politely and backed away.

Sita closed the door and read the note several times:

The person you are seeking will be at the Mandarin Chinese Restaurant on Gulshan Avenue between 9:00 and 9:30 p.m. this Friday. He will be with his family. Make a reservation for yourself at 8:30 p.m. When he arrives, there will be only a few of his men present. This is one of the few times when his guard is down. Through the kitchen, there is a back door that will allow you to make an escape. Good luck.

Sita studied the note, her pulse quickening. It was Thursday. Her waiting was nearly over.

She picked up the weapon and checked again to see if it was loaded. She then raised it up and aimed it in the direction of the mirror. Her scalp was still almost bare, just the barest fuzz shading it. Her eyes, large and almond-shaped, didn't flinch from the sight of the barrel pointing at her.

The next evening, Sita arrived at the restaurant at exactly 8:30 p.m. As requested, she was given a small table near the kitchen. Knowing that this might be her last meal, she ordered two of her favourite dishes: egg fried rice and chicken with cashews. She also ordered a beer to calm her nerves.

When Mr Khan entered the room, the full strength of his presence was immediately apparent. He and his family took the place by storm, conversing loudly with one another, as if they were in their own home. The table reserved for them was in the centre of the space, not far from where Sita was seated.

Mr Khan looked much older, and the years had not been kind. He no longer had the appearance of strength and power that she remembered. It was disorienting, watching this faded old villain play the role of the loving family man.

From where Sita was sitting, she could easily see Mr Khan at the head of the table. It looked as though the gathering included uncles and aunts, along with his own adult children and grandchildren. There were at least twenty family members in all, and the table spanned the entire width of the dining room. The mood was lively and festive, as amusing statements were made by the children that caused the entire group to laugh as one.

The blood of her parents was on his hands. Yet he laughed fondly at his granddaughter, then kissed his wife on the cheek.

She shook off her confusion. It was time to make her move. While the presence of his family members added a disturbing element to the task, she might never get a chance like this again.

With her right hand firmly grasping the pistol under her shawl, she began to walk in the direction of the Khans' table. With her white dress and shaved head, she should appear harmless enough to Mr Khan's bodyguards, who were positioned strategically throughout the room.

Sure enough, they ignored her. She managed to get within two metres of Mr Khan. His back was to her, making an ideal target. But when she willed her arm to rise and line up the shot, it remained frozen by her side. She had dreamt about killing this man, dreamt of watching his body twitch in a pool of blood. But now, when the moment finally presented itself, she could not do it. Her own father's death had devastated her. She couldn't curse the children at this table with a vision that would haunt them all their days.

Several family members looked over at her. Moments later, everyone, including Mr Khan, turned to see what this strange woman was doing standing behind him, staring.

Noticing them watching her, Sita finally smiled, nodded her head and then walked away. A moment later, the conversation was up to full steam again as the family continued to enjoy each other's company.

Sita paid her bill and left, passing by the Khan family one more time on her way out the door. They had no idea that a violent death had almost ripped their world apart.

22

Mr Kumar's servant led her out to the veranda this time, which overlooked the gated garden. Beneath the four-metre-high stone walls, Mr Kumar's greyhounds chased one another around a rose garden.

"I'm very surprised to see you again," said Mr Kumar, who greeted Sita with a pleased smile. "Your hair is growing back. And that sari is very becoming on you," he said, nodding at the beautiful turquoise cloth that Mrs Shrestha had brought her the day she was released from the hospital.

The servant motioned her to a throne-like chair, then poured them both tea from a steaming metal samovar. She cradled the delicate cup in her hands, punishing herself with the scalding heat.

She waited till the servant had left, then said, "I was in the restaurant, standing just a few feet away from him. I could have easily walked up and killed him. But I couldn't do it. When I looked at his family sitting around that table, I kept remembering how I felt the night I witnessed my own mother and father being killed. I couldn't do that to these people. I just couldn't."

"And what if those others had not been there, could you have done it then?"

"No, I guess I will never be a killer."

"So, you are a pacifist," replied Mr Kumar with a smile. "That is not such a bad thing to be. We need more people in this world like you. Perhaps we'd be much better off if this were the case."

"But being this way does nothing to bring this man to justice. It is eating me up inside. For weeks now I have been obsessed with this idea of forcing him to pay for his deeds. I had my chance, and I let it slip between my fingers. I will have to always live with this regret."

"You should not give up so easily, Sita. Consider another approach. Killing him is only one option. In some ways, if you had done this, it wouldn't have brought justice to Mr Khan. It would have been revenge. There is a big difference."

"What do you mean?"

"In a so-called civilised society, justice comes from taking a person to court and trying them in a formal setting. This is what your father did with Mr Khan. If a person is convicted in this formal setting, then this is justice. Like I said, killing him would have merely been vengeance."

"What are you suggesting?"

"Why not take him to court and try to get a conviction against him?"

"That would never work. No one wants to take on a case like this, it's too dangerous. Look what happened to my father. Besides, it's an old case. Who would bother with something like this?"

"Why don't you do it," Mr Kumar suggested.

"Where would I find a willing barrister?"

"I'm not suggesting that you find a barrister, I'm suggesting that you become a barrister."

"I can't. I haven't attended school for many years. I can't go back now, after all this time."

"Why not? You're a brilliant young woman. All you'd have to do is get into a university, finish your course work and then enter a good law school. With your passion and initiative, you'd shine above the rest."

"I can't get into a law school without any formal schooling. It takes many years to complete these studies."

"Didn't you once tell me that you and your sister home-schooled yourselves when you were working at the boys' school?"

"Yes, but..."

"What class did you get up to?"

"Class 12."

"Then I am sure you'll be as good as any other student, merely a few years behind, that's all."

Inside the house, a phone rang, and she heard the soft murmur of the servant's voice taking a message.

"But you need excellent test scores," she said, resuming her argument. "A person needs to compete to get a placement. There are thousands of young people out there vying for only a few seats."

"I wouldn't worry about that. I can get you a placement into any university you choose."

"How can you do something like this?"

"Just because I'm involved in organised crime doesn't mean I don't know people who are not involved in what I do. My daughter went to law school. At the time, I offered a handsome donation to the school. She wasn't much of a student. But she graduated with honours and is now practicing law in Calcutta. I'm very proud of her."

"Does she know what kind of business you do?"

"You mean does she know I'm a criminal? Yes. But I'm still her father. Unlike other bosses, I will never pass my present business to any of my children. I will hand it off to someone else. My family is going straight. I don't want my sins to be on their heads. But like you, I had nothing. Like you, I lived off the street. My mother was a prostitute like you and my father a pimp. Until I was seven years old, I never owned a pair of shoes. Two years later, with both my parents dead from tuberculosis, I was alone in this world. I worked my way up through the system. I have made it this far without a single day of school. But now I am on the top. Most people assume that I am an educated man. And I am. I'm self-educated. I learnt how to read and write on my own. I read hours every day, much more than so-called educated people. I'm sure I know more about this world than the average university professor. Education does not always have to come formally. It's what you make of it."

"But what about money? There's no way I could pay for this. I still have to support my brother and sister."

"If you had followed through with your plan to shoot Mr Khan, you would be dead now. How were you planning on supporting them under this circumstance?"

"I have set aside some money in savings. It is enough to cover at least another year of school for them both. At some point they need to be on their own. They have been too dependent on me."

"Don't worry about the money then. I have so much money, I don't know what to do with it all. I'll pay for everything."

"I don't understand. Why would you do this for me?"

"Because I like you. And I've come to really dislike Mr Khan. It used to be that the bosses of the big cities worked together. We had our own code of conduct. But over the years, Khan has abandoned any presence at civility or humanity. I wouldn't mind him spending some time in jail." He paused for a few moments, watching the greyhounds. The dogs had stopped running some time ago and now lounged in the shade. Somewhere close by, a peacock screeched.

Mr Kumar sipped his tea. "Perhaps another reason is that I myself have done many bad things to people. When a person gets older, they begin to think about these things with regret. Maybe by helping you, I can somehow balance the books a bit."

"I understand. But I can't do this. I don't want to do this."

"Sita, you are forgetting something."

"And what is that?"

"When I agreed to provide you with the gun, I said you'd owe me a favour. Remember?" His smile held a hint of something dangerous. "Well, I've now decided that this is what I want from you. You will go to law school and then convict Mr Khan in a court of law. You owe me. And I expect you to honour your commitment." His tone had become harsh, brutish. His business voice, she suspected.

"Are you really serious about this?"

"Absolutely serious. But first, some changes must be made. First, we have to make sure that there is no connection between you and me. This could discredit you in the future. Second, what name are you going by now?"

"Sita."

"I mean your full legal name. What is your husband's last name?"

"Dutta.'

"This is what you need to do. Have your name legally changed from 'Sita' to 'Seeta.'

"Why?"

"It will allow you to answer to your own name without suspicion and at the same time, make it harder for anyone to make a connection. They are the same name, just spelled differently. And continue using your husband's last name. From this day forward, your name will be Seeta Dutta. Do you understand?

"Yes."

"Are you sure?"

"Yes."

"If you are going to eventually file a case against Mr Khan, he must not suspect that you are the Sita Sharma who escaped from their little fire. The moment he does, your life and the lives of your brother and sister will be in grave danger. This information has to come as a surprise very late in the process, if at all."

She nodded, slowly. "That much, at least, should be easy enough. From now on, my name is Seeta."

"Good, then we have a plan."

"But the rest, all the schooling, I have to think about..."

"Stop thinking so much," Mr Kumar cut her off, setting his teacup down with a sharp rap. "Let me do the thinking on this one. You owe me a favour. This is what I want. Like I said, I expect those who owe me to pay up."

His idea had appeal. It just seemed impossible. Finally, she nodded. "Do you think it will work?"

"Yes. I have no doubt in my mind. The next semester starts in about two weeks. This is excellent timing. I'll make some calls immediately. You'd better start making plans. You're going back to school."

23

Mr Kumar came through with his promises. Within a week, Seeta had a letter of acceptance from the university inviting her to begin attending classes in five days. The school was small but very prestigious and conveniently located, not far from the centre of Delhi.

Walking into her very first class, Rhetorical Argument, it was obvious that she would not be blending into the student body. Surrounded by classmates in blue jeans and T-shirts, her sophisticated Indian ensemble stood out. She was better dressed, in her opinion, but she certainly felt less prepared. When the professor gave them the syllabus, Seeta flipped to the list of related reading on the back, wondering how many of these titles she could finish by the end of the week. Her fellow students stuffed the syllabus into their binders, sketched in their notebooks as the professor lectured, stole moments to flirt with one another when he wrote on the chalkboard. Seeta kept her attention rigidly focused, taking notes the entire time. The others were fools to waste this opportunity. They didn't know how quickly fate could turn the wheel.

At the end of class, a girl approached her, a small flier in her hand.

"There's a party in my dorm this evening, if you'd like to come." She gave Seeta a curious but friendly look.

Seeta looked it over, briefly tempted, then handed it back. Mr Kumar had made a huge investment in her. He'd have a low opinion of her partying it away. "Thank you, but I need to study."

The girl handed it back. "You might finish early," she said.

Seeta was touched that she was making this effort. "I took some time off, between studies. I really have to catch up."

The girl simply nodded. "Well, good luck. I'm sure you'll be caught up in no time."

By midterms, the girl had proven to be right. Seeta was at the top of almost every class and enjoying it. Her main concern was just that Mr Khan would die before she had the chance to convict him.

When she wasn't studying or working, she spent much of her time researching the important crime figures that ruled the biggest cities throughout India. She spent hours in the library poring over old newspaper articles and magazines. This research helped her understand how the course material she was learning related to the case she wanted to one day bring against her parents' killers. While Mr Khan and his associates were often cited in newspaper articles, Mr Kumar was also regularly mentioned. The media portrayed her benefactor as a cold, calculated mobster with a "hollow soul." Try as she might, she couldn't reconcile this version with the man she knew.

At the start of her second semester, Krishna readily agreed to meet her for lunch.

"Chang's?" he suggested. Their old favourite.

"How about Samosas?" Seeta countered. The cafeteria-like atmosphere was better suited to the conversation she had in mind.

They met the next day, the bouquet of purple orchids he brought distinctly out of place in the cavernous room of long, stainless steel tables. It had been months since she'd seen him; he was thinner, his smile uncertain. They ordered at the counter and sat down to wait.

"I'm glad you finally decided to see me," he said. Their food was delivered then, in a desultory manner.

"Binod is doing well in school," he said, falling back on his old habit of filling the silence. "He's being offered a place at a better school, his test scores were quite high."

She merely nodded.

"And how is Ravi? Chandra?"

She dunked the samosa in mint sauce, though she had no intention of eating it. "Well, so far, I've bailed Ravi out of jail twice this year. He's dropped out of school, found some hoodlums to run around with and started drinking and shooting drugs." She glared at him, as if this too were his fault. She took a deep breath. "Chandra is doing fairly well. She says she's forgiven me. We talk now and then, but there's still a lot of distance between us."

"Give her time. You two will be close again, I'm sure. Everything can be mended with time."

Seeta stared at him. She knew what he was doing.

"And Ganesh?" he prompted when the silence had gone on too long.

"I've hired a private detective in Mumbai. I can't pay him much, so he's working on the case part time."

Krishna reached his hand toward hers. "Let me pay for it."

She pulled her hand back, rested it in her lap.

"I thought you should know that I changed the spelling of my name. I am now Seeta, not Sita. Also, I'm going to law school."

Conflicting emotions played across his face. "Law school? That's great, but why change—"

"I want a divorce." She hadn't intended to just blurt it out, but there it was. The real reason they were having this awful lunch.

His expression closed, the light in his hazel eyes dimmed. "No. We're not getting divorced. I'm not giving up on us."

"You gave up on me once, that was enough. I can't take another betrayal."

"I wouldn't—"

"How can I ever believe you?" she asked, tears threatening.

"Darling—" Krishna visibly sagged as she stood up. "We're not getting divorced," he reiterated.

She hurried out, leaving the bouquet on the table. It would all have been so much easier if she didn't still love him.

The four years required to finish her Bachelor of Law degree and the All-India Bar Examinations went by very quickly. By taking extra courses and attending classes over summer breaks, she was able to complete her degree a year and a half early. After graduating at the top of her class, she took her exams and was quickly hired as an assistant public prosecutor in New Delhi. Unlike her initial placement into the university, she managed to get this job on her own, without the help of Mr Kumar. She took great pride in this personal accomplishment. Perhaps she did deserve to live. Thoughts of suicide receded, only pricking at her in her darkest moments.

Within a short time, Seeta became an important player in the public prosecutor's office. Often taking the cases that no one else wanted, she began to develop a reputation as someone who was hard-working, committed and always compassionate. One of her most often remarked upon characteristics was her vociferous quest for fair play and justice, not always based on the laws themselves but on what she believed qualified. She judged every case not just on the facts but also on the conditions that lead up to a crime being committed or reported. For example, when it was clear that someone of influence was wrongly accusing someone else, she was not afraid to speak out against this in court. As a result, more than a few of her cases were thrown out, despite tremendous political pressure being applied.

While most successful barristers were men in their middle age, she was never intimidated by them. To her, what a person said and did in court was all that mattered, certainly not their age or gender. It was their performance that she valued, not whether they were male or senior or somehow well-connected. She expected no less from others. While there had been many before her who had tried to maintain this level of indifference, most failed. She pulled it off by never involving herself in office politics and never taking sides.

While her unwavering integrity was highly respected by most of her colleagues, it also made her a target among some who liked to cut corners. She made them look bad. She could not be bought or influenced, which constituted a real threat in their minds. On several occasions, she went after law enforcement officers and politicians who had been caught accepting bribes or using their influence on behalf of criminals. While most of her colleagues turned a blind eye to these cases, based on her own personal experiences, she would not allow it. This made her very unpopular and even feared among those within the system who chose to break the law.

One Friday afternoon, Seeta received an urgent message stating that the chief public prosecutor himself wanted to meet with her immediately. She grabbed a handful of her current files and raced down the wood panelled halls to his office.

"Seeta, please sit down," said the prosecutor as he removed his glasses and placed them on his desk. With his silver hair and chiselled features, he had a look of integrity that instilled confidence. Most days he wore a warm smile. On this occasion, his expression indicated that he had something very serious to discuss.

Without hesitation, she took the seat.

"Seeta, I don't know how to say this. So I will just come out with it. Two days ago, I received an anonymous letter stating that you once worked as a call girl here in Delhi. While I do not believe that this is ..."

"Excuse me, sir, for the record, it is true," she replied, without allowing him to finish his statement. She made this confession matter-of-factly, as if she had nothing to hide. "When I was much younger, I found myself in a situation in which I was forced to sell myself to survive. This went on for a number of months. I did this discreetly and was never arrested. It was not by choice. It was by necessity. I cannot change the fact that this happened, so I will not try to do so."

There was a long pause in the conversation. He looked dumbfounded.

"Unless there are any more questions about this matter, while I have you here, sir, could we talk a bit about the Sunil case?"

"Excuse me? But...well, I suppose."

"When I went through the case folder, I realised that the witness list was incomplete. When I went to..."

After spending a half-hour discussing the details of several of her cases, Seeta left the prosecutor's office. The subject was never brought up again.

One afternoon, Seeta was sitting at her desk reviewing the list of upcoming cases on the roster when she noticed a familiar name: Sangeeta Banik, the woman who recruited her into the sex trade. She froze, with a cup of tea halfway between the desk and her lips. She set it down with a splash and hurried down the first-floor hallway to her colleague's office.

"Kisan, do you have a few minutes?" asked Seeta, with the case list in her hands. He sat before his computer, several to-go containers scattered across his desk. Kisan was about her age, and though he'd worked at the prosecutor's office much longer, he didn't seem to care that her career was taking off faster. A round-faced man with little ambition, she suspected his mother had expected him to become a barrister, and he'd never thought to do otherwise.

"What do you need?" he asked, seemingly pleased to be interrupted.

"Can you tell me about this case involving a woman named Sangeeta Banik?"

"Sure, she was arrested on solicitation charges. She is an older lady."

"Are you the one handling this case?"

"Unfortunately."

"Is this her first offence?"

"No, if I recall correctly, she had a couple of other charges against her. When she was much younger, maybe sixteen, she was arrested for the same thing.

That time it was something to do with a hotel. There may be other charges as well."

"Where is she now?"

"She's still in jail. She wasn't able to find anyone to get her out."

"How long has she been there?"

Kisan picked up a file and scanned it. "Nearly ten days."

"She has been in jail all this time on a mere solicitation charge?" asked Seeta. Prostitutes were normally booked and released within 48-hours.

He continued scanning the file. "No, she also has a drug charge. When she was picked up, they found some heroin in her possession. The last time I saw her, she was in pretty bad shape. The withdrawal had her trembling from head to toe."

"Do you mind if I take this case off your hands?" asked Seeta.

He looked as if someone had just announced a holiday he'd forgotten about. "Please, be my guest! I would consider it a favour. I am overwhelmed with so many other things," he said, with a vague sweep of his hand that seemed to take in both files and food containers. "What do you want in return?"

"Nothing."

"Then it is all yours. Thank you."

The interview space at the jail was tiny and very cramped, with only a small table and two wicker chairs. She waited for the prisoner to be brought into the room, her heart filled with vengeance. She could taste the poetic justice that went along with this accidental discovery. She couldn't wait to see the expression on Sangeeta's face when she learnt who was prosecuting the case.

But when Sangeeta entered the room, Seeta hardly recognised her. Once a woman with poise and refinement, Sangeeta was now reduced to nothing more than a scaffold of bones draped with folds of skin. There were dark circles under her milky eyes and hair much akin to mop strings, it was clear she was suffering from some insidious illness.

The officer escorted her to a chair. The prisoner glanced at her visitor for a moment before turning away.

"Hello, Sangeeta. Do you remember me?"

She looked up and carefully inspected Seeta's face for several seconds before barely shaking her head "no." Her hands trembled as she held them clasped in her lap.

"It was not so long ago that I worked for you. My name is Sita Sharma. Do you remember me now? My sister needed an operation, and you gave me the money? That is when you made me...That's when I started to work for you."

Sangeeta looked up again and met Seeta's eyes. This time her memory served her.

"What are you doing here?" she asked, appearing confused.

"I am now working in the public prosecutor's office. I am the one who will try your case in court. Your life is now in my hands."

"How...what...?"

"Yes, despite the terrible things I might have done in my past life, I was able to go back to school and become a prosecutor. And now, after all these years, I am trying a case against you. Isn't life amusing?"

"So, I guess this is your chance to get back at me," Sangeeta mumbled, her head lowered.

Seeta had mentally prepared herself to take on the brash, arrogant madam she had once known, not some ailing and pathetic drug addict. She had worked out in her mind what she was going to say. Now, she was at a loss for words. To buy herself time, she opened up Sangeeta's file and began to study it carefully.

"Tell me something, what happened to you when you were sixteen?" asked Seeta. "Your file says that you were arrested on a solicitation charge for the first time."

"Why do you want to know about that?" Sangeeta asked, embarrassed. "That is ancient history. Who cares?"

"I'm just curious."

"I don't want to talk about it. That was a long time ago. You'll only use it against me."

"Just tell me. I promise, I won't do anything with this information."

Sangeeta sighed, as if too tired to argue. "I was working in a brothel that got raided," she finally replied with a soft voice. "Because of my young age, I was taken away from that place to a government 'remand' home. There, I was repeatedly used by one of the guards. When I threatened to tell on him, I was let go and then immediately arrested again on some phony charges. They had me in that awful jail for nearly three months. At the end of this time, they sent me back to the brothel. It was all for nothing."

"Who sent you back?"

"The police. They sold me to another madam, one they controlled. I watched as the money changed hands."

"How did you originally end up in the brothel?"

"What difference does that make?"

"I want to know," Seeta replied, suddenly seeing a different side to this woman. Her sense of compassion was beginning to overshadow her anger.

"I was tricked into it. I went with a friend to audition for a part in a movie. At least, that's what I thought we were going to do. When we arrived at the place, they forced us both into a car and drove us to a brothel."

"How old were you then?"

"Fourteen."

"You couldn't get away?"

"No. We were locked up in small rooms for many months. They said they'd kill me if I tried to run off."

"So how did you eventually come to be a madam?"

"I spent many years in the brothel. In time, I became clever. To pay me back for the life that was taken away from me, I decided to get as much out of people as I could. Why shouldn't I do this? Everyone had cheated me. It was my turn to get something back. After a while, the madam and some of the others who worked for her noticed me and gradually helped me to move up in their business. For a long time, I was on top."

"So what's wrong with you now?"

"Nothing."

"I don't believe you." Seeta reached out and grabbed Sangeeta's arm. It was covered with track marks. "How long have you been using?" She knew a few things about drugs, having watched her brother's slow descent into addiction.

"What are you talking about?"

"How long have you been shooting up heroin?"

"I don't use drugs!" Sangeeta snapped, folding her arms away and pouting.

"Stop playing silly games with me. When did you start using?"

There was a long pause. Sita could sense that she wanted to talk about this with someone.

"I used pills for a long time. I only started using heroin about eighteen months ago," Sangeeta finally confessed, still looking at the floor. "I met a man. We became lovers. He was the one who gave me the drugs at first. Within a short time, I couldn't get along without them. They've ruined me, but I can't stop. I lost all of my girls. I couldn't manage them anymore. The money started to dry up. When I reached a point where I had nothing else to sell, I tried to sell myself. That was when I got caught. They found..."

"What did they find?"

"Nothing, I have already said too much."

"How can I help you if you don't answer my questions?"

"Why would you want to help me after what I did to you?"

"Because you saved my sister's life," replied Seeta, surprised at the words even as they came out of her mouth.

"You don't feel angry that I made you enter the sex trade?"

"Yes, of course I do. But at the same time, you told me from the beginning what I would have to do. It was I who decided to accept your money. At least you offered me an option. There were no others willing to do the same for me. Chandra is alive today because of this. I cannot deny that."

Sangeeta studied Seeta for a long time, not knowing what to think. Finally tears started rolling down her face.

"I have to get out of here," said Sangeeta, grabbing Seeta's hand. "I will die if they send me back to jail. I am sick and weak. They will prey on me like cats with a skinny mouse. Please help me!"

Seeta stared at this woman, another ghost from her past who she had hated for so long.

"I'll make a few calls. Maybe I can get you into one of the treatment centres. That would at least keep you out of jail. But if I do this, you have to promise me that you'll stay at the centre the entire four weeks."

"I will. I can't do this anymore. I want out."

"And what will you do after you've been released?"

"I will go and stay with my sister. She's the only one in my family that knows what's happened to me. She will help. I just need some time to pull my life together again. I need another chance."

"Okay then. I'll see what I can do. I will do this once and only once. Do you understand me?"

"Yes, I understand. Thank you. Thank you."

After calling in a few favours, she was able to admit Sangeeta into a treatment facility. She had successfully convinced the court officers that the woman was not fit for trial in her current condition.

A full month passed, and Sangeeta made it successfully through the full programme, but after her release, she disappeared. Seeta never heard from her again.

After two years of applying for a position at the public prosecutor's office in Mumbai, Seeta finally got her wish. This time, she wasn't sure if she got the position on her own or whether Mr Kumar had used his influence once again. Having mentioned her frustration to him over the phone a week earlier, she'd received the letter in the mail two days later. She suspected that it was not happenstance but wasn't about to question her luck.

While the idea of leaving Delhi after all these years was very troubling, there was no other choice. It was time to fulfil her ultimate destiny. She'd never given up her hope that she'd one day be able to take on Mr Khan in a court of law.

The two months that followed were filled with a series of tearful send-off parties given by those who had become very fond of Seeta. She was surprised by the number of people who made a special effort to offer kind words on her behalf. The experience only added to the confidence she had slowly built in herself, brick by brick.

The person most affected by her departure was Krishna. Over the years, while they had remained husband and wife on paper, they had never returned to living under the same roof. Over time, they'd managed to become friends again. On some level, Krishna understood Seeta's need to sort out her past. Patient by nature, he'd vowed to wait as long as it took, always hoping that one day she would return to him as his wife. Their final goodbye kiss was tender, lingering longer than either of them expected. Seeta broke away when her old passion for her husband began to tug at her.

After saying many tearful goodbyes to her colleagues, friends and family, she embarked on the next chapter of her journey. Upon arriving in India's business capital, having retraced her previous path, she quickly located a small apartment on the third floor of a three-family building. The space had a large comfortable sitting area, a single bedroom and a small kitchenette. Since she had been accustomed to living a simple lifestyle, she did not require anything else. It was time to begin her new life in Mumbai, and the less distracting amenities, clutter and luxury in her life, the better.

24

During her first week at the Mumbai prosecutor's office, Seeta made it clear that she was very interested in going after the high-profile criminals. Since many of these people were connected with specific political parties or somehow insulated from police scrutiny, most were considered untouchable. Instead, those who were arrested and prosecuted often included lower-level henchmen who took the fall for their bosses. Even in these cases, they seemed to fall into two basic categories: those that were politically hot and therefore potentially damaging to a barrister's career or those that were high-profile and somehow acceptable because the accused was considered dispensable by the criminal network. Because Seeta was too junior to be assigned the higher-profile cases, she was forced to focus on the "less sought after" ones. While this came with its own set of baggage, it allowed her to gain valuable experience and collect useful information about the city's crime syndicate hierarchy and infrastructure.

During the first eight months, Seeta found the work to be unrewarding. Her immediate supervisor felt that she was too aggressive in her approach and totally oblivious to the "big picture." This was his way of telling her that she couldn't simply go after connected people because there would be political consequences for them all. While she regularly argued with him about these things, she was seldom able to make much headway.

Her fortune changed when her supervisor was promoted to a higher position in another department.

She was reassigned to work directly under Mr Chetri, the chief public prosecutor himself. Having followed her progress from the time she arrived, he had been impressed by her commitment to the law and her indifference to the politics. This change in assignment allowed Seeta direct access to the person in charge and helped her gain status among her colleagues. While many tried to endear themselves to Mr Chetri, by not playing this game, Seeta was selected over all the others primarily because he admired her independent spirit.

As the months passed, Seeta nurtured a close working relationship with her new boss. She often anticipated what he wanted, providing it before he knew himself what he needed. This made her so indispensable that he seldom did anything or went anywhere without her by his side.

The weekly staff meeting that Friday afternoon was finally coming to a close after nearly two hours of detailed discussion. The long wooden table was littered with notes and sweating beverages and almost everyone was gathering up their papers or looking at their watches. Outside, the sky was blue and mild, fall having arrived earlier in the week. Everyone seemed eager to get outside and enjoy the fine weather. She couldn't blame them, yet Seeta left her agenda and files spread open.

"Okay, I have one more agenda point before we break up," said Mr Chetri as he studied his notes. "Over the past three weeks, I have received a number of phone calls from high-level elected officials. They're complaining that we're not doing enough to go after organised crime. This is an election year. They want publicity to help themselves in the polls." He smiled, then shrugged. "Or perhaps they are finally serious about changing the image of this town as crime central. Stranger things have happened. Whatever the case may be, they want us to do something about this, and soon. With that in mind, I want you all to review your cases to see which ones we can focus on so that we can give the impression that we are aggressively fighting crime in this city. If you know of any other way to help me respond to this issue, please send me a memo or bring it up during next week's meeting. That's it for this week." He tossed everything inside his briefcase and snapped it shut.

While everyone else bolted from the room, Seeta remained behind.

"Mr Chetri, do you have a few minutes for me?"

"Not really, Seeta," he replied, looking at his watch. "I have an appointment in about twenty minutes."

"I want to talk to you about an idea I have for a high-profile case."

He stopped what he was doing and gave her a sharp look. She hadn't quite managed the neutral tone she'd hoped to achieve.

"You have one in mind."

"Yes."

"A big one."

"Yes, very big. But I'd prefer to discuss this in your office if you don't mind. It needs to be handled confidentially."

"Very well. You have ten minutes."

Mr Chetri and Seeta moved to his private office and closed the door. She sat in a green leather chair and took a deep breath.

"Did you ever know a prosecutor named Prakash Sharma?" asked Seeta, already knowing what his answer would be.

"Of course. He and I graduated from the same university, one year apart. We worked on a number of major cases together, including the one that he won right before he was killed in that fire. Why do you ask?"

"Because I think Mr and Mrs Sharma's death could be your big case."

She had his full attention, his dark eyes boring into her. In the silence that followed, the heavy Friday evening traffic filtered through. In the distance, she could hear the train whistle.

"Their deaths were accidental."

"They were not accidental. They were murdered."

A troubled expression crossed his face. "That's not what the investigation concluded."

"I know this, of course," she said, trying not to lose her patience. "But didn't you feel it was a bit strange that he suddenly died the night after convicting the notorious Raju Khan?"

"It could have been a coincidence," he replied, almost wishfully.

Perhaps he'd had to believe as much to be able to go on with his own work prosecuting criminals, to not quit in fear of what might happen to him and his own family. Softening her tone, Seeta said, "Off the record, didn't many people find it bizarre the way he and his family died?"

He nodded, clearing his throat. "There was talk, but they never found any conclusive evidence."

"If someone were to provide proof that it was not an accident, that it was a murder, would our office investigate it?"

"Of course! But do you really have evidence of foul play?"

Seeta looked at the jade plant on his desk rather than him. "An eyewitness saw the murder take place."

"What did this anonymous source say really happened that night?"

"Four men entered Mr Sharma's home," replied Seeta, a slight tremble in her voice. "In their living room, both Mr and Mrs Sharma were beaten and tortured before being stabbed to death. This was done to pay him back for his role in the conviction. But before they could go after the children, all four of them were smuggled out of the house to safety. They did not die."

"The newspapers all reported they were killed in the fire, along with the nanny."

"They never found any of their bodies," Seeta countered. "One of the newspapers tried to explain that this was because several explosions and the intensity of the fire had destroyed all evidence of them. But we both know how unlikely that is. They didn't find the bodies because the bodies were not there."

"You're telling me you believe the children all survived? And could be witnesses?"

"Yes."

"Are you sure about this?"

"Absolutely."

"But what happened to them? Why didn't they ever surface?"

"They were afraid to come forward. All this time they have been hiding from the men who killed their parents."

His desk phone rang, they both jumped a little. He made no move to answer it.

"Who supposedly carried out this crime?" he asked, when the call had gone to his answering service.

"The actual murder was carried out by Mr Khan himself."

"Which Mr Khan?"

"The brother, Mr M.S. Khan."

"What?" asked Mr Chetri, shocked. "You're telling me that he went to Mr Sharma's home himself and killed these people, and someone actually witnessed this?"

"Yes, he did it, along with someone from this very office and two policemen, or men wearing police uniforms. He is a very proud man. He wanted to do this job himself. It was his way of getting revenge."

"Who was it from this office?" Mr Chetri's eyes bulged, and he leaned over the desk. He'd run a hand through his steel grey hair, which now stood straight.

"Mr Khanna."

He exhaled audibly, then sank back into his seat, shaking his head. "He's retired now. Everyone knew he was corrupt, but I never would have imagined he'd be involved in a murder. He had a stroke nearly a year ago and can't move the left side of his body."

"I know that too."

"Seeta, I'm finding this all very hard to believe. Tell me, who is this so-called witness?"

"One of the daughters – the eldest."

"Are you absolutely sure that it's her?"

"I'd bet my life on it."

"What is her name?"

"Same as mine—Sita."

"And where is this namesake of yours now?"

Her heart was pounding so hard she was afraid her boss could hear it. She was afraid she might pass out.

"Well, where is she?" he demanded.

"Actually, she is standing directly in front of you, sir."

"Excuse me?"

"It is me. My name is Sita Sharma, daughter of Prakash Sharma. I was the one who witnessed the murder."

Mr Chetri's mouth opened, but no words came out. Then, after a few moments, he picked up the phone.

"Nila," he barked at his secretary. "I want you to cancel all my appointments this afternoon. Everything. I do not want to be disturbed for any reason. I don't care who it is."

"Does anyone else know about this?" asked Mr Chetri, hanging up the phone. "Anyone at all?"

"No," she lied. "You're the first person I'm telling. For a long time, I've wanted to see Mr Khan go to jail for what he did to my parents. That's why I became a barrister in the first place. Based upon what you said today in the meeting, I decided to take a chance and tell you about this case. The timing feels right. I only hope I haven't made a huge mistake and misjudged your passion for justice."

Walking over to the coffee pot, he poured them both a cup, then settled in his chair like he planned on being there quite some time. "I want you to start from the very beginning. I need you to tell me everything, every tiny detail: what happened to your folks, what happened to you and the rest of the family, everything. We have as much time as you need. No one will disturb us."

For the next four hours, Seeta described the entire story of her life from the age of fourteen. She talked about what happened that night, how she and her brothers and sister had fled, what they did to survive; everything. She even told him about her work as a prostitute. Knowing that all of the facts would someday come out anyway in trial, she decided to be totally transparent with Mr Chetri. The only details she did not talk about were her associations with Mr Kumar. This was something she felt could never be acknowledged. No one would understand, and it would put him in jeopardy.

"So do you think there is much of a case here after all these years?" asked Seeta.

"I can't say for sure," replied Mr Chetri honestly. "This happened a long time ago, and you were the only eyewitness. Seeta, Mr Khan is one of the most powerful men in Mumbai. After what he did to your parents, do you really want to take the risk?"

She sat up straighter in her chair, her jaw tight. "I have waited for years to bring him to justice. Now is the right time. I want to try this case, Mr Chetri. I need to do it, and I deserve the chance."

"He'll attack your character. This business about you working as a prostitute will ruin your credibility in court. And when it gets into the newspapers, and it will, it could ruin your career. The general public can be very judgemental."

She looked at the red carpet on the floor, tracing the geometric flower with the toe of her shoe.

"I know all of this," she said, more softly. "But I don't care. I am determined to see this through to the end. Please, let me do this."

"When his people find out you're still alive, they may come after you and your family."

"I have a plan to deal with all of that."

The overhead lights dimmed, it must have been after nine. Far off, a lone pair of high heels clicked down the hallway towards the lift.

"You do realise that you can't try this case if you're the primary witness."

"Well, yes and no. I'd like to begin trying the case and then, when my identity is revealed, I'll hand it over to a second chair. I've figured out a way to avoid revealing my identity until after the trial starts. You must understand. I've been thinking about this for a long time now."

"Your chances of getting a conviction on this are very slim."

"I know. But whether we win or not is of no consequence. Mr Khan will get justice. Because of his nature, he can't help but pay the consequences for his actions. I can promise you that. So, Mr Chetri, will you allow me to move forward on this case?"

"Slow down, Seeta. I can't make a decision like this on my own. Losing a big case like this could damage the credibility of our entire office. Not to mention putting all my people at great risk. Can I speak to Mr Roy about this? He was a close friend of your father. He is a man of integrity and a great barrister."

Seeta nodded, and Mr Chetri called him. He'd left the office but said he'd come back.

"Seeta, I have to agree with Mr Chetri," said Mr Roy, shaking his head. With his long silver mane, he looked like an old lion. "The only evidence is your own eyewitness account which is tainted by many things: your age at the time of the supposed crime, the time that has passed, and your bias. Based on what you've told me, I think they would rip you apart on the stand. He has the money and the power to not only win this case, but to crucify you."

"Mr Roy, you were my father's friend, weren't you?" asked Seeta, struggling to stay calm.

"Yes, I was. He was a great man. I also remember you as a child."

"What do you think he would have done in a situation like this?"

"We both know the answer to this question but he was a man. I do not..."

"You answered my question," replied Seeta, holding up her hand and not allowing him to finish. "Someone must investigate this case. If this office doesn't agree to move this action forward, I will file it myself, not as an assistant public prosecutor but as a citizen of India. Either way, the case will be submitted for consideration."

"But what…"

"Please, Mr Roy. I know you mean well, but you have to stop making excuses. I know what I'm doing. Mr Khan must pay for his crime. And one way or another, he will. I have a plan to move this process forward. I have always had a plan. Let's talk about it, shall we?" She'd regained control of herself, so she held her chin up. The men turned to her, ready to listen.

At the end of a lengthy discussion, it was decided that they'd move forward in initiating a case. The men were far less convinced of success than she was, but she had made her case. They were left with no further grounds for objection.

The three of them began to meet regularly in various locales outside the office. From the first meeting, it was decided that there had to be two basic elements: strict confidentiality with no leaks and as much evidence as they could possibly gather. Every step in the process was done according to the letter of the law, with an emphasis on total secrecy. To prepare for the case and to make progress, they gave themselves a time frame of two months.

25

Seeta was struggling to finish some paperwork at home one night. The secondhand lamp she'd bought had begun to flicker some hours back. Now her eyes were tired, and she had a splitting headache. It was nearly eleven o'clock, and she needed another two hours to complete the task at hand. The carved bench she sat on, with its silk tufted pillows, had never felt so comfortable. The urge to lie down for just a moment was overpowering. They had only a few days left to file the formal charges against Mr Khan, and it seemed they'd never get everything done. The phone rang, startling her.

"Can I please speak to Seeta?" The man's voice sounded familiar, but she was too tired to place it.

"Speaking."

"It's me, Ramesh from Mumbai, the private detective. How are you doing?"

"Ramesh! It's been nearly a year. What's this about?"

"I sent two letters to you in New Delhi, but I never received a reply. I only found out you were here in town today." He paused. She could hear the smile when next he spoke. "I have some good news for you."

"Are you serious? What kind of news?" She so rarely got good news, there must be some mistake.

"During one of my last visits to the private schools, a nurse who works in a clinic told me she had a birthmark match. After I went and checked it out, I'm convinced that this one is genuine."

"Really?" Seeta stood. Tears immediately began to stream down her face. "Do you have a name and an address?"

"Yes. Jasmin and Kamal Jain. They live near Juju Beach at 1432 Hyderabad Road."

"Are you sure it's the right family?"

"Yes. Everything seems to check out perfectly."

"Did you talk to them about this?"

"No. I wanted to wait until after I spoke with you. I know it is a very sensitive matter."

"So they don't know anything at all?"

"Not from me."

"I can't believe it, after all these years."

"Sorry it took me so long. It was kind of like finding a tiny minnow in a giant pond filled with minnows."

"It doesn't matter. I'm so excited, I'm trembling all over."

"Well, after all you've been through, it doesn't surprise me. What do you want me to do now?"

"Nothing. If you don't mind, I'll take it from here. I've noted down the name and address. Thank you so much. I will always be indebted to you for this. Always."

After hanging up the phone, Seeta called the station house and told them she was a public prosecutor. Not willing to wait another minute, she immediately made arrangements with the police to have them pay a visit to the Jains on the following day. She wanted them brought into the police station for questioning.

"The Jain family arrived a few minutes ago," stated one of the police officers after entering the office Seeta was occupying within the station house. "Where would you like me to put them?"

"How many are there?" asked Seeta. She sat bolt upright in the metal rolling chair, fingers tapping nervously beneath the desk. She had not slept a wink, yet she was wide awake.

"Three. Father, mother, and their son."

"Place them inside interview Room 2. Tell them that I will be there shortly. And I also want you to make sure

I have Room 1 open as well. I need them both over the next hour or so."

Little waves of electricity shot through her. She had been waiting for this moment for many years, and now it had finally arrived. She stood up, straightened her sari, and took a deep breath. It was time.

"Hello, Mr and Mrs Jain, thank you for coming in," said Seeta, as she entered the small interview room. Her three visitors were huddled close together at one end of the table. "My name is Seeta Dutta. I am one of the assistant public prosecutors, and I work here in this station."

The couple sitting across from Seeta appeared totally out of place in the station house. They were both in their late thirties, dressed as though they had just returned from a formal reception. The woman had well-coiffed black hair down to her shoulders. Her wide-set eyes looked intelligent, the smile lines around her mouth gave her an air of approachability. She reminded Seeta of one of her favourite professors. The father was older by a few years, still handsome, though a bald spot was appearing on the crown of his head. He had a concerned look that consumed all his features as he waited for someone to explain the meaning of this unexpected summons. They were obviously unaccustomed to dealing with the police.

Sitting between his parents was a boy of fifteen years. He was tall for his age, and thin, with light brown eyes like their father's. Seeta searched his face for other signs of their parents, but he was his own person, a unique blend of characteristics. From his lanky appearance, it looked as if he was just beginning to grow into his body. His adopted parents each held one of his hands, the three of them comforting one another in a way that spoke volumes about their happy home life.

"Please, Mrs Dutta, can you explain the meaning of this visit to us?" asked the father. His tone was reasonable, though grave. "My family and I were having breakfast at a local restaurant when your two officers approached us and insisted that we come with them. They wouldn't explain what was going on."

"Before I answer your questions, I'd like to ask a few of my own if you don't mind," said Seeta in a cold voice. Every now and then she'd glance over at the boy, trying to reconcile the teenager she saw before her with the infant she had carried away from their home. Her mind was filled with a jumbled mixture of elation, anger and love, all competing. At any given moment, one of these feelings predominated in her mind.

"Certainly, anything," replied the father, politely. He said it humbly, seeming as though compliance was very much a part of his nature.

"Is your husband's name Jamil Jain?" asked Seeta, addressing her questions to the mother.

"Yes, that's his name."

"And is your name Jasmin Jain?"

"Yes."

"And what's your son's name?"

"Kamal Jain," replied the mother looking up at her husband with anxious eyes.

"Tell me, how old is your son?" asked Seeta, without taking her eyes off the boy. He kept looking back and forth between his parents.

"He's fifteen years old, going on sixteen."

"And where was he born?"

"Mumbai. Why are you asking us these questions about our son?" asked the mother. She squeezed his hand with both of hers, leaning against him as if scared someone might try to pull him away.

"Please, just answer my questions."

"I'm sorry. Certainly."

"What is your son's birth date?"

"March 11th."

"Are you certain of this?" asked Seeta, looking up to gauge her answer. Once again, her eyes remained fixated on the boy.

"Yes."

"Mrs Jain, did you deliver Kamal yourself?" As Seeta was asking the question, she began to wonder if she should discontinue the interview until after Kamal had been removed from the room.

"No, he was adopted," she offered freely.

"How old was he when he came to live with you?"

"We believe he was approximately eighteen months old," she answered, with tears in her eyes. "Why are you asking me these questions about my son?"

Kamal freed his hands so he could wrap his arms around his mother.

"If you don't mind, I think we should continue this talk in private. There is a room next door where Kamal can wait."

"But what..."

"Please, I think it is for the best."

"Very well," said Mr Jain. "Kamal, I want you to go next door while your mother and I sort this out. We will be there in a short while."

"I don't want to leave you," he replied, stiff with fear. "Please don't make me go."

"You must. Don't worry, we'll sort this out. Everything will be fine." Mr Jain placed his hand on his son's head and gently stroked the boy's hair. It was then that Seeta noticed the swirl of hair, the unruly cowlick that had always stuck up on the crown of Ganesh's head.

"Take him to Room One," Seeta said, trying to hide her emotions. The guard who had been standing inside the room quickly escorted the boy out.

"Well, let me explain myself," said Seeta, as she turned towards the parents. "I am investigating a case that goes back many, many years. A small baby named Ganesh was kidnapped and sold to an adoption agency, the same one that you used to adopt your 'son'." She made quote marks in the air, and her voice dripped with sarcasm.

"Are you saying that you think our son was this kidnapped boy you are referring to?" asked the mother, horrified.

"That is what I'm trying to determine here, Mrs Jain."

"How could this be?" she asked, appalled by the accusation. "We went through the formal adoption process. We even used a barrister to ensure that everything along the way was done legally. You must be mistaken."

"Did you meet Kamal's birth mother?" asked Seeta, as she studied every aspect of the parent's response.

"Yes, her name was Mrs Guha. She said she had several other young children and couldn't take care of yet another. She herself signed all the papers. Our barrister was present when this took place. I'm sure it was all legally done."

"How could you be sure she was the mother?"

"I...I guess because the child was with her. She said it was hers—who would lie about such a thing?"

"Well, for your information, Mrs Guha is presently in jail serving a ten-year sentence for seven counts of child exploitation. For many years, she was a human trafficker, buying and selling children for profit."

The father leaned forward, covering his eyes with his hands.

"What...what would happen if my Kamal was found to be this baby you referred to?" asked the mother.

"I can't say for sure. But there is a chance that he might be taken away from you."

Hearing these words spoken, both parents began to cry.

"I think I should consult a barrister," the father said, a gleam of defiance in his damp eyes. "No one is going to take my son away from me."

Seeta held her hands up, placating. "If you don't mind, before we take this complaint any further, I'd like a chance to talk with your son alone for a few moments."

"Why would you want to do something like that?" enquired the mother. "He will not remember anything that happened back then. He was only an infant. What could he possibly tell you?"

"I just want to talk to him. It is not my intention to break up this family. We are just carrying out an investigation into a possible allegation. I am just doing my job."

"Will this help?" asked the father. "You talking to him?"

"Yes, it will."

"Then go ahead. We have nothing to hide. Whatever it will take to sort this out, we will do it. But you have to understand, no one is going to take our son away. He is our life."

Seeta entered the other interview room. Kamal was sitting in the corner, his head lowered, his feet tapping nervously.

"Hello, Kamal. My name is Seeta."

He did not respond. Instead, he sat there with his legs bobbing back and forth under the chair.

"Kamal, how old are you?" asked Seeta with a warm smile. Her little brother was finally here.

"My mother already told you that. I am fifteen," he replied with his head still lowered.

"Can you do me a big favour and lift your left shirt sleeve so that I can see your shoulder?"

"Why do you want me to do this?" he asked shyly, placing his hand over the exact spot.

"I just want to see something. I promise, it will not hurt you. Please?"

Kamal used his right hand to slowly pull his sleeve up to expose his shoulder. Seeta immediately recognised the red birth mark that resembled the shape of India. She had finally found her Ganesh.

Her first impulse was to take him into her arms, but she restrained herself. This gesture would only frighten him. He had no idea who she was.

"Kamal, are you in school now?" asked Seeta, with tears running down her cheeks.

"Yes, I attend class nine," replied Kamal, taken aback by her reaction.

"Do you like school?"

"Yes, very much."

"What do you like most about it?"

"Playing cricket with my friends."

"Are you a good player?"

"Yes, I am one of the best players on the team. I'm also the captain."

"And where are you living now?"

"We have a house outside the city."

"Is it a nice house?"

"Yes, it's very big. I live there with my parents, two uncles and my grandparents."

"Are there any other children?"

"Yes, my three cousins."

"Did you always know that you were adopted?"

"My parents told me when I was very little."

"Do you know anything about your mother or father?"

"No, just that my mother was too poor to take care of me. I never knew anything about my father."

Seeta had to stop and turn away to compose herself. For a moment, a wave of love for her parents passed through her body. While it lasted only a millisecond, its residual effect lingered on.

"Do you ever think about her? I mean your mother?"

"No, I have my mother. I don't need another one. Can I see my mother and father now?" asked Kamal, anxious to end the discussion.

Seeta did not respond at first. She wanted the moment to last forever. Having finally found him after all these years, she wasn't sure what to do next.

Should she confess to the parents that he was her long-lost brother? Should she insist that he come live with her? Should she go after the parents legally for their role in his being kidnapped and taken from her? As she stared into the boy's eyes, she sought answers to these questions, wondering also if he would despise her for taking him away from the only parents he remembered.

"Please, can I go be with my parents?" asked the boy with a hopeful expression. He stood up in anticipation.

At that instant, Seeta had her answer.

"Kamal, can I ask you a big favour before I bring your parents back inside the room?"

"What do you want?"

"Can I have a hug from you? Just a small one?"

"A what?"

"A hug. If you give me a hug, I will bring your parents in here now and you can go home."

For a long time, he stood there not knowing what to do. The request seemed so awkward and out of place, he couldn't bring himself to do it. Understanding his hesitance, Seeta walked over and wrapped her arms loosely around him while he stood as stiff as a stick. Feeling his heart beat against her chest, Seeta lost all control. He awkwardly patted her back, waiting for her to calm down.

A few minutes later, they returned to the room where his parents were waiting.

"Thank you for allowing me to talk to your son," said Seeta as she wiped the tears away. The parents looked from her to their son, more confused than ever.

"What do we have to do now?"

"Nothing. I have reviewed the facts and have decided that there is no need to pursue this matter any further. You are welcome to leave now. However, I do need you to promise me that if you ever decide to leave this area that you report this to me directly. Do you understand?"

"What about the person who made the complaint? Are you certain that this won't come up again?"

"All I can say is that there is no chance that your family will ever be split apart. You have my word. But having said that, I might need to meet with you from time to time. It is just part of the routine follow-up process."

"Are you sure about this? We don't need a barrister?"

"No, as far as I'm concerned, this case is closed."

"Thank you very much," said the father as he shook Seeta's hand vigourously. "Thank you."

After the family left, Seeta sat down and cried. As much as she wanted Ganesh back in her life, it would be selfish to try to insert herself into his world. He was fifteen years old and in a loving, caring family. He had his school and his friends; he didn't need confusion and upheaval in his life. And with the case against Mr Khan coming up in a matter of days, she didn't want to do anything that might put Ganesh in danger.

She'd had a chance to see him. She'd had a chance to hold him. She knew he was all right. This would have to be enough for now.

26

When Mr Chetri felt that the time was right, a formal complaint against Mr M.S. Khan was finally made to the magistrates' court with two complainants: Sita Sharma and Mr Sushanta Gurung, the night guard who had once worked for the Sharma family. Seeta had been able to locate him in Mumbai with the help of Ramesh, the private detective. Since he had once worked for the government as a security guard within a health post, he received periodic cheques from the district. Knowing this had allowed the detective to track him down quite easily. They'd found him working as a night guard for a small garment factory.

Having been a heavy drinker and smoker throughout much of his life, Mr Gurung was in very poor health when they found him. While he was initially opposed to getting involved in any case against Mr Khan, Seeta explained that all he had to do was hand over some documents to the court and then make one very brief statement on the stand. In exchange for this, she promised to provide him with free medical care and medicine, along with a sum of money to help him to return home to his ancestral village immediately following his part in the trial. She also appealed to his sense of responsibility to the family that had employed him for so long, by helping to put their murderer behind bars. He finally agreed.

To protect him, throughout the process he was taken to a secluded hotel and guarded 24 hours a day. Since Seeta couldn't submit the papers herself without revealing her own identity, Mr Gurung was given this task. The idea was to have Sita Sharma be a complainant but to have her remain a mystery to everyone until the trial actually commenced.

After the complaint was officially filed, a petition was granted by the Judge to move forward with the case. Because of the person being accused and the nature of the case, instead of sending a directive to the concerned police station to carry out the usual investigation, the higher court appointed its own investigator to perform a judicial investigation. This was rare, but sometimes done with sensational cases. Once completed, the results were passed on to the district court.

After reviewing the findings, the District Judge agreed to file the case against Mr Khan, and a set of charges were detailed. To avoid complicating the trial, it was decided that the three other Defendants would be approached only after Mr Khan's case was completed.

The day the arrest took place, Mr Chetri made sure that reporters had been tipped off and were on hand to photograph the event. Mr Khan was picked up at the Mandarin Restaurant while he was enjoying a convivial meal with his family. He was so infuriated by this insult that it took four burly policemen to prevent him from attacking the arresting officer. It was a bonus for the prosecutors that when he was arrested, Khan was concealing an illegal weapon, adding to the charges against him.

This unprecedented event made it onto the front page of nearly all the local newspapers and a few of the national ones as well.

As the days built up to the trial, Mr Khan's team of high-priced barristers did everything they could to locate Sita Sharma and Mr Gurung, but with no success. Since most people believed that Sita and her siblings were deceased, there was a lot of speculation in the papers as to whether or not these mysterious witnesses were real or imposters. Many doubted their existence and believed there was a vendetta being staged against Khan. This just added to the suspense that surrounded this case.

The trial began midmorning on a Friday. Approaching the Mumbai High Court for the first time since her return to Mumbai, Seeta's knees were weak. The last time she had walked across the oval lawn toward this building, she'd been fourteen, walking beside her mother. The Gothic building, with its conical towers and mansard roof, was just as forbidding as she remembered. The dark, massive structure seemed to dare anyone to question the justice dispensed within. Seeta prayed that justice would be on her side.

The interior was as she remembered it, the clean white walls lined with pointed, arched windows. The long wooden benches, filled to capacity with reporters and spectators, reminded her of church pews in a cathedral. Mr Roy had arrived already, and he waited on one side of the great dais on which the Judge would sit, in a carved wood throne. On the other side were Mr Khan's four legal representatives. Two of them were well-known in the legal field and considered major players. Mr Khan joined them, escorted in by an armed guard.

"Miss Dutta? I am from the Delhi Post." A woman appeared from nowhere, walking alongside her, a small microphone in hand. "This is a huge case, can you tell us why you, a junior prosecutor, have been entrusted—"

Another reporter, a man, accosted her from the other side. "Did Prakash Sharma actually survive the fire?"

Seeta ignored them both and passed into the area reserved for those involved in the case. A bailiff stepped in front of the wooden gate she'd passed through, cutting off the reporters.

Upon the Judge's entrance, everyone in the room stood as protocol required. The man had a stern face and completely white hair, despite not looking much past fifty. His reputation was good, he was said to be fair. After he sat down, those who had seats followed his lead.

To begin the proceedings, the case description was read aloud, and the proceedings started. After making their opening statements, during which the prosecution promised conviction and the defence promised acquittal, the testimony of witnesses commenced.

"Good luck," Mr Roy whispered.

Her hands were shaking, her cheeks burning. She took a breath and stood. It was time.

"If it will please the Court, I would like to call upon our first witness, Mr Sushanta Gurung."

A moment later, Mr Gurung timidly shuffled through the door and up to the polished mahogany witness box. She'd been surprised, seeing him for the first time after so many years. As a child, she'd thought of him as a large man, but time had diminished him. Time and alcohol. He was rail-thin now, except for an enormous paunch, and his shoulders sagged. His greying moustaches were yellowed from constantly smoking hand-rolled cigarettes, the whites of his eyes yellowed as well. Liver cirrhosis probably. She was fortunate she'd found him in time.

"Would you please state your name for the Court's records?" asked Seeta.

"My name is Sushanta Gurung."

"Mr Gurung. Could you please explain to the Court your association with the Sharma household?"

"I used to be their guard when they lived in Pune."

"How long were you employed by the family?"

"Nearly five years."

"During this time, did you have an opportunity to get to know the family well?"

"Yes. I was provided a small room on the compound, so I was there most of the day ... almost all the time."

"Can you tell me what happened the night of September 13th, 1988?"

"The night of the murders?"

"Yes."

"Objection," yelled one of the Defence Barristers. "I ask that the Court strike this statement. It is misleading. There is no evidence that a murder ever took place."

"Sustained," replied the Judge. "You may proceed, Mr Gurung, but limit your responses to the facts."

"Yes, sir. Well, Sahib had a big party that evening. There were many people attending from his office. They all came to celebrate Sahib's big court victory. Everyone seemed happy. I remember it well."

"What happened then, after this party took place?"

"After everyone left, I went to my room to sleep."

"And what time was that?"

"It was a little past 1:00 a.m."

"Then what happened?"

"Later, in the middle of the night, four men came to the house."

"Do you recall what time this was?"

"It was about 3:30 a.m."

"Did you let them into the compound?"

"No, the gates were locked, I always made certain of that. It was my responsibility. They came in somehow by themselves but made enough noise that they woke me."

"Did you know who these men were?"

"One of them I did recognise. He was a regular guest at the house."

"Could you please tell the court the name of this person?"

"His name was Mr Khanna. He worked for Sahib's office."

Upon hearing this statement, the audience erupted in conversation.

"Silence," said the Judge, as he banged his gavel.

"What about the other three men?" asked Seeta, having waited for the room to quiet down.

"One of them I also knew, but from the newspapers. His name is M.S. Khan. The remaining two were police officers who I had never seen before."

"And how do you know they were police officers?" Seeta asked.

"Because they were wearing uniforms," he answered, as though that should be perfectly obvious.

"Do you see any of these men sitting in the courtroom today?"

"Yes, the one over there, that's Mr Khan." He pointed a bony finger at the Defendant.

Upon hearing this, the audience erupted a second time. Mr Khan smiled coldly, undaunted. Mr Gurung's finger trembled.

"Silence, silence," ordered the Judge, banging his gavel repeatedly. "If there is one more outburst like this, I will clear the room."

He waited for compliance before nodding to Seeta to continue.

"Can you tell me what happened after that?" asked Seeta. "What did these four men do?"

"About twenty minutes after those men arrived, Nilopha, the nanny, came to her window and asked me to get a ladder and come up. I thought it was a funny thing to ask me to do, but I did it anyway. After climbing up to the window, she explained that Sahib and Madam had been murdered."

"Why did she ask you to come up there?"

"She wanted me to help her save the children. All four of them were hiding in her room. She gave me some money and told me to take them to New Delhi to meet Sahib's sister."

"How did you get the children out of the house?"

"They climbed out the window and then down to the ground. I then took the four of them through the park and over to the train station."

"Did you then take them to New Delhi?"

He looked down without answering.

"Go ahead, please tell what happened next," Seeta urged.

"No. Since I didn't have enough money for all of us to travel on the train, I didn't go with them. I bought food for them, put them on the train and left. Their Auntie was supposed to meet them in Delhi. That was the nanny's plan. She repeated this to me over and over again."

"Do you know what happened to the children after this?"

"No, they left, and that was the last I ever heard from them. Until..."

"What happened next," interrupted Seeta, not allowing him to embellish his answer just yet.

"I returned to the Sharma house. By this time, it was fully engulfed in flames. When I saw this, I ran. I left town."

"Why did you do that?"

"Because I knew who Mr Khan was."

"Were you afraid for your life?"

"Objection, leading the witness."

Without waiting for the Judge to rule on the objection, Seeta asked, "Mr Gurung. Tell me, why did you not stay?"

"I was afraid for my life. Everyone knows that Mr Khan is a powerful man in Mumbai. Being a mob boss..."

"Objection, Your Honour," stated the Defence Barrister.

"Sustained," replied the Judge. "There should be no more references to the Defendant in those terms."

Seeta paused for a moment. With a slight smile, she turned to the Defence. "Your witness."

The Defence Barrister, Mr Ali, paced back and forth for several minutes before asking any questions. His long black robe and distinguished features commanded respect, whether or not he deserved it. The streaks of grey at his temple were so perfect, she had to wonder if he dyed them.

"Mr Gurung. Tell me, after the party that took place in the household, did you ever see Mr and Mrs Sharma again?"

"No, but I..."

"Just answer the question, yes or no," the Barrister insisted.

"Yes, sir."

"So did you see the Defendant do anything against Mr and Mrs Sharma?"

"No."

"Are you aware that the police report states that this fire was an accident and that those in the house died as a result of smoke inhalation?"

"I do not know what inhalation means."

"It means that they couldn't breathe because of the smoke they inhaled."

"Yes, I had heard that this was what the papers said. But this was not what really happened."

"So, what makes you think my client had anything to do with their deaths?"

"Because the nanny told me so."

"The same nanny that died in the tragic fire?"

"Yes."

"Mr Gurung. Is it true that you like to drink alcohol?"

"Yes, I drink now and then. But…"

"Just answer, yes or no."

"Yes."

"Did you have a drink last night?"

"Yes."

"What about the night before?"

"Yes."

"Is it safe to say that you drink every night?"

"Yes, but…"

"Just answer the question, yes or no."

"Then yes."

"Did you have a drink the night the fire took place?"

"I don't remember."

"You remember everything that the nanny had to say, but you don't remember if you had a drink? How convenient. Could it be that you got it wrong? A fire started in the house, and the nanny brought the children to the window to save them?"

"No."

"How can you say this? You were drinking. How do you really know what happened?"

"I do not know if I was drinking."

"If you can't be sure about this, how can you be so sure about anything else?"

"I know what I know."

"Okay, Mr Gurung. If you say that the children actually escaped that day, once again, how is it that this was never reported to the police? And even if they did survive, how do you know they are really alive today?"

Mr Gurung looked over to Seeta as if to get a sign from her.

"I am over here, Mr Gurung," said the Defence Barrister, noting this gesture. "Don't look to the assistant prosecutor to help you out with your answers. You are bound by the truth. So please just answer the question honestly."

"Because, I have met with Sita Sharma. I have also seen pictures of Chandra and Ravi. I know that they are all alive."

"Oh, really? So you are telling me that these children weren't killed in the fire the way the police report stated and that these four long-lost children have suddenly surfaced after all these years?"

"Yes."

"Mr Gurung. Did you have anything to drink today?"

"Yes. I had something to calm my nerves before coming here."

"It is 10:30 in the morning, and you have already had a drink?"

"Yes, but..."

"Yes or no."

"Yes."

"I have nothing further," stated Mr Ali, returning to his seat, a smug smile on his face.

"If the Court will permit me, I'd like to ask a few more questions of this witness," Seeta said, standing.

"Very well," replied the Judge.

"Mr Gurung," said Seeta, as she went toward the witness box again. "In some ways, you did not answer Mr Ali's question. Tell me how you know that the children are alive."

"Because you told me so."

"And why would I have this kind of information?"

"Because of who you are."

"And who am I?"

"You are Sita Sharma, the daughter of Prakash Sharma."

For a split second, the courtroom went completely silent. A moment later, the entire place exploded in outcries. Mr Khan jumped to his feet, angrily speaking to Mr Ali, the smug grin wiped from the Barrister's face.

"Quiet, quiet!" shouted the Judge, as he slammed his gavel down hard. "That's it! I want all of those who are standing to be taken out of this court. And if this happens again, everyone will be asked to leave. If you continue to act like children, you will be treated as such. I demand respect in my court!" His face had turned a vivid shade of red and a vein pulsed at his temple.

"You may step down, Mr Gurung," said Seeta with a smile. "And thank you for saving our lives."

"I would like both counsels to approach my desk," stated the Judge, breaking the court's usual protocol. Flustered, he turned to Seeta. "What is the meaning of this? I've been a judge for thirty-five years and never have I witnessed such a stunt. This is completely unorthodox. Explain yourself."

"I am Sita Sharma, correctly spelled S-i-t-a. It was my father and mother who were killed. I witnessed the murder myself many years ago, when I was fourteen-years-old."

"Rubbish," stated Mr Ali, clearly angered and embarrassed by this turn of events. "I object to this ridiculous antic being used in this courtroom. Why is it that we did not know about this?"

"You saw the transcripts for Sita. If you had looked into the matter, you could have figured out that it was me. This was never hidden from anyone."

"Your last name is Dutta. And you spell your first name S-e-e-t-a, not S-i-t-a."

"I am married, Dutta is my husband's name. As for the change in the way I spell my first name, I decided I preferred Seeta over the other spelling. I made this change through a legal process. Had you asked, we would have admitted that this was the case. We have nothing to hide. But you never made the effort to ask."

"How could we have known to ask?" Mr Ali said, frustrated.

"I'm afraid this is all highly irregular," stated the Judge, lips pursed. "If what you say is so and you are a witness, you can no longer try this case."

"That is fine. My colleague Mr Roy is here, and he can take over my prosecutorial responsibilities. There is nothing in the law that prevents this trial from moving forward. Everything that I have done has been within legal limits."

"Based on what just happened here, I suggest this trial be stopped this very minute, your Honour," declared Mr Ali. "We cannot..."

"Let us proceed," stated the Judge, ignoring his request.

"Very well," replied Seeta, pleased that her plan had made it this far. Her introduction to the Court had been memorable. The surprise would work in her favour.

The two barristers returned to their benches. From her seat, Seeta could see Mr Khan looking daggers at Mr Ali.

"Mr Roy, are you prepared to take over this case?" the Judge asked.

"Yes, your Honour."

"Then let us proceed."

"If it pleases the Court, I would like to now call Mrs Seeta Dutta to take the stand."

Seeta walked over to the witness box. She had waited for years for this moment, for a chance to go after her parent's killer. She was ready.

"Mrs Dutta, prior to your marriage, could you please tell me what your maiden name was?"

"Sita Sharma."

"Are you related to Mr and Mrs Prakash Sharma?"

"Yes, they were my parents."

"When was the last time you saw your parents?"

"September 13th, 1988. No, actually, it was really September 14th since it happened in the early morning hours of September 14th."

"Under what circumstances did you last see your parents?"

"They were being brutally murdered in the living room of my home in Pune."

"Did you witness this happening?"

"Yes, my nanny saw the attacks taking place and woke us all up. As she led us to her room, past the stairway, I looked down from the top of the stairs and saw my father lying on the floor dead. At the time, my mother was still alive. But she had been severely beaten. They repeatedly told her she was going to die. The person committing the crime said over and over again that this was to pay my father back for his role in convicting his brother."

"And who was it that carried out this heinous act?"

"It was Mr M.S. Khan, that man sitting right over there."

Oh, how she had waited for this moment. It was infinitely more delicious than shooting the man at close range in a crowded restaurant.

Mr Khan maintained direct eye contact with Seeta as this statement was made. The hatred he harboured for her at this moment was felt by everyone in the courtroom.

"Could you please provide a detailed account of everything that happened that night?"

For nearly three hours, she provided an exhaustive description of almost everything that happened from the night her parents were killed to the present. Knowing that they'd attack her character as part of their cross-examination, she didn't hold back. She wanted the story to be out in the open, no secrets. This strategy was decided upon because the team felt that she might get the public's sympathy if she demonstrated her courage in admitting all that she had been through due to her parents' murder.

At times, Seeta was unable to hold back her tears. The audience hung on her words, captivated. When she talked about her baby brother, Ganesh, who was now living with an adoptive family, several in the courtroom openly wept.

Mr Khan editorialized at different points during the interview. Whenever Seeta made a statement that he didn't like, he responded by calling her a liar or by laughing out loud. At times, the Judge had to intervene, threatening to remove him from the courtroom. The man couldn't seem to help himself.

"Thank you, Seeta," said Mr Roy, after completing his questions. He was clearly pleased with her answers. "Your witness."

"Under the present circumstances, I think we should stop the proceedings today," stated the Judge. "We can start up again at 9:00 o'clock sharp Monday morning. I suspect that the defence team might want to regroup. Court is adjourned." The gavel banged to close the session, and everyone rushed from the courtroom.

"Seeta, you were wonderful," stated a beaming Mr Roy.

"Thank you, but I'm totally exhausted," said Seeta, noticing the crowd of reporters gathering.

"The outcome of this case will be known over the weekend when the newspapers come out. They'll either accept your testimony or reject it. Without public opinion on your side, you'll never win this case. It's hard to know which direction they'll go. All I can say is that you did your best. I'm proud of you."

"Thank you."

On Monday, it became clear that the defence team had been busy. Seeta cringed as the manager of the five-star hotel in Delhi took the stand, the hotel where she had run into trouble. Though the Judge's stern face remained impassive, the audience whispered and cast reproving glances her way as the manager recounted her drunken, unseemly behaviour. She had known this would happen. Still, there were hours where it felt like she'd forgotten to breathe.

"They seem to forget that you aren't the one on trial," Mr Roy growled, as a nurse took the stand and testified that Seeta had run into traffic in an attempt to commit suicide. Another witness lived in Seeta's apartment building in Delhi. She talked about how Seeta shaved her head and wore a white sari for weeks. She described that many of the tenants thought that she was crazy, and some were even afraid to have their children be around her.

In addition to these witnesses, the defence team recruited a number of sympathetic barristers who Seeta had taken on in court. Their role was to provide examples of things that she had supposedly said or done while trying cases. Although some of what they described was true, most took liberties in telling the truth, stretching stories into unrecognisable shapes. Feeling confident that Seeta's career would not survive this public assault, they'd agreed to participate in the trial.

Seeta watched in horror as her credibility crumbled.

Once Mr Ali and his team had accomplished this goal, they began trying to prove that Mr Khan was a successful businessman, a family man and a pillar of the community. The defence team introduced an impressive list of influential people from different walks of life, each praising him as a model citizen. These people included prominent captains-of-industry, entertainment icons and well-known elected officials.

To create doubt that a murder had even taken place, some of those who supposedly handled the fire investigation were asked to provide their own testimony. While most of these individuals were not even directly involved, their questioning further confused and clouded the few facts offered. Most implied that there was no tangible evidence to support that Mr and Mrs Sharma were murdered.

Finally, Mr Khan himself was put on the stand. During his questioning, he indicated that he couldn't have been involved in the crime since he wasn't even in the city of Pune that day. To support this statement, he produced a number of documents and names of eyewitnesses who confirmed that he was visiting Calcutta during the time the supposed murders were taking place. With his unlimited power and influence throughout Mumbai, it would have been no trouble for him to fabricate such evidence.

As Mr Khan listened to the damning testimony against his accuser, along with the tributes offered on his behalf, he smiled and regularly nodded his head. At times, he'd brazenly look over at Seeta to see her reaction. She kept her face mask-like, her chin high. Her placid demeanour infuriated him, and watching his rage only made her more determined to brave everything they threw at her.

At night, returning to her apartment, she would find the newspapers gathered on her doorstep: "Public Prosecutor Call Girl" and "Sharma Suicide Scandal." Mr Khan apparently had friends in the media too. These vicious attacks on her character revealed nearly all of Seeta's shortcomings in such a way that it was hard to believe she could possibly be a credible witness. Even the editorial pages were filled with different opinions about the case and Seeta's character. While a small minority appeared to be sympathetic to her situation, many joined in the attack. One article summed it up nicely:

> *Since when does our legal system allow prostitutes to try substantial cases? What is next? Will burglars and terrorists soon be filling in as our barristers? We rely on our public prosecutors to be honest, moral, ethical professionals. How can we put our faith in the hands of a person who has lived an immoral lifestyle? It is not right. I agree that she should be taken out of that office immediately before she pollutes the entire system.*

Another editorial read:

The Khan case never should have been brought to trial. The courts should not have allowed this good man's name to be slandered by someone like this. She is the criminal. She should be the one standing trial now. Not someone like Mr Khan who is well-respected by all. When this unjust trial is over, she should be disbarred and then thrown out of that office.

The trial itself lasted a total of nine days. After the closing statements had been made, the Judge's verdict came quickly. In his remarks, which lasted only a few minutes, he stated that there was insufficient evidence to convict Mr Khan of the crimes against him. Mr Khan was acquitted of all charges and allowed to leave the courtroom a free man.

After this verdict was read, the entire courtroom erupted in an uproar. Reporters dashed out to pass the word on to their hungry editors, while bystanders stood in animated clusters offering their own opinions on the merits of the case.

Seeta remained in her seat. Although a few of her colleagues had come up to offer some supportive words, she forced a smile and did her best to keep the conversations short. All she wanted was to be left alone, to creep away into anonymity.

After thanking his barristers and waving to his supporters, Mr Khan walked up to Seeta and whispered into her ear.

"You are even more pathetic than your father was," he taunted. "At least he knew how to try a case."

Seeta turned and casually replied, "Mr Khan, your people may have painted a false picture of you as an upstanding citizen, but everyone in this courtroom knows the real truth. You are nothing more than a depraved, uncivilised animal. In fact, I would go as far as to say that you are one notch above a common rat and several notches below a street dog. And one other thing. You went to my father's house to kill him, my mother and us children. But you failed to finish the job. We outsmarted you. I guess this just goes to show that you are not as competent as you make yourself out to be. When little children can defeat you, I guess you are not as clever as you think you are."

This comment so infuriated Mr Khan that he couldn't stop himself from shouting his response.

"How dare you say that to me? We'll see what happens to you after this trial. You are finished. Do you hear me? Your career is over."

"Thank you for confirming my last statement," Seeta replied, as she stood and exited the courtroom through a side door.

As Seeta entered the apartment that evening, the phone was ringing.

"Hello."

"Seeta, is that you?" asked Chandra, her sobs making her difficult to understand. "Is the trial over?"

"Yes."

"What happened?"

"We lost."

"How bad was it?"

"Very bad. But this is not over yet."

"I can't believe all of the awful things they are saying about you. It's so unfair. You should have let me testify with you."

"I told you, that was never a possibility. There is no way I'd drag the rest of our family into this mess. It's too dangerous. Besides, you didn't witness the murders. Your testimony would have been seen as merely one sister supporting another."

"Are you going to be all right?"

"Yes, I'll survive."

"Do you think you're going to lose your job over this?"

"I submitted my resignation late this afternoon to beat them to the punch. The pressure being placed on the department was getting to be too much. And besides, if they start really looking into my past and find out that I managed to get into university without finishing my formal schooling, this will raise all kinds of questions. It is much better if I leave before things get even uglier."

"What will you do? How will you make a living?"

Seeta wondered if her sister was concerned about her, or herself. "I don't know yet."

There was a long pause.

"Seeta, this is not the only reason I'm calling. I'm so sorry to bother you. There is something else, something truly awful."

She had just been publicly humiliated and lost her job. What else could be heaped upon her shoulders?

"I didn't want to tell you in the middle of the trial, but I can't handle it by myself anymore. It's too horrible."

"Spit it out, Chandra. What happened?"

"It's Ravi. He was in a terrible accident with his motorcycle. He got drunk and went off the road. His bike slammed into a tree."

"When did this happen?"

"Three days ago. I wanted to call you, but I saw how badly the trial was going. I decided to wait until it was all over. There was nothing you could do anyway, but now that it's over, you need to know."

"Did he survive?" asked Seeta.

"Yes, but he has both head and back injuries. He's still in critical condition. No one knows if he's going to make it."

"Is he going to be paralysed?"

"It's too early to say. He's still unconscious. I need you, Seeta."

Seeta dropped onto the nearest chair and hung up the phone. She couldn't handle yet another crisis. She just couldn't. In the surrounding apartments, voices echoed through the thin walls. It was dinnertime. They were probably gossiping about her, about the trial. The scents of ginger and cumin made her stomach rumble, but it was an automatic response. She wasn't hungry. She didn't recall the last time she had eaten. Maybe she would just never eat again. Curling up on the carved bench, she hugged a pillow to her chest and wept.

27

Several hours later, Seeta sat stiffly in a high-backed chair positioned directly in front of the television. With a glass of scotch in hand, she had just finished watching the 10:00 p.m. news coverage of the trial. Following the short segment that offered a not-so-flattering post-case editorial, she turned off the sound and just watched the picture. Scotch on an empty stomach made her lightheaded, but maybe that was for the best.

The phone rang.

"Hello," said Seeta, answering reluctantly.

"Khan and two others have just entered your apartment building."

Seeta put down the receiver, then continued to stare at the television. She did not have the inclination or energy to move. Yet, she roused herself, angling the high-backed chair so that, as the men entered the room, it would appear that she was sitting in it, watching television, unsuspecting. Then she slipped out onto her balcony. The nearby hallway window was open, and from there, she could hear them talking.

"I don't think you should be here, sir. We can do this job on our own. You are just asking for trouble. If someone sees us, it could get you into trouble again."

"Shut up." She recognised the voice of Mr Khan. "I want to do this job myself. That bitch tried to put me away. She can't say what she said to me without paying a price. She is going to get what's coming to her, just like her stupid father did."

"But what about the police?" A third man spoke.

"What about them? They are insignificant worms in my pocket. With the amount of money I pay them each month, they had better not get in my way."

"Do you think she's armed? What if she's expecting us?"

"Good. Let her try to put up a fight," said Mr Khan. "That will only add to the excitement. Now, whatever you do, let me take the first shots. Go ahead, kick the door down."

She heard the hollow door break as she climbed onto her neighbours' balcony, and from there to the building's hallway window. She heard shots in rapid succession. As her chair was blown to smithereens, she slipped down a different staircase than the one the men had come up. At the landing, she heard an angry shout of surprise — Khan, realising he had been fooled. More shouts of surprise followed as the trio encountered the police who had been waiting for them. The sounds of gunfire filled the halls as she ran down to the street.

Her ultimate plan had worked. She knew he wouldn't be prosecuted but also understood that his nature would not allow him to ignore a personal insult. After poking a stick at this bear, he fell for the bait.

28

The phone in Mr Chetri's luxurious apartment rang. Seeta sat rigidly on the plush sofa, another tumbler of scotch in her clenched hand. Heart in her mouth, she snatched up the receiver.

"They fell for it, just as you said they would," said the chief public prosecutor. "All three of them were killed."

"Did any of our men get hurt in the raid?" asked Seeta.

"Yes, two of them. But they will both be all right. Their injuries are not life-threatening."

"I told you that his ego would force him to go over to my apartment. His taste for revenge would not allow for any other alternative."

"You were absolutely right. I can't believe how arrogant and stupid he was."

"Human nature is like that. We are all creatures of habit."

"If you'd like, you can remain at my apartment. Your place is a mess. It looks like a practice shooting range."

"I think I'll do that. Thank you again for everything."

"No problem. By the way, Seeta, now that it's over, will you take back your resignation?"

She finished the scotch and wandered into the small library, full of gold-leafed law books and literary classics.

"No, I'm done prosecuting cases for a long time. I need a break. Besides, I must travel up to Delhi. My brother has been seriously hurt in a motorcycle accident. My sister needs my help. I plan to take a flight out early tomorrow morning. I'm going to continue my life as Sita Sharma. Seeta Dutta is no more."

"Your brother, Ravi? Is he going to be all right?"

"I don't know yet. We'll have to wait and see."

"Good luck. And please use the time to reconsider my offer. We don't want to lose you."

"My mind is made up. But thank you for asking. It means a lot to me that I have not lost your respect."

29

The following morning, Sita went directly to the airport to take the first scheduled flight up to Delhi. From the moment she entered the crowded street surrounding the airport, people stared. Some were surreptitious, some obvious and bold. She longed for the days when she had been invisible in a crowd. They must all loathe her.

From the time she purchased her ticket to when she entered the waiting area to board the plane, countless people tracked her every movement. Finally, after she had taken a seat at the boarding gate, someone came up to her.

"Are you Sita Sharma?" asked a young college-aged woman with a disarming smile.

"Yes," replied Sita, as she looked around for a means of escape.

"I just wanted to say that I thought what you did in that courtroom was very brave. I am a student at Mumbai University, and I read about your case in the newspapers every day. Our professor even brought it up in class on two occasions. I wanted to tell you how much I admire what you did. This morning I read about what happened to Mr Khan last evening. What an evil man he was. Everyone knew it, and now he is gone forever. Thank God."

As the young woman was talking, others wandered over, encouraged that someone else had made the first move. Before long, there were at least a dozen people surrounding Sita.

"I too want to congratulate you," stated a middle-aged woman who stood beside her young daughter. "What you did on that stand was inspiring. Few people would confess all the awful things that happened to them the way you did. Everyone knew that Mr Khan was a criminal, yet you went after him by yourself. Everyone I know has been talking about it. You are a heroine."

As these statements were being made, others nodded their heads in agreement. Sita looked from one face to the next, stunned at the acceptance and admiration they expressed.

"I don't know what to say," Sita replied, as she looked into the many eyes of the people standing in front of her. "After all the terrible things that have been written and said about me, I thought everyone hated me. I just don't know what to say." She pulled a tissue from her pocket and dabbed at her eyes.

"Don't believe those scandalous newspapers," declared a third woman with conviction. "Mr Khan probably owned those editors. He had nearly everyone in his pocket, including the police. Everyone knows what he was. We are sorry about your father and about all the terrible things that you had to go through. The fact that Mr Khan was caught in your apartment yesterday demonstrates what kind of man he really was. I'm glad he's finally gone. He brought misery upon all who came in contact with him. Mumbai is a safer place now."

"Flight A9 to Delhi is now boarding" came an announcement over the intercom.

"Thank you all for your kind words," Sita said, standing and picking up her carryon bag. "That's my flight. All I can say is that I'm truly touched by your support."

After each day in court, Sita had hurried to escape the reporters. As a result, she'd had no direct contact with the general public until now. Through the remainder of her trip, she was astonished by the number of strangers who greeted her with kind words. Some asked for her autograph, while others just wanted to shake her hand.

After landing, Sita headed toward the terminal's exit. As she made her way outside, she noticed a large crowd of people standing off to one side. In their hands were balloons and flowers and banners. Wanting to avoid this group, she walked in the opposite direction to locate a taxi.

"Sita," shouted out a familiar voice. "Sita, over here!"

Mrs Shrestha pushed her way through the crowd, carrying a banner that read, "Welcome home, Sita!"

Sita stepped forward, focusing in on the group. They were all there for her, with banners and balloons that said, "We love you, Sita," and "Congratulations!" Cheers greeted her astonishment.

"Sita, welcome home," Mrs Shrestha shouted, reaching over the rail to give her a big hug. "We are so proud of you. It is so good to have you home again, where you belong."

Sita kissed her friend's well-powdered cheek, then pulled back to look around them. They were surrounded by former customers, vendors and designers she had known. Each of them reached out to squeeze her hand or kiss her on the cheek.

"Yesterday I thought everyone despised me," she admitted, choking on tears. She smiled even as she started to cry. Before long, the entire crowd was sobbing too.

"How did you know I was coming here today?" asked Sita, after regaining some composure. "I didn't mention it to anyone."

"Your sister called Krishna, and he called me. I know you always like to take the first flight out," Mrs Shrestha added with a smile.

"Where is Krishna?" Sita searched the crowd.

Mrs Shrestha pointed to him, standing patiently off to one side near a baggage carousel. It had been a year since she had seen him. He looked better than she remembered, though there was a touch of grey in his hair. They were getting older. They'd wasted so much time. His eyes locked on hers, those kind hazel eyes, filled with longing.

With the hatred she had harboured for Mr Khan gone from her heart, the love that she had always felt for Krishna rushed in to fill the void. With total abandon, she ran to him and leaped into his arms. Without the slightest hesitation, he buried his face in her hair, wrapping his arms tightly around her.

30

Two days after Sita arrived in Delhi, Ravi woke up from his coma. For the first two weeks of consciousness, he was dazed and incoherent. In time, as he regained his strength and began to take solid nourishment, he gradually took control of his memory and his thoughts. The good news was that he would completely recover from his head injury. There was no permanent brain damage. The bad news was that he was paralysed from the waist down from the severe spinal injury.

Sita and Chandra remained by his side. They read to him, talked to him and cried with him. Upon learning the truth about his legs, Ravi became his old angry and defiant self. For weeks, he was obsessed with the idea of killing himself. Once, when he was left alone for a short period, he rolled himself out of bed and tried to crawl over to the window. His goal was to use his arms to climb through the opening so that he could fall to his death six stories below. He was too weak to succeed; he did not try again.

Twice during his stay in the hospital, his hoodlum friends came to visit him: once before he learnt the news of the severity of his spinal injury and once after his condition had been revealed. After discovering that he wouldn't walk again, they never returned. That was too much reality for them to handle. Their abandonment only added to his feelings of total despair.

During the days and weeks that followed, Sita devoted nearly all her time to her brother. To keep his mind off his injury and his altered future, she spent hours talking to him about anything and everything. They chatted about his friends, his view of the world, his many adventures at school and their experiences following the death of their parents. Sita also used the time to talk about what she had been through, including her own attempts at killing herself. During one of these discussions, Sita learnt that Ravi had known that their parents had been killed well before Sita finally told him. He said he pretended not to know because it seemed to make it less real.

What she came to realise most about her brother during these discussions was that, beneath his exterior of a tough, angry teenager, there was a very frightened insecure boy. The inquisitive, friendly, sometimes-shy person he had once been was still very much there, but dominated by this superficial shell he had fashioned for himself. She also came to realise how emotionally affected he had been during the period when they were moving from place to place.

After two months in the hospital, Sita was able to move him to her new apartment. There she hired a nurse to help tend to his needs until he could fully heal. To keep his mind occupied, she bought him a secondhand computer. With nothing else to do all day but watch TV, Ravi mastered the machine in a short time. He became obsessed with this toy, spending hours teaching himself all there was to know about its many functions. He devoured the books she brought him from the library, constantly begging her for more. When he finally discovered the Internet, his entire world changed. With nothing but time on his hands, he began to explore every facet of this technology. The new challenge gave him a reason to wake up in the morning and opened up the world beyond the windows of the apartment. He was no longer confined but free to roam and explore anything and everything that interested him.

Sita unlocked the door of the first-floor apartment. The apartment was quiet, with only the soft buzz of a rotating floor fan that could be heard. Krishna was still at work, and Ravi was sprawled on his bed, fast asleep from the pain medications as he often was at this time of day. In the late afternoon light, he looked peaceful. She closed his bedroom door so as not to wake him, then set the bag of groceries on the counter. The ringing of the phone jarred the tranquil space. She hurried to pick it up before it woke her brother.

"Sita?" The woman's voice was unfamiliar.

"Yes, and who is this please?" asked Sita.

"It is me, your Auntie Nadia. Your father's sister."

For a moment she said nothing. It could be a trick. She was famous now—or infamous—and her notoriety was sure to attract a few scammers.

"I hope I'm not disturbing you? I have had a terrible time trying to reach you these past weeks since the trial ended."

"How did you find me?" Sita finally responded.

"Well, when I first heard about the trial in Mumbai, I was absolutely furious. I thought someone was pretending to be you in order to get some kind of publicity. But when I read the newspaper accounts of Mr Khan's attempted murder and subsequent demise, I realised that it was really you. After that, I left many messages with people at your office in Mumbai. Did you ever receive them?"

"During the trial period I received a lot of hate mail. I told the staff to just destroy all personal mail to me. I'm sorry, I never received your message. Where are you calling from?"

"I'm calling from my home here in Delhi."

"Is Uncle with you?"

"No, he passed away two years ago. I'm alone now, I'm afraid."

"I'm so sorry to hear that. Our poor family, it seems, is shrinking at an alarming rate."

"That is true, my dear. But he was very sick for a long time." It was the grief in her voice that convinced Sita. This was her Aunt Nadia.

"How did you track me down in Delhi?"

"One of the many articles written about you in the local papers said that you once worked in a dress shop here in town. I called the owner, Mrs Shrestha, and she told me where to find you. She worships you. You would not believe the wonderful things she said about you."

"I feel the same way about her. So, Auntie, can we meet?"

"Of course. How about today? I can't wait another minute."

"Just give me your address."

"243 Park Road. It is near the British Embassy."

"I know the area well. I'll hop into a cab and be there in twenty minutes."

"Can you bring your brother and sister with you?"

"Unfortunately, no, not today. Another long story I'm afraid."

"Well, come alone then, just hurry! It has been far too many years."

As Sita made her way up the flower-bordered walkway to her Auntie's home, she found an aged and fragile Nadia standing on the front doorstep waiting. The warm, much overdue embrace that followed lasted several minutes.

Nadia was in fact only fifty-years-old, but her hair was completely grey, her face a moonscape of wrinkles. As the only survivor of Prakash's immediate family, Sita wondered if she had somehow given up on life.

"Come in, dear," said Nadia as she stood back to get a good look at Sita. "You look so much like your mother. You have her beautiful eyes and hair." She touched Sita's hair lovingly as they entered the dark, old-fashioned salon.

The two of them sat down on a Victorian brocade couch of ancient vintage, a family heirloom no doubt. Sita's tastes in furnishings were more modern and contemporary styles, sleek and clutter free. Her aunt's home was the opposite, layered with doilies, knick-knacks, dusty rugs and heavy draperies.

"I still can't believe you're here with me," Nadia said, beaming at her. "Never in my life have I received such a precious gift. And after all that you've been through.

Tell me, why weren't you able to locate me here in Delhi all those years ago?"

"Nilopha, our nanny, was supposed to contact you the night that we escaped. We were expecting you to be at the train station to collect us. But you didn't show up."

"I never got the message, Sita. I'm sorry. The day after the fire, I was told that everyone was killed. It was one of the worst moments of my life. I wept for days."

"I guess she died before she could make the call." Sita lowered her head as she remembered her beloved Nanny and how she had saved their lives. "We didn't have your address, and I didn't know your full name. I didn't know how to find you. Then something awful happened that forced us to leave the city. Many years ago, I did send out letters to hundreds of people in Delhi who had the first name Nadia in an attempt to find you."

Her Aunt's eyes widened. "Years ago, I received a short note asking if I was related to Prakash. It also mentioned something about the fire. I responded, but I never heard back."

"That was my letter. We must have left the school by then." She took a deep breath. "If we had received a reply earlier, our lives would have been much different."

"I read what you did for your father, Sita. I'm so proud of you. I also read about what happened to you and your sister and brother. The three of you had to face so many awful things. I cried when I read the details. Please tell me about Chandra and Ravi. I am dying to see them."

For the next two hours, Sita talked at great length about Ravi's accident, Chandra's schooling, her husband Krishna and her brief visit with Ganesh.

"It's almost too much to be believed," said Nadia, exhausted after hearing the details. "Can we all get together?"

"Of course. You're our only family, Aunt Nadia. Chandra and Ravi will be thrilled to see you."

"I can't wait to see them." There was a short pause in the conversation. "Sita, there is one other thing I should mention."

"What is that?"

"When your father died, his inheritance went to me as the only surviving family member. Now that you and the others are here, I'd like to see that it goes to you four."

"Don't talk about that now," said Sita, not wanting to get into such details. And what she would do about any inheritance for Ganesh was a problem she wasn't yet ready to consider.

"But we have to talk about it soon. I am not getting any younger. There are legal papers that must be drawn up and signed. Your father and I both inherited a great deal from our own parents, your grandparents. Most of that can be divided up. I also have the plot of land in Pune. I rebuilt the house with some of the money that belongs to you and the others. It's not nearly as grand as it once was, but it is a nice house. The rest can be distributed equally among you children. Based on what you said about Ganesh, I think we need to think about how to provide him with his share as well. After listening to what happened during your visit with him, I am sure that the Jains know the identity of their son by now. With so much written about you and the others, it must be pretty obvious to them."

"Please, can we talk about this later? I'm so tired of talking about legal matters. Right now, I just want to enjoy your company."

"Yes, you're right. I just wanted you to know. By the way, do you remember what your mother and father looked like?"

"Yes, but I haven't seen a good picture of them for many years, only the formal ones they keep using in the newspapers over and over again."

"Your mother used to send me pictures of the family once a year. I still look at them often. They are one of my few real treasures."

"Can I see them?"

"Of course," said Nadia, reaching over to a set of albums that she had pulled out of trunks for this occasion. She reached over and snapped on a floor lamp next to the sofa, which cast a soft glow over the room.

As Sita turned the pages, a feeling of warmth came over her. It was so good to see her parents again, standing in front of the school, smiling as they held baby Ganesh, at a bazaar buying vegetables. It brought them back to life, refreshed her memories. The photos also helped to wipe away the images of that awful night. The love they'd felt for their children radiated out from the pictures, captured for all time.

Sita's notoriety did not end with the trial. The general public had embraced her as a symbol of defiance against all that was wrong and corrupt in the country. Not long after settling into the new apartment with Krishna and Ravi, she was offered a job at a prominent law firm that specialised in human rights issues. After reading the job description, she immediately accepted it even though the salary was much smaller than she had earned in Mumbai. Her role was to take on issues involving child labour, human trafficking and violence against women. Having experienced all of these phenomena in her own life, it seemed as though the job description had been crafted with her in mind.

Life with Krishna was wonderful once again. At last, Krishna knew everything about her and accepted her. She had not realised how much anxiety she had lived with before, not allowing herself to fully trust his love. Now, at last, the trust was there.

PART THREE:

"A PROMISE KEPT"

31

It was a quiet Saturday morning. Sita sat on one of the two matching living room couches as she read her morning paper and enjoyed a cup of sweetened black tea. She had furnished the apartment with money provided from her inheritance, splurging at the chicest furniture and accessory stores in the city. White leather, chrome and glass gleamed throughout the contemporary interior, and every surface sparkled with simplicity. Krishna occasionally voiced his preference for the heavy drapes and velvet furnishings of his childhood home but not with any vehemence. His one contribution to the decor, one to which Sita could not object, was the bouquet of fresh flowers that he brought home daily.

After scanning the headlines, she turned to the local section to see if her latest case had received any coverage. There was a small, one-column article about a move to change the dowry burning laws. Her name was mentioned three times. As always, she would have preferred if they had spent more time on the issue than on her involvement in the case, but the firm believed that without her involvement, these issues would have received no attention at all.

Krishna played on the floor with Maya, their curly haired two-year-old daughter. Whenever he had a spare moment, he loved getting down on the Kashmiri carpet, which Sita had allowed in deference to the child's knees. She was an easy-going child who laughed readily at everything her father did. Every now and then Sita looked up and smiled at the tableau. Krishna was a great father, one of the many things she loved about him.

"I see you are finally out of bed," said Sita, as Ravi wheeled himself into the room. "Were you up all night again on that bloody machine of yours? I'm sorry I ever introduced you to the world of computing." She smiled to let him know she was teasing.

"I was up until 3:30, I had two websites to build. These customers seem to want everything to be a certain way, but they don't ever really know what way that is. They're driving me crazy. If they didn't pay so well, I'd drop them in a heartbeat."

"Do you want to go out today?" asked Sita.

"No, I'm tired. If you don't mind, I'll stay around the house." Ravi turned toward his niece. "Aren't you going to give your old uncle a hug?"

Maya raced over to Ravi, climbed up on his lap and gave him a big hug and a kiss. He spun his chair around in tight circles, causing her to squeal with laughter.

Turning to the entertainment section, Sita glanced through the text to see if there was anything of interest. From the upper right-hand corner, a photo sent a shock through her, causing her to jump to her feet.

"What is it?" asked Krishna.

"How many hours is it to Jaipur?" asked Sita.

"I don't know exactly. Four hours? Why?"

"We need to go there today. Now. All of us. Quick, quick!" She clapped her hands. "I'll explain in the car. Hurry. I need to call Chandra. Get the car ready and make sure you get the bag for the baby and plenty of drinks. And also pack some snacks. If we hurry, we can get there before noon."

Ravi wheeled himself over to the couch and picked up the paper she had been reading. With more excitement than she had seen from him in years, he clapped as well.

"Krishna, you heard Sita," he said. He rolled himself off in the direction of his room. "We have to leave immediately. Hurry!"

Within twenty minutes, Sita, Chandra, Ravi, Maya and Krishna were all packed up in their Tata Safari and on the road heading toward Jaipur.

"Sita, this whole idea of yours is completely ridiculous," said Krishna, as he shook his head in exasperation. "This is like locating a particular grain of sand on a beach that spans for miles. There's no way you'll find what you're looking for by just spontaneously driving to Jaipur like this."

"Please trust me, Krishna." She'd find them, she just knew it. "This thing will happen. I can't say how I know this, but I do. If you put a desire out there and you wish it to manifest with all your heart, it will happen. I know this from experience. Destiny conspires to make it happen. Since you don't believe in this, you'll never understand. But I do believe with all my heart. I have wished for this day for many years, and today it has come to me, like so many wishes in the past. You have to trust me. I know what I'm doing. All things in life eventually come full circle. This has always been true in my life. This is the one last thing that has remained outstanding. It will happen."

"But what if..." asked Krishna.

"Stop asking questions, Krishna," said Chandra, cutting him off. "I too believe. And you know how Sita is. When she's determined, it's settled."

With the heavy traffic that they encountered along the way, the journey took nearly five hours. It was two o'clock in the afternoon when they arrived in the centre of Jaipur, known as the pink city. Having only stopped once, everyone was already tired. Even the sweet-natured Maya was getting restless.

"Pull over," Sita shouted suddenly, pointing to the side of the road.

"Here?" Krishna asked, slamming on the brakes.

"Yes, just stop in front of that bazaar." She couldn't help herself; she was bouncing up and down in her seat.

Sita jumped out of the car before it had fully stopped, newspaper in hand, and began approaching strangers and showing them the picture she had found. While the first three people shook their heads to indicate that they didn't know anything, one man nodded and pointed farther down the road.

"We need to go to the end of this road and find the street to a football field," said Sita as she climbed back into the vehicle. "There we need to take a left."

"Are you sure about this?" asked Krishna. "I really don't think—"

"Yes, just drive."

For nearly four hours, they drove from location to location, following every lead. With a blind determination, she forged ahead, though Krishna was convinced they were going in circles.

"Sita, it's nearly six o'clock," Krishna complained softly. "We have hardly eaten anything, and we're all tired. It's time to get a hotel room or go home. It's time."

"That man back there said that we should try the northern highway. This could be the place."

"No, Sita," said Krishna, finally holding his ground. "I'm putting my foot down now. We tried our best. We came all the way out here and have found nothing. I told you this was impossible. I'm sorry, my love, but enough is enough."

Krishna turned the car around and headed in the direction of the highway they had travelled in on. Sita merely shook her head. It would happen today. After all she had been through, she no longer believed in coincidences. Life provided omens and signs to those who were open to recognising them. Every cell in her body told her so. The energy was there, and she could feel it drawing her near.

As they reached the first crossroad out of Jaipur, it happened.

"There it is!" shouted Ravi, full of excitement. "There, behind those buildings."

"Stop," Chandra chorused.

Maya began chanting, "Thop, thop, thop, Papa!"

"What? Where?" asked Krishna, confused.

"There, next to those wagons," Sita ordered. "Please hurry and park."

Krishna turned the car around again and pulled up beside a quaint collection of old tattered red wagons that were parked in the shadow of a large building. The sides of the wagons were painted with faded images of the great buildings of India and important gods and goddesses. Krishna grabbed the newspaper photo and compared it with the wagons. Sure enough, these were the same ones the photographer had caught. Sita was right. The caption underneath the photo read "An example of a rural circus visiting Jaipur."

Off in the distance, Sita could see a large circle of people. From the centre of the circle, loud Hindi music filled the air. As Krishna helped Ravi from the car and into his wheelchair, Chandra grabbed Maya up into her arms and slung the diaper bag over her shoulder.

"Sita, where are you going?" asked Chandra, surprised that her sister wasn't running toward the crowd. Instead, she seemed to be walking toward some laundry that was hanging between the wagons. It included several colourful dresses that swayed in the evening breeze.

"I'll be there in just a moment. I need to do something first. Go and watch the performance, just save me a good place to stand."

She watched them walk through the crowd. At the centre of the gathering, she could just make out a dancer. The woman was tall, strong, proud and full of life. She performed in the centre of the circle as if she were alone in the desert, dancing in the light of a full moon. Her dance was uninhibited, full of passion. She represented the essence of freedom as her head and body twisted and turned to the beat of the music.

Sita pulled the colourful dress over her head and hurried forward to join her.

For a brief moment, Maya stopped and stared. But when Sita began to dance, Maya smiled and regained her composure. The two of them began to turn and spin. It came back to her, the movements of the dance, her hips carving figure-eights through the air, her feet shuffling forward and back, her arms moving sinuously above her head. The beat of the music coursed through her; for one beautiful moment, she held the moon in her hands. Then the music ended. The crowd clapped wildly, then reluctantly moved away.

Sita turned to face Maya, studying her old friend as night fell. Time seemed to have collapsed, like the folds of an accordion; she looked just the same. A cool, desert breeze tugged at their hair, and for a moment, they seemed alone in the world.

"You kept your promise," Maya said at last.

Sita hugged her, unable to resist another moment.

"Come," Sita said. "There's someone I want you to meet."

The star-crossed women walked hand in hand to meet Maya's tiny namesake.